15427

Bright
Wind of the
Spirit

Bright
Wind of the
Spirit

PENTECOSTALISM
TODAY

by
STEVE DURASOFF

PRENTICE-HALL, Inc.

Englewood Cliffs, New Jersey

Bright Wind of the Spirit: Pentecostalism Today
By Steve Durasoff
Copyright © 1972 by Steve Durasoff
All rights reserved. No part of this book may be
reproduced in any form or by any means, except
for the inclusion of brief quotations in a review,
without permission in writing from the publisher.
Printed in the United States of America
Prentice-Hall International, Inc., London
Prentice-Hall of Australia, Pty. Ltd., North Sydney
Prentice-Hall of Canada, Ltd., Toronto
Prentice-Hall of India Private Ltd., New Delhi
Prentice-Hall of Japan, Inc., Tokyo

Library of Congress Cataloging in Publication Data
Durasoff, Steve.
Bright wind of the spirit.
Includes bibliographical references.
1. Pentecostalism. I. Title.
BX8763.D87   289.9   72-6536
ISBN 0-13-083089-5

Dedicated to all
whose hearts and minds
are open to the
"Bright Wind of the Spirit."

Acknowledgments

BRIGHT WIND OF THE SPIRIT is designed for the man on the street who knows little or nothing about Pentecostal persuasions, practices, or people. So it was a wise move on the part of the publishers to assign a Catholic, completely new to the subject, to undertake as an editor the difficult task of helping me to write this story so it could be readily understood. Miss Carol Cartaino has done her level best in this task and, if there are traces of dissertation stuffiness, I am to blame.

Dr. William Jernigan and Juanita Raudszus, colleagues at Oral Roberts University, suggested that I would be able to write such a book and I thank them for their confidence. My gratitude goes to Dr. Carl Hamilton, Academic Dean of ORU, Juanita Raudszus, and Anna Bell Collins for reading the entire manuscript in early draft form. And to Evelyn Roberts and Wayne Robinson I owe appreciation for assistance on the Oral Roberts chapters. Nadja, my wife, is invaluable as a constant consultant. It is impossible to mention all the ministers, colleagues, and friends who have contributed their thought to this book and my sincere gratitude is extended to them.

Thanks to Roberta Hurlbut for her diligent research, a burden made lighter by having the world's best Pentecostal collection located on campus. Final acknowledgment is due to Ellen Vaughn and Lequinta McKaig for their capable typing.

Of course, the views and conclusions drawn are solely the writer's and the buck ends there.

CONTENTS

I

Pentecostals – Who Are They?

PENTECOSTALS BELIEVE in miracles. They expect the supernatural most anytime, anywhere.

Often called the Billy Graham of Africa, lean, black Nicholas Bhengu was in Toronto addressing the Pentecostal World Conference. He told about preaching to the people of South Africa on the theme of Jesus. Suddenly a cripple jumped up, threw his crutches away, and ran about creating an uproar. No one had prayed for him. "Jesus healed him. . . . When we preach Jesus He saves souls, He heals sick bodies. . . ."[1]

Pentecostals live right. They are dedicated to holy living.

Before the nation of Chile voted in a Marxist president, the Pentecostals had earned the reputation of being the workmen most sought after by management. Why? Their Pentecostal beliefs caused them to be sober, hard-working, salary-saving and non-wife-beating men, all of which impressed employers in a country where four out of every five Protestants are Pentecostal.

Pentecostals pray in unknown languages–they are glossolalics. They worship with the heart as well as the head.

Today even Catholics are praying in tongues. In the United States Catholic Pentecostals from all walks of life regularly hold Pentecostal prayer meetings. Such groups range from a handful of seekers in a city apartment to several hundred who attend weekly events at a Catholic student center in Ann Arbor, Michigan. Conservatively estimated, 30,000 American Catholics have experienced glossolalia, or speaking in tongues. Recently, a distressed priest stated that he did not believe the Holy Spirit was "going to play the foolish game of speaking in foreign languages" when communicating with people. He was surprised to find his fellow priests the first to disagree.

Pentecostals seek to share Jesus. They are zealous witnesses.

Even the so-called hippies respond. This was emphasized in January 1971 on an NBC "First Tuesday" telecast featuring the controversial young people who call themselves "Children of God."[2] Others call them "Jesus Freaks" and resent their exclusivity, but most of them have experienced cataclysmic conversions, leaving behind sordid lives of promiscuity and drug addiction. Disillusioned and empty, they were awakened to new life through the testimony of similar youth now sold on Jesus. Swinging to the other extreme, they set up Christian communal boot camps where disciplined daily work schedules and Bible study are conducted in an atmosphere of love and respect for each individual. After they have memorized four hundred Bible verses, they set out in groups in all directions, stopping wherever young people gather so they may witness and share the good news of Jesus and His love. Following conversion, the men's long hair is shorn and water baptism is administered. Then they pray to be filled with the Holy Spirit in order to have greater power to witness for Jesus.

Pentecostals challenge traditional churches. They are disquieting.

A few years ago the American Lutheran Church gave a cautious endorsement of speaking in tongues, admitting that the phenomenon was one of the several gifts of the Holy Spirit mentioned in the Scriptures. Charismatic ministerial groups among Presbyterians and

Methodists are growing and even God's "frozen people," the Episcopalians, have continued to melt before the Pentecostal fires kindled by Father Bennett back in 1960.

Pentecostals evoke criticism. They are misunderstood.

The critics of Pentecostalism are many. Most are sincere and some most severe. They invariably get hung up on the issues of divine healing and speaking in tongues, viewing Pentecostals as fanatical crackpots caught up with chasing after miracles and uttering meaningless gibberish. Others have labeled Pentecostal believers schizophrenics and a few have concluded that their utterances in tongues are not divine but demonic.

A Jesuit priest, Father Damboriena, suggested a good approach for those trying to place the Pentecostals into proper focus. He said, "We shall never understand Pentecostal beliefs and practices until we grasp the centrality of the Third Person of the Trinity in their lives."[3] Damboriena, a constructive critic, feels that Pentecostalism is one of the most powerful and dynamic religious movements of our day.

Just who are the Pentecostals? Why are they important? What do they mean by the "baptism in the Holy Spirit" and the "supernatural gifts of the Holy Spirit"? Where may they be found and how many Pentecostals are there in the world today?

Pentecostals are Christians, most of whom believe in all the historical doctrines of Christianity. What makes them *Pentecostal* Christians is their earnest desire to recapture the early practices of the first followers of Jesus of Nazareth. They are Spirit-filled Christians who claim it is possible to duplicate the dynamic lives of the disciples, to know Jesus as a powerful person in the present, through the enablement of God the Holy Spirit.

An estimated twenty million Pentecostals may be found in all parts of the world, including Communist

3

China and Red Russia. They have accepted Jesus Christ as personal Savior and have experienced the "happy day when Jesus washed their sins away." They believe the miracle of salvation from sin is the greatest of all miracles, for without this crisis experience they would still be as dead men—dead to God and to abundant life. A small percentage of Pentecostals have so highly exalted Jesus in a "Jesus Only" concept that they have rejected the biblical, historical teaching of the Trinity.

A second experience common to Pentecostals, the "Baptism in the Holy Spirit," is so unusual that it rarely fails to attract attention. It is overtly more dramatic and obvious than the first, essential experience of salvation in Christ, but never more important. When this supernatural baptism occurs in answer to the humble, believing prayers of earnest Christians, when they voluntarily meet Jesus in a new dimension as Baptizer in the Spirit, Pentecostals are confident that they will respond by speaking in tongues and praising God in languages neither understood nor acquired.

Baptism in the Holy Spirit is a spiritual experience not to be confused with water baptism, be it by sprinkling, pouring, or immersing. Nor can it be considered the same as the sacrament of confirmation, though this rite is believed by many in Christendom to convey the Holy Spirit to the participant.

Pentecostals maintain that no clergyman can ever perform this baptism, for there is only one Baptizer in the Spirit. His name is Jesus. All four Gospel writers—Matthew, Mark, Luke, and John—support this position by presenting the words of John the Baptist who declared, "He shall baptize you with the Holy Spirit."[4]

This is nothing new. In fact it first happened 1900 years ago when the Christians received this baptism and spoke in tongues in a Jerusalem upper room. It created an uproar then and it is creating a great stir in many places today.

What actually takes place when a person is baptized with the Holy Spirit? What goes on in his mind and heart and how does he feel? He may be praying alone, or more often with a group in a home or at a church altar. He may be standing, sitting, kneeling, or prostrate. Posture does not produce Pentecost. Ideally his thoughts are centered not upon the baptism but upon the Baptizer, Jesus—in worship, adoration, and praise. He is very much aware of the presence of his Lord and he finds his vocabulary woefully inadequate to express the gratitude in his heart for the Person who loved him enough to die in his stead.

The Baptism in the Spirit may be a hushed experience with prayer ascending in little more than a whisper, it may be conversational in tone, or it may be an ecstatic, explosive outbreak accompanied by waves of joyful exhilaration. Human responses vary greatly, but Pentecostals maintain that each will speak in tongues upon receiving this spiritual baptism. Most will sense the nearness of Jesus as never before and will receive added power to serve the Savior. One thing is certain: recipients become more effective witnesses of the reality of Jesus in their everyday lives. This is a positive result of the Pentecostal experience. Baptism in the Holy Spirit is not an end; the baptized Christian is not a finished product. Rather, it is an open door, a beginning of greater experiences in God. The Pentecostal becomes a channel through whom the supernatural gifts of the Holy Spirit may be transmitted to help others at their moments of greatest need. Nine of these charismatic gifts are listed in the Apostle Paul's first letter to the Church at Corinth: the word of wisdom, the word of knowledge, faith, gifts of healing, working of miracles, prophecy, discerning of spirits, tongues, and the interpretation of tongues.[5]

Because it is so spectacular, speaking in tongues is the spiritual gift that usually strikes the neutral observer as being awesome, mystical, fanatical, or foolish. In 1927 Colgate University's President, George B. Cutten, wrote his scholarly *Speaking with Tongues.*[6] He believed that the experience was almost entirely for those of low mental ability and that none of the large Christian denominations would attempt to cultivate the experience. How times have changed!

Today the outbreak of tongues and other gifts of the Spirit has been so widespread that several distinguishing labels such as "Classic Pentecostals," "Protestant Neo-Pentecostals," and "Catholic Pentecostals" are helpful, necessary, and much in vogue.

The Classic Pentecostals are those Christians active in churches readily identified as Pentecostal, most of which came into existence early in the twentieth century. Among these are the Assemblies of God (the largest group), the Church of God, the Church of God in Christ (black membership), the United Pentecostal Church (non-Trinitarian), the Pentecostal Church of God in America, the International Church of the Foursquare Gospel (founded by Aimee Semple McPherson), the Pentecostal Holiness Church (from which Oral Roberts emerged), and dozens more. These are the Classic Pentecostals, in whose regular worship services the supernatural gifts of the Holy Spirit are welcomed.

Then there are the Protestant Neo-Pentecostals, members of historic Protestant denominations who have recently experienced speaking in tongues. This frequently happens as these seeking individuals join friendly, informal prayer meetings held in homes or apartments. Other spiritually hungry persons discover far more than a pleasant dinner at the monthly meetings conducted by active Pentecostal laymen known as the Full Gospel Business Men's Fellowship International (FGBMFI). Its members joyfully share their Pentecostal experience and pray with anyone who desires the same. And who can tell how many historic Protestants have been introduced to Pentecostalism and the parti-

6

cipation of the gifts of the Spirit by attending small prayer groups or services in Classic Pentecostal churches? Or by the large crusades, the nationwide telecasts, and Pentecostal broadcasts such as Revivaltime? Baptist seminary professors have stated, ". . . even if the movement started somewhat spontaneously . . ., Pentecostals certainly deserve credit for helping to fan the sparks into a vigorous flame."[7]

Although Protestant Neo-Pentecostals enjoy the same supernatural blessings, they continue to worship and serve in their own churches, many of which would be considered far too liberal in theological beliefs by the Classic Pentecostals. You will discover Protestant Neo-Pentecostals among Episcopalians, Lutherans, Presbyterians, Methodists, Reformed, Baptists, Brethren, Congregational, Church of Christ, Disciples of Christ, Mennonites, and other Protestant groups. This unexpected phenomenon probably began in the mid-fifties, but was not dramatically publicized until April 3, 1960 when Father Dennis Bennett arose before his congregation at the Van Nuys Episcopal Church and confessed from his pulpit that "the Holy Spirit did take my lips and tongue and form a new and powerful language of praise and prayer that I myself could not understand."[8] Seventy of the 2,500 members understood—they had already spoken in tongues. But the late Bishop Pike saw in the movement a "heresy in embryo," banned tongues from confirmation services, and advised Episcopalians to desist from the practice in churches, homes, and elsewhere. Spirit-filled members who remain in these historic denominations are apt to emphasize the fact that Pentecost is not a denomination but an experience.

Harald Bredesen, a Lutheran minister often heard at FGBMFI banquets in plush hotels across America, had just left a breakfast session when he chanced upon the Egyptian heiress, Marie Khayat, in the lobby. It didn't

7

take long for Bredesen to strike up a conversation, hoping to share his faith in Christ with the sophisticated Moslem, but no opening presented itself. Before parting, he startled her by asking, "Have you ever heard this language?" And immediately he began to pray in tongues. She looked at him in amazement and said, "Where did you possibly learn archaic Egyptian?" She explained that there are certain tones that no one but a native can acquire; "Foreigners study it for years and we laugh at their accent. You sound just like a Bedouin saying his prayers." After he explained the biblical basis for the phenomenon of glossolalia, she remarked, "When I go back to Egypt I'm going to gather my friends around the Bible and we're going to study it."[9]

The number of Protestant Neo-Pentecostals is impossible to estimate because so many of them worship in this supernatural manner beyond the limits of their church walls. Pastors may be unaware of the frequent gatherings in home prayer groups for Pentecostal worship. The nation is crisscrossed with Protestant Neo-Pentecostal Bible studies and prayer groups.

Recently the United Presbyterian Church has given a cautious endorsement of the supernatural gifts of the Holy Spirit. The special committee headed by John H. Strock reviewed the biblical, theological, and psychological aspects of this charismatic experience of speaking in tongues. Because the chairman, himself a glossolalic, declined to leave his church and instead remained loyal to his denomination, he was able to play a key role in causing this favorable response.

The greatest surprise to appear on the Pentecostal world scene was the emergence of the Catholic Pentecostals. Since 1967, when a few professors and students gathered together at Duquesne and Notre Dame universities to seek God for a renewal of Pentecost, many thousands of Roman Catholics have been filled with the Holy Spirit and speak in tongues. Most claim that since they received this spiritual baptism they have a greater appreciation for the sacraments and loyalty to Catholic teachings. More important, Jesus has become intensely real to them and they have become involved Christians.

In the national Catholic magazine *Ave Maria*, Father Edward O'Connor wrote about a large number of undergraduates and several professors who attended the Pentecostal prayer meetings at Notre Dame. The Catholic theologian noted significant changes among those who received the Spirit-baptism. For one thing, they had an instant love for reading the Bible "such as one rarely finds in priests or religious people, let alone college students. They read it eagerly . . . as souls hungry for the Word of God, devouring and savouring every word. . . ."[10]

Had such unexpected events occurred before the Second Vatican Council, the participants would likely have been condemned for heresy and fanaticism. But a little man prayed, "Renew your wonders in our time, as though for a new Pentecost . . ." Pope John XXIII opened the window to the wind of the Holy Spirit. The Classic Pentecostals don't know what to make of this Catholic breakthrough. It wasn't supposed to—it couldn't—happen within Catholicism. But it did and there is no end in sight.

Of course, some old-timers in Pentecost have grown cold and sour. Having experienced rejection in past decades from the historical Protestants and Catholics, they tend to react negatively to the current charismatic movement. Perhaps they have absorbed too much of the elder brother's sullen attitude shown in the story of the Prodigal Son. As the father rejoiced when his youngest son returned, so the joyful celebration for these charismatics who have returned to receive the Pentecostal "promise of the Father" may also have awakened envy among older Pentecostal brothers. Then, too,

9

many of the new tongue-speakers haven't become members of the Pentecostal churches as expected.

But no one is happier about the present move of the Holy Spirit upon all flesh than David du Plessis, the congenial gentleman often called Mr. Pentecost. A real old-timer in Pentecost, when asked if tongues was not considered the least of all the gifts, he surprises people with, "I believe it is, and that is why I suggest that everyone begin with this manifestation of the Spirit."[11]

By this time you may have wondered why most tongue-speakers are called Pentecostals, be it Classic, Neo-, or Catholic. The Pentecostals are so labeled because the initial outburst of tongue-speaking took place 1900 years ago on a Jewish feast day called the Day of Pentecost. It had been celebrated for centuries by all adult male Jews who were able to be present in Jerusalem for the annual commemoration of the occasion. On that very day the followers of Jesus were gathered together in earnest prayer. The New Testament account declares that, "when the Day of Pentecost was fully come, they were all with one accord in one place. . . . And they were all filled with the Holy Spirit and began to speak with other tongues, as the Spirit gave them utterance."[12] Today the word Pentecost is associated more frequently with charismatic tongue-speakers than with the ancient Jewish feast day.

While one major denomination after another report declining memberships and incomes, and even as their overseas missionary staffs are hit the hardest, Pentecostal churches, to the contrary, have made impressive and even startling gains. Pentecostalism has developed into the world's fastest growing Christian body of believers, a "third force" in world Christianity along with Protestantism and Catholicism.

In 1970 U.S. News and World Report observed that the fastest growing of all churches in Latin America was the Pentecostals, ranking second only to Roman

Catholicism in many areas. In Brazil they surpass all other Protestant groups combined, amounting to millions.[13]

During the decade of the sixties the Assemblies of God, the largest group of American Pentecostals, saw its number of stateside adult members advance from 515,000 members in 1963 to 645,000 in 1971, while its number of believers abroad soared from less than a million to almost three million.

This can be better understood by observing Pentecostal zeal in witnessing to the unchurched and uncommitted. Pentecost is practical. It has a "go" in its gospel. Every member is urged to become an evangelist to his neighbors and friends. After the mountain-top experiences received during prayer, these believers find an urge to enter the valley of human suffering and sin with the compassion of Jesus, bringing supernatural assistance to people who face problems without knowing that God loves them and desires to meet their needs.

The urgent priority of receiving the fullness of the Holy Spirit was stressed by none other than Jesus Himself. His last command to His disciples was to tarry until they received power from above,[14] for then only would they be dynamic Christians, equipped to deliver the good news of God's love and supernatural graces to mankind. Human power is unable to accomplish the task, but human beings endowed with power from on high—the power of Pentecost—could turn the world upside down. The early Christians did.

As David du Plessis explained, "The reason why Pentecostals have been so successful . . . is because they are Pentecostal. I did not say it is because we speak with tongues, for if that was all we had from the experience . . . we would have been a forgotten issue long ago. However, Jesus said: 'Ye shall receive power,' and that is the secret of our success."[15]

Like du Plessis, the Pentecostals believe that the New

11

Testament is not simply a historical record of an unusual generation of believers, but a blueprint of exploits that should be repeated in every generation. And it is being repeated in the most unexpected places. A skinny Pentecostal pastor in the relative obscurity of a Pennsylvania town was led one day to enter the dangerous, drug-infested asphalt jungle of New York City. David Wilkerson had neither funds nor contacts, but his love and faith communicated a Christ Who could set hooked gang leaders free—free from all hellish forces and addictions. Today there are centers in many major American cities modeled after Wilkerson's Teen Challenge Center in Brooklyn. His vivid account of God's concern for troubled youth is known around the world as the best-seller *The Cross and the Switchblade*. Even readers in Communist nations such as Czechoslovakia and Yugoslavia enjoy the revelation of apostolic power dwelling in contemporary Christians as they thumb through the story translated into their own languages.

A theologian formed part of a team of anthropologists who studied Pentecostalism over a period of three years. In the course of this research Catholic Kilian McDonnell observed the effectiveness of Wilkerson's Teen Center in Brooklyn. He noted that 90 percent of the addicts seeking deliverance were nominal Catholics and most became members of the Pentecostal churches by the time they completed the nine-month program at the Rehrersburg, Pennsylvania, farm. During McDonnell's two-week visit to Brooklyn he observed a "good deal of handclapping, some loud praying, occasionally some tears," but at no time did he judge the emotional level to be excessive. He rejected the hypothesis that mass hysteria was the cause of Teen Challenge's effectiveness. Instead, he concluded that the project was effective because the staff members had "taken seriously the imitation of Christ and because they live

12

Spirit-filled lives."[16] The former drug addicts absorbed the whole biblical message, which was "simple, direct, and eminently personal" as the Pentecostals believed it.

The star performer of the film adaptation of *The Cross and the Switchblade* is a Christian who speaks in tongues. Pat Boone, a former member of the Church of Christ, is among the many thousands of Protestant Neo-Pentecostals. In an interview by Walter Wagner in *Christian Life,* Boone related that although he is a graduate with honors from Columbia University he was "still an illiterate ignoramus when it comes to trying to speak to God." He didn't have the words to express what he felt within his inner self. Boone believes that through tongues, the prayer language, God is saying, "I'm bigger than you are, I understand your problems, and I will communicate with you in a way that maybe you wouldn't understand except inwardly and in a spiritual way. You won't understand it intellectually, but . . . I understand your needs and I will minister to them."[17] Unfortunately, speaking in tongues coupled with their belief in miraculous healings cost the Boones their membership in the Church of Christ. In a disciplinary action following a year's review, the Church of Christ "disfellowshipped" Shirley and Pat Boone in February of 1971.[18]

The insistence of the Pentecostals that all of the supernatural gifts listed by the apostle are available today sets them apart from other Christians who either deny this possibility or chronologically restrict the charismatic gifts to the apostles' century. Pentecostals believe their experiences to be part of the normal life for all Christians in all nations today. Their desire is to see all the supernatural gifts of the Holy Spirit renewed and properly functioning in the lives of contemporary Christians.

Father Kilian McDonnell is of the opinion that both Classic and Protestant Neo-Pentecostals simply do not

13

receive a fair hearing and, as a result, the public image of Pentecostalism has suffered. He feels that to the general public Pentecostalism "conjures up images of emotionalism, fanaticism, religious mania, illiteracy, messianic postures, credulity, and panting after miracles." But he is convinced that this public image "no more reflects the true nature of Pentecostalism than . . . the Inquisition [and] the massacre of St. Bartholomew's Day . . . reflect the essential quality of Catholicism, though all belong to Catholic history."[19]

In spite of all the obstacles, the Pentecostal movement is growing in some countries about ten times as fast as the historic churches. The goal of the Pentecostals is a lofty one. They are most fulfilled when their resurrected Lord is powerfully portrayed in their individual lives—lives which are becoming physically, psychologically, and spiritually whole.

II

Where It All Started

AS WE HAVE SEEN, contemporary Pentecostals do
not claim to possess a new set of beliefs originated by a
twentieth-century denomination. Rather, they maintain that their beliefs point back to the early church
and its exercise of the supernatural gifts of the Spirit.
These gifts were the order of the day, the norm,
not the exception. What were some of these experiences? What did happen on the Day of Pentecost and
succeeding days?

An explosion of 120 voices bursting forth in foreign
languages pierced the Jerusalem air at the startling
inauguration of the Christian Church. Literally thousands of pilgrims already in the city were irresistibly
drawn to this unexpected event. Not by formal invitation, but by the voluminous, multilingual praises of
the followers of Jesus, the man crucified less than two
months before and subsequently reported to be very
much alive. The New Testament book of Acts records
the details.

From time to time in the course of His forty post-
resurrection days while yet on earth, Jesus appeared to
His apostles and disciples. On one occasion more than
five hundred believers assembled in a single gathering.
The Gospels contain very few recorded conversations
during this brief period of time. It is important to note
that on the evening of the first Easter, when Jesus met
the disciples cringing in fear behind closed doors, he
said; "Peace be with you; as my Father hath sent me,

even so send I you." And when He had said this He
breathed on them, and said to them, "Receive the Holy
Spirit."[1] In this initial reception of the Holy Spirit the
Scripture does not declare that the disciples were
"baptized with the Holy Spirit" or that they were all
"filled with the Spirit." In His new relationship to the
disciples and believers, the Holy Spirit was now the
divine resident of each follower of Christ. But they had
yet to be endued with the Holy Spirit's power in a
dynamic baptism.

Keeping this in mind, notice that Christ's final declaration to the apostles forty days later, on the very day
he ascended, was in the form of both a command and
a promise: "He charged them not to depart from Jerusalem, but to wait for the promise of the Father, . . .
for John baptized with water, but before many days
you shall be baptized with the Holy Spirit.

"But you shall receive power when the Holy Spirit
has come upon you; and you shall be my witnesses in
Jerusalem and in all Judea and in Samaria and to the
end of the earth. And when he had said this, as they
were looking on, he was lifted up, and a cloud took
him out of their sight.

"Then they returned to Jerusalem from the mount
called Olivet, which is near Jerusalem, a sabbath day's
journey away; and when they had entered, they went
up to the upper room, where they were staying, Peter
and John and James and Andrew, Philip and Thomas,
Bartholomew and Matthew, James the son of Alphaeus
and Simon the Zealot and Judas the son of James. All
these with one accord devoted themselves to prayer,
together with the women and Mary the mother of
Jesus, and with his brothers."[2]

The matter of replacing Judas, the betrayer of Jesus,
was settled by the appointment of two candidates,
Justus and Matthias. After further prayer, "They cast

16

lots for them, and the lot fell on Matthias; and he was enrolled with the eleven apostles."[3]

Strangely enough, although Jesus had showed Himself to many hundreds of believers since His resurrection, only a small segment, a distinct minority, was found in that upper room. This prayer band was composed of 120 people who found faith in their hearts and the time in their schedules to tarry in Jerusalem. Theirs is the distinct honor of composing the charter membership of Christians.

Thus on the day of Pentecost the Christian Church was presented to the world as a company of Spirit-baptized men and women. But careful preparation for its presentation had been going on for more than three years—a transitional period which was to bring down the curtain on the Old Testament system of revealed commands and promises which long had regulated Israel's human affairs. Now New Testament grace and truth were to appear: "For the law was given through Moses; grace and truth came through Jesus Christ."[4]

During this time of transition Jesus had summoned His twelve apostles, giving them power over unclean spirits and power to heal every sickness and disease. He dispatched them to the lost of Israel alone, instructing them to preach that the kingdom of heaven was at hand, and further to "Heal the sick, raise the dead, cleanse lepers, cast out demons. You received without pay, give without pay."[5]

Later, the Lord commissioned seventy other disciples, dispatching them in pairs to every town and place He intended to visit. Their marching orders were to heal the sick in the cities that received them and to proclaim the kingdom of God.

When the seventy returned they were overjoyed. Flushed with success, they exclaimed, "Lord, even the demons are subject to us in your name!"[6] The disciples, or learners, were reminded rather to rejoice that their names were written in heaven. In effect, Christ was teaching them and His future followers that the power of God in a ministry of miracles and instant success must always be tempered by the humility and centrality of the cross. Their new life, heavenly citizenship, and hope beyond the grave were made possible only through Christ's death and resurrection.

They learned this lesson well, for their successes were counterbalanced with dismal failures. Topping all their errors and failures in the school of discipleship was the haunting memory of their cowardly retreat when Jesus was arrested in the Garden of Gethsemane. True, Peter had tried to split the skull of Malchus as he clumsily wielded a sword in defense of Jesus. But this same Peter cursed and swore as he denied any knowledge of his Lord shortly thereafter. A hasty trial was followed by the ignominious crucifixion of Jesus of Nazareth outside the city limits of Jerusalem. But the disciples' paralysis, fear, and failure were turned into a tremendous triumph because of an empty tomb.

Doubts and despair were replaced by new hope and expectation as they met their Master, very much alive in His tangible resurrected splendor. The first to feel the warm glow of forgiveness was the impatient, impetuous apostle, Simon Peter.

"Simon, do you love me more than these?" asked Jesus, referring to the disciples. Burning with shame as he recalled his boast of loyalty to the death, Peter painfully accepted three such pointed questions from his Lord, and his quiet, affirmative answers served to erase his threefold denial. Happily restored, the fisherman was present in that upper room on that famous Sunday, the Day of Pentecost.

The Day of Pentecost was one of the three annual Jewish feast days in which all Hebrew males within traveling distance made a pilgrimage to the Holy City.

The Jewish followers of Jesus who gathered in the upper room made up the gamut of human temperaments, but despite the variety of personalities there was a unity of purpose. What followed was a unique evidence common to each one seated in this sacred gathering: "When the day of Pentecost had come, they were all together in one place. And suddenly a sound came from heaven like the rush of a mighty wind, and it filled all the house where they were sitting. And there appeared to them tongues as of fire, distributed and resting on each one of them. And they were all filled with the Holy Spirit and began to speak in other tongues, as the Spirit gave them utterance."[7]

The biblical account is clear. They did not speak in tongues *in order* to be filled with the Spirit. They spoke in tongues *as a result of being filled.* No one attempted to mechanize the experience by introducing prompting techniques such as "repeat after me." No, their minds were neither on tongues nor on a baptism, but on the Baptizer Jesus. Christ, the risen Lord, had become their Baptizer as prophesied by John. It was none other than the Spirit of God, the Third Person of the Trinity, who supplied the patterns of speech which passed over their tongues.

Mary, the mother of Jesus, spoke in other tongues. James and John, volatile sons of thunder, spoke in tongues. Thomas, dismissing his doubts, likewise spoke in another language. Matthew, formerly a despised tax-collector, was spiritually enriched by this phenomenal occurrence, as was guileless Nathaniel. Multiply the uninhibited prayers and praises a hundredfold and it is not difficult to understand why a massive audience quickly gathered and surrounded the upper room asking, "What does it mean?"

Boldly facing the people, especially the scoffers in the crowd who sarcastically remarked, "They have had too much new wine," Peter reminded them it was only

19

mid-morning. The exuberant Christians were not drunk as some supposed. On the contrary, the disciples were experiencing the initial fulfillment of the prophecy of the Old Testament prophet Joel, who had foretold that a spiritual "latter rain" was destined to fall upon all flesh. In that upper room the Spirit was saturating them. The overflow experience brought praises to God from their lips in languages they never before learned. These tongues were readily understood by the pilgrims in Jerusalem representing many countries far and near. It startled them. Peter then stood up to preach in the common language understood by all. So powerful and persuasive was the new Peter under the anointing and enduement of the Spirit of God that his words struck as an arrow, leaving the crowd conscience-stricken. In response to his pungent, provocative message the audience cried out to Peter and the rest of the apostles, "Brothers, what can we do?" Peter then answered: "Repent, and be baptized every one of you in the name of Jesus Christ for the forgiveness of your sins; and you shall receive the gift of the Holy Spirit. For the promise is to you and your children and to all that are far off, every one whom the Lord our God calls to him."[8]

The results were amazing! At the close of the sermon on that memorable Day of Pentecost, three thousand persons accepted the good news of Jesus Christ's substitutionary death, burial, and triumphant resurrection. They now became eager candidates for both water baptism and the baptism in the Holy Spirit. Having been witnesses to the supernatural and having heard the Scriptural basis for what had just transpired, they eagerly responded to Christ's Baptism in the Spirit, unconditionally promised to all believers. The identical promise was given to all people who would accept Christ in the generations and centuries to come.

The Book of Acts should be read and reread by all

of us who profess Christianity but are prone to be
unconcerned or compromising Christians. If we would
catch the fire and faith—the dynamic love—of those
forerunners of the Gospel, watch out world! Their list
of accomplishments is staggering, yet it merely suggests
the scope of their miraculous ministry to the men and
women of their generation.

Here are a few examples—the healing of a man lame
from his mother's womb, the instant deliverance of a
demoniac, the deacon who forgave his accusers as they
stoned him to death, the cataclysmic conversion of the
most dreaded persecutor of Christians, his blindness
healed when a layman prayed for him, Gentiles accepting a risen Christ and the new Christian religion, the
beaten and imprisoned apostles blending voices in
praise to God at midnight, the voluntary book-burning
which shook the sorcerers' economy, the courage of
Christians occasionally crowded by admirers but more
often threatened by mobs. Examples could be multiplied indefinitely.

The power of God radically transformed sinners to
saints, caused the blind to see, the deaf to hear, the
lame to walk, the diseased to be made whole, and even
the dead to be raised. Under the administration and
empowerment of God, the Holy Spirit, Christians
became channels of the supernatural. This becomes
unmistakably clear when we realize that the supernatural events recounted in the New Testament Book
of Acts could be nothing other than the dramatic acts
of the Holy Spirit Himself manifested through the
disciples in the infant Christian Church. And in a very
real sense the same Holy Spirit is producing new
chapters in our day through contemporary Christians
fully dedicated to serving Jesus Christ.

This exciting Book of Acts introduces a faithful
deacon named Philip, suddenly cast into the role of a
dynamic evangelist to share the mind-changing news of

21

Jesus' death and resurrection. Philip's Spirit-filled ministry in Samaria was so successful that people repented and were brought to God. Divine healing was brought to the sick and the afflicted, demons were cast out, and the long-standing prejudices between the Samaritans and the Jews were temporarily shelved. Philip's leaving Jerusalem in the first place had been a strange thing. Great persecution against the Christians had suddenly erupted and it became too dangerous to remain in the Holy City. The followers of Jesus at this time were the special targets of the misguided zeal of a certain Saul of Tarsus, a persecuting Pharisee absolutely convinced that he was carrying out God's will. The Christians were scattered in all directions, but by preaching the Gospel wherever they stopped they were obeying their Lord's Great Commission to go into all the world and propagate the good news.

It was under these circumstances that Philip arrived in Samaria. It was then as routine for Jews and Samaritans to enjoy each other's company as it is for Israelis and Arabs to attempt socializing today. No doubt the miraculous deliverance of suffering humanity which followed Philip's preaching of the Scriptures played a significant role in pulling down the walls of intolerance. So prevalent were the healings that accompanied his mission that "there was great rejoicing throughout that city."[9]

In Jerusalem the apostles learned of Samaria's spiritual awakening and dispatched Peter and John to the scene of action. Shortly after their arrival, the two Jewish apostles prayed, laying hands on the people of Samaria who had welcomed the deacon's message. The expectant Samaritans promptly received a visible manifestation of the Holy Spirit, for it is the consensus of Bible commentators that these Samaritans were speaking in other tongues! Before this event took place, healings and exorcisms were readily apparent. An

22

opportunist named Simon the Magician was so impressed by the striking results of the Samaritan tongue-speakers after the laying on of the apostles' hands that he offered them a sum of money for the key to this power. His selfish attempt to duplicate the phenomenon was futile. Peter pulled no punches as he declared, "A curse upon you and upon your money, for thinking that God's free gift can be bought with gold."[10] To this day the word "simony" is used to describe an attempt to purchase a spiritual gift or office.

Another account of glossolalia is lucidly depicted in the tenth chapter of Acts. A Roman military officer, a centurion named Cornelius, invited the not too ecumenically minded Peter to grace his home in order to introduce the Christian message before a receptive audience. That Peter accepted this invitation may seem strange, for if the Jews were loathe to have any dealings with the Samaritans, who were half-Jewish, they most certainly avoided contamination through contact with the *goyim,* or Gentiles. Peter's action, however, is explained by the fact that when he had been engaged in prayer at noontime he received a most disturbing vision in which God was directing him to eat animals considered unclean by all orthodox Jews. He recoiled at the very thought. Perplexed and pondering over the implications of this vision, he was interrupted by two men seeking him at the door. Representing their captain, the soldiers invited Peter to the centurion's household in Caesarea. Sensing God in this, Peter relinquished his ingrained religious prejudices and agreed to accompany them.

Once Peter arrived, he tried to forget the discomfort of a Jew in the midst of Gentiles and began preaching to Cornelius' family and friends. Soon he was glad he came, for the attentive, avid congregation hung on his every word. Suddenly the unexpected happened. It must have shocked Peter. He was cut short, unable to complete his sermon, for as he proclaimed the forgiveness of sins through Jesus Christ's substitutionary death and shared the report of a Savior who had come forth alive from the grave, "The Holy Spirit fell on all who heard the word. And the believers from among the circumcised who came with Peter were amazed, because the gift of the Holy Spirit had been poured out even on the Gentiles. For they heard them speaking in tongues and extolling God."[11]

The Jews who had accompanied Peter were as astonished as he, but without hesitation they unanimously accepted the validity of the experience. Why? Because of the supernatural sign, the divine barrier-breaker which could not be denied or dismissed—the congregation was yielding praise in God-given tongues! It was exactly as they themselves had praised God on the Day of Pentecost. Call it a Gentile Pentecost if you will, it certainly served to remove the invisible sign which read "For Jewish Members Only." How else were these Hebrew Pentecostals to cope with the jubilant, ecstatic Italians? Peter then offered a rhetorical question: "Can any one forbid water for baptizing these people who have received the Holy Spirit just as we have?"[12]

Even when changes are God-ordained and divinely directed, religious traditions prove difficult to abandon. Upon Peter's return to Jerusalem, explanations were very much in order. Happy and relieved that he had witnesses who could verify his fantastic story, Peter simply and logically reasoned, "As I began to speak, the Holy Spirit fell on them just as on us at the beginning. And I remembered the word of the Lord, how he said, 'John baptized with water, but you shall be baptized with the Holy Spirit.' If then God gave the same gift to them as he gave to us when we believed in the Lord Jesus Christ, who was I that I could withstand God?"[13]

There it was. Anyone who wanted to persist in the status quo which excluded everyone outside the commonwealth of Israel would have to argue with the Holy Spirit Himself. Instead of debate and dissension, these early Christians broke forth in a doxology. The Gentiles were definitely in on the charismatic blessing. A contemporary analogy may be drawn as Roman Catholics in ever increasing numbers enter into the Pentecostal experience to the bewilderment and wonder of the earlier twentieth-century recipients, the Classic Pentecostals.

Another clear example of supernatural speaking in tongues occurred under the Apostle Paul's ministry. Formerly a terror to the Christians, Paul was now a Pentecostal leader as he met a group of disciples from Ephesus. In the course of the conversation, the apostle asked, "Did you receive the Holy Spirit when you believed?" He learned that they knew only of John's baptism: they were completely ignorant of the existence of the Holy Spirit as a Person and knew nothing of Pentecost.

But with hearts already prepared, the twelve Ephesians readily accepted Paul's teaching about Jesus and the Holy Spirit. So responsive were they that when Paul laid hands upon them in prayer, "The Holy Spirit came on them; and they spoke with tongues and prophesied." [14]

These are four recorded examples of different groups who received the Pentecostal experience in the first century; they were baptized in the Spirit and they spoke in tongues. They were among the first, but they were not God's special favorites. They were earnest Christians, intensely devoted to Jesus Christ. The supernatural multipurposed gifts of the Holy Spirit functioned frequently in and through their lives.

The supernatural gifts of the word of knowledge and the word of wisdom provided lucid solutions to perplexing problems. Both these gifts are miraculous manifestations of the Spirit, not to be compared with the efforts of human reasoning and deduction. The decision to receive Gentile converts without imposing the rite of circumcision upon them is an example.[15] Prophetical exhortations reinforced the truths of Scripture and in some cases foretold times of persecution, as did Agabus to the apostle Paul in Caesarea. He dramatized his prophecy by taking Paul's belt, tying up his own hands and feet with it, and stating: "This is what the Holy Spirit says: The owner of this belt will be tied up in this way by the Jews in Jerusalem, and they will hand him over to the Gentiles." The believers who heard the prophecy begged the apostle not to go to Jerusalem, but although Paul accepted the validity of the prophecy he felt it was God's will that he go. He explained, "What are you doing, crying like this and breaking my heart? I am ready not only to be tied up in Jerusalem but even to die for the sake of the Lord Jesus." Unable to dissuade him, they acquiesced, saying, "May the Lord's will be done."[16]

By the empowerment of the Holy Spirit, the disciples were able to reproduce the works which Jesus performed when He walked with them. They healed the sick and wrought miracles in Jesus' name as they exercised mountain-moving faith. Even Tabitha and Eutychus were raised from the dead![17] The demon-possessed were set free as the command to "Come out" was issued by these Spirit-filled men, who were able to detect the presence of demons. This was the gift of discernment of spirits. Exorcism was not uncommon, and at times repercussions followed. Consider the example of the seven sons of a Jewish High Priest named Sceva. The nineteenth chapter of Acts indicates that these men were not Christian believers but were attempting to exorcise evil spirits with the following formula: "I command you in the name of Jesus, whom

Paul preaches." One day they faced a rebuttal from an evil spirit who answered through the possessed person saying, "I know Jesus and I know about Paul; but you—who are you?" The Scripture goes on to say, "The man who had the evil spirit in him attacked them with such violence that he defeated them. They all ran away from his house wounded and with their clothes torn off." Both Jews and Gentiles living in Ephesus heard about this and were filled with fear, but "the name of the Lord Jesus was given greater honor. . . . Many of those who had practiced magic brought their books together and burned them in the presence of everyone. They added up the price of the books and the total came to fifty thousand dollars. In this powerful way the word of the Lord kept spreading and growing stronger."[18]

On another occasion the apostle Paul and his companion Silas were confronted by a fortuneteller who had earned a great deal for her masters. The girl dogged their steps for many days shouting, "These men are servants of the Most High God! They announce to you how you can be saved!" The words were commendable but the Satanic source was recognized by means of the gift of the discernment of spirits. This disturbed Paul no end until he "became so upset that he turned around and said to the spirit, 'In the name of Jesus Christ I order you to come out of her!'" The deliverance was immediate. "The spirit went out of her that very moment." When the owners realized that their pawn for lucrative gain was gone, "they grabbed Paul and Silas and dragged them to the authorities in the public square" on a trumped-up charge that they were trouble-makers teaching illegal customs. When the crowd joined the attack against them, the Roman officials "tore the clothes off Paul and Silas, and ordered them to be whipped. After a severe beating they were thrown into jail. . . ."[19]

The Bible makes it clear that the supernatural minis-

27

try did not always pave the way for simple solutions to the problems of the day. For instance, when the Christians at Corinth received an added dimension in their worship by the exercise of speaking in tongues and the interpretation of tongues, they also found themselves faced with new problems of spiritual pride and undisciplined emotionalism. But these were the results of the abuse and not the use of the vocal gifts of the Spirit. The apostle Paul outlined clear instructions for the proper use of these gifts so that the utterances would edify and not horrify those listening. Unless the foreign tongues were followed by interpretations, the tongues-speakers were to be silent. And a limit of three utterances in tongues with interpretations was set for each service.[20]

The apostle encouraged the proper exercise of glossolalia in the church and gave no carte blanche for the elimination of tongues. On the contrary, he said "Do not forbid speaking in tongues," and "I thank God that I speak in tongues more than you all!"[21] If Paul spoke in tongues more than all the Christians in Corinth, where excesses were admitted, then this reveals the valuable use of tongues in private devotions as well as in public services. The apostle tells us why. "One who speaks in a tongue speaks not to men, but to God."[22] The charismatic Christian is strengthened in such a devotional practice. But in public worship tongues must be followed by the companion gift of the interpretation of tongues so that not only the speakers but all the hearers will be edified. Paul was being more than a cautious Christian when he insisted that everything be done decently and in an orderly way. Desiring supernatural gifts not only to operate in his own life as a charismatic Christian, he also urged and encouraged other Christians to exercise the supernatural gifts in an atmosphere of love and understanding. The charismatics were not puppets, unable to

28

exercise will and won't power. Tongues and prophesies could be controlled. They were subject to the wills of the speakers, who could remain silent or speak at the proper time for the benefit of all present.

Ira Jay Martin III, a non-Pentecostal, believes there were two extreme types among those Corinthians who publicly spoke in tongues. On the one hand was a transformed person with an improved moral standard of living; on the other was a proud, boastful, and conceited person. Martin feels that the majority of the glossolalists in the Apostolic church were not the kind of persons who "intentionally sought the gift for its own sake as a manifestation of divine favor and human approval." He draws a sharp and interesting contrast between the person motivated by God's love—the "Agape Christian"—and the "Glossolalia Christian," by which he means the negative extremist. Taking Paul's famous "Love" chapter (I Corinthians 13) and applying the instructions given in Chapters 12 and 14 to the conceited extremists, Martin comes up with some startling contrasts.

> *Love is longsuffering*—but the glossolalist is impatient;
> *Love is kind*—but the glossolalist is unmerciful in his feeling of superiority to those who call themselves Christians; but who cannot "speak in tongues";
> *Love is not jealous*—but the glossolalist is envious of much in his desire to be superior to others;
> *Love is not boastful*—but the glossolalist boasts of his gift and is proud;
> *Love acts not unbecomingly*—but the glossolalist loses all control and moral restraint;
> *Love seeks not its own*—but the glossolalist seeks the respect and honor of men, and especially his fellow Christians;

Love is not provoked—but the glossolalist cannot stand criticism;

Love rejoices not in unrighteousness, but rejoices in the truth—but the glossolalist rejoices in his ability to speak with tongues, which has no profound truth to reveal or to teach;

Love bears all things, believes all things, hopes all things, endures all things—but the glossolalist offers only his apparent gift of tongues, and knows nothing of Christian courage, patience, tolerance, or willingness to suffer in behalf of others.[23]

Surely Paul did not suggest a mutually exclusive choice: he did not mean choose tongues *or* love, but accept tongues, prophecy, miracles, healings, *and* love—the love of God shed abroad in Christian lives. All these gifts were made possible by the Holy Spirit Who was resident in the lives of the disciples. Through them, God wished to display not only the power of Christ but His compassion to the people of their generation. The transformation in their lives was so great that these mortal men challenge all twentieth-century Christians to duplicate the depth of their devotion and deeds.

Billy Graham put it this way: "They had no Bibles, no seminaries, nor Bible schools. No radios or telephones. No printing presses. No churches. Nothing! However, they turned the world upside down in one generation. What did they have? They had an experience with the living Christ. They had the filling of the Holy Spirit."[24]

III

Supernatural Traces
Through the Centuries

AS THE SPIRIT-FILLED Christians continued to
multiply, their phenomenal growth posed an increasingly serious challenge to the pagan faiths of the Roman
Empire. Christianity was banned by the Roman state,
which wanted no rivals for the allegiance of its subjects.
Christians refused to offer incense on the altars dedicated to the genius of the Roman emperors during the
imperial period from Caesar Augustus to Constantine,
confirming suspicions of their basic disloyalty to the
state.

Persecuted by their own parent Judaic religion, the
Christians continued the struggle for their existence
during periods of pressure from Nero's reign to A.D.
313. General and violent persecutions began under
Emperor Decius in A.D. 250, when he ordered each
citizen to obtain a certificate called *libellus* from
government officials. This document affirmed that its
holder had sacrificed to the emperor's image. Multitudes of Christians who refused were painfully tortured. They would not serve two masters. Some
surrendered, while others bribed officials to issue them
the *libellus* without offering the sacrifice at the Roman
altars. In the eyes of the loyal, suffering Christians
these defectors were apostate, and when the persecution ended, schisms arose in the churches regarding
their readmission to the church.

During the reign of emperors like Diocletian, the
persecutions reached inhuman heights. This ruler fed

31

Christians to the lions, burned them alive, and tortured them in the most sadistic ways known to the empire. Diocletian not only destroyed the churches, he burned the Scriptures as well. Finally, however, the climate changed and Christianity was granted toleration by the edict of Milan issued by Emperor Constantine in A.D. 313. The Church's lost properties were restored and Sunday was made a legal holiday. The emperor built new churches and ordered others built at the expense of the pagans. It wasn't long before Christianity was declared the imperial state religion and all loyal subjects were expected to become members of the Christian Church. In protest against this amazing turn of events, which amounted to a forced Christianization, many believers withdrew themselves from all worldly contact for fear of being smothered by the garlands of prestige and popularity. More than all else, they wanted to preserve the spirituality of the Church and the growth of monasteries was the result.

The need for an authoritative list of writings of the New Testament, a canon, became evident after Diocletian's burning of Scriptures and during the rise of Gnosticism. The Gnostics commonly held that Jesus was ushered onto the stage of human history as an apparition masquerading in a body and that He did not actually come in the flesh. The Gnostics also maintained that the Jehovah of the Old Testament was an inferior being and that the Old Testament must be rejected as useless.

In the second century the Gnostic view was also advocated by a rich Roman shipowner named Marcion, who repudiated the continued use of the Old Testament and held that its conception of God was misleading. In his attempt to provide a scripture for his followers, Marcion deleted all passages linking Jesus with the God of the Old Testament. He also broke away from the Church and organized a new congregation. The Chris-

32

tian Church, convinced that Jesus came to fulfill and
not to destroy the Old Testament, found it necessary
to point out clearly that these teachings violated the
plain meaning of Scripture. Marcion's error emphasized
the need to supply a canon which could be accepted
with confidence.

The criterion for the work to be included in the New
Testament canon was this: Does the writing agree with
the teachings handed down from the apostles? Irenaeus,
Bishop of Lyons, wrote *Against the Heresies,* in which
he set forth this guideline: Teachings not in agreement
with those of the apostles' as transmitted in the Gospels
and in the Epistles were to be excluded. By the close
of the second century most of this canon was recognized as authoritative and these writings became the
doctrinal norm. But it wasn't until A.D. 367 that they
were fully sanctioned.

Were the supernatural gifts of the Holy Spirit withdrawn from the Christian Church during these difficult
centuries of persecution and transition? I do not
believe so. Many Christians living in various parts of
the world today believe that the miracles in the early
Church were displayed for a brief period of time—only
long enough to substantiate the Gospel message. They
maintain that when the New Testament canon was
completed, there was no further need for the supernatural gifts of the Spirit and they simply ceased to
exist. But Church historians have uncovered, admittedly
in meager measure, miraculous events that occurred
during the early centuries of Christianity—a clear indi-
cation that the supernatural gifts of the Holy Spirit
never did cease. Bernard Bresson mentions more than
twenty charismatic movements and sects between the
late second century and the middle nineteenth, and
the *Encyclopaedia Britannica* maintains that glossolalia
"recurs in Christian revivals of every age."[1]

Although legality, prestige, and secular power lulled

33

the Church to sleep, from time to time seasons of spiritual awakening and revival stirred believers within a slumbering Church which had forsaken the exercise of the gifts of the Spirit. Renewals would cause it to come alive again with the power and compassion of Jesus. Today these same supernatural gifts are bursting forth once more, crossing all denominational lines and major branches of Christendom.

Many Protestants who are chronically in doctrinal disagreement with each other somehow manage to stand firmly together when it comes to the question of their opposition to the Pentecostal Movement. They are quick to quote the words of Apostle Paul when he addressed the Corinthian Church and said, "Prophecies shall fail and tongues shall cease."[2] But they have a blind spot concerning the conclusion of the same statement, which goes on to declare that "knowledge shall vanish away." The apostle indicated that all three— prophecy, tongues, and knowledge—will terminate when the perfect One returns—which is understood by most evangelicals to mean the personal return of Jesus Christ.

The meager historical references to the supernatural gifts of the Spirit beyond the infancy of the Christian Church have led many to conclude that the decline of these gifts was inevitable. Upon the completion of the New Testament canon, the argument goes, the spiritual gifts became superfluous; they were no longer necessary, for their purpose in launching the Church's phenomenal growth and proliferation had been fully served. Some go so far as to say that the continued practice of the gifts would have proved detrimental to the Church because the fanaticism displayed by overzealous participants would have frightened away potential converts. Carry this logic a step further and the result is a host of miracle-denying Christians who have been brainwashed to reject any and all contemporary appearances of the supernatural gifts of the Spirit as nothing more than the emotional outbursts of the naive and misguided or the craftiness of charlatans. Contemporary Pentecostals prefer to advance the theory once proposed by Methodism's founder, John Wesley. He suggested that the supernatural gifts diminished because of the decline of love and the subsequent dead formalism of a frigid Church that rejected all such manifestations.

The writings of men called the Church Fathers enable us to trace the continuity of the spiritual gifts in the second and third centuries. "It is possible now to see among us women and men who possess gifts of the Spirit of God," stated Justin Martyr (ca. 130-200) who found it necessary to remind doubters of his day who asserted that the gifts had disappeared after the death of the last disciples.[3] Bishop Irenaeus (115-202), who studied under Polycarp, a disciple of the Apostle John, shared this personal observation: "In like manner we do also hear many brethren in the Church, who possess prothetic gifts, and who through the Spirit speak in all kinds of languages."[4]

In an effort to recapture the supernatural manifestations recorded in the apostolic church, a Phrygian named Montanus stirred up a wave of enthusiasm for a Pentecostal renewal, and the result was a sect called the Montanists which flourished for several centuries, beginning about A.D. 154. As late as the sixth century a Montanist group still existed in North Africa. The followers of Montanus, who called themselves Pneumatics because they were possessed by the Pneuma, a Greek word referring to the Spirit, were determined to escape the clammy hand of institutionalism. Montanus encouraged them to express their spiritual longings freely and without inhibition. Unfortunately, as might have been expected, this action precipitated the kind of services in which there were wrong emphases and harmful excesses. Their intentions were noble, but their practices became bizarre. Apollinaris, Bishop of Hierapolis (ca. 170), described Montanus as "one beside himself, babbling and uttering strange things, prophesying contrary to the custom of the Church."[5] Eusebius Pamphilus pictured Montanus as one "wrought up into a certain kind of frenzy and irregular ecstasy, raving, and speaking and uttering strange things."[6]

Tensions arose over the question of whether to accept these dramatic prophecies as valid. If the Church leaders acquiesced, they risked the loss of their influence; conceivably a movement like this could place the prophets in a position of greater esteem and honor than the bishops. The decision was obvious: Montanism was declared schismatic and ultimately was labeled a heresy by synods and gifted church writers alike.

Montanus was also charged with the heresy of vaunting himself as God, because he used the pronoun "I" when he exercised the supernatural vocal gifts such as the interpretation of tongues and prophecy. It is quite likely that Montanus was a passive human instrument moved by the Spirit of God when he engaged in these utterances. If the accusation leveled against Montanus were used today, I'm afraid that contemporary Pentecostals would be equally guilty, for many use the personal pronoun "I" instead of "He" when referring to God as they interpret tongues and prophesy. There is no attempt, however, to play God.

A Roman lawyer before conversion, Tertullian (ca. 160-220), the highly esteemed Church Father, emerged as the most famous convert of Montanism and became its chief apologist during the second-century revival. He objected to and challenged apostolic succession and ecclesiasticism by maintaining that the power conferred on the Apostle Peter by Christ was also passed on to all who were filled with the Holy Spirit. While acknowledging the presence of spiritual gifts, he nevertheless was cautious and wise. Tertullian required that all new revelations be in accord with the traditional faith of the Christian Church. Opposing bishops, however, could see no spiritual value in the movement and the Montanists, weighed in the balances, were found wanting. They were charged with violating the spirit of orthodoxy by encouraging dangerous excesses of fanaticism.

It was at this early time in church history that Origen (ca. 185 - ca. 254), a great Christian scholar, wrote about the diminishing signs of the gifts of the Holy Spirit. His definition of speaking in tongues included not only the utterance of a strange language, but also the speaker's knowledge of that language for the purpose of preaching and spreading the Gospel. This understanding of the function of the supernatural gift of tongues was also reflected by the Church fathers Jerome and Augustine. The great majority of today's Pentecostals, while not limiting the sovereignty of God, refuse to accept this interpretation of the tongues gift. Why? Because the Scriptural accounts of speaking in tongues never indicated that the speakers were preaching. Rather, they were praising and glorifying God in prayer.[7] Contemporary instances of the utterance of tongues heard by foreigners in their own native language have occurred during services among Pentecostals. The glossolalic speaker usually is surprised to learn that his utterance in tongues was understood. He is more delighted to learn that its effect has been to sweep away all doubts and unbelief, pointing to the reality of Jesus Christ. Often conscience-stricken, the hearer is ready to seek God in earnest.

Following the legalization of the Christian faith and its favored position as the state religion in fourth-century Rome, the spiritual gifts apparently faded into oblivion as far as recorded history is concerned. John Chrysostom and Augustine flatly state that the spiritual gifts were no longer observed.

Although legendary layers have been added to some of the accounts of the medieval church, men such as Anthony of Padua (1195-1231), the monk Vincent Ferrier (1350-1419), Francis Xavier (1506-1552), and others are mentioned as having the gift of tongues. They were enabled to utilize these languages, received instantaneously from God, in their missionary endeavors among foreign people.

The historian Sauer makes the sweeping declaration that Martin Luther, the leader of the Protestant Reformation, "was a prophet, evangelist, speaker in tongues, interpreter, and in one person, endowed with all the gifts of the Spirit."[8] Evidence of this from Luther's own writing, however, is nowhere cited by Sauer.

During the sixteenth century the glossolalia appeared among the Camisards in France. Under pressure of being forced back into the Roman Catholic Church after the revocation of the Edict of Nantes in 1685, the Camisards exhibited frequent outbursts of ecstatic phenomena. "An infectious ecstasy seized people of all ages and both sexes. Children of the tenderest years were subjects (Little Prophets of the Cevennes) of the most extraordinary manifestations." For instance, among these French Protestants (Huguenots) Henry M. Baird observed the following: "From the mouths of those that were little more than babies, came texts of Scripture and discourses in good and intelligible French, such as they never used in their conscious hours."

Not only children, but feeble-minded people prophesied among the Huguenots. Jacques Mazel mentions a woman, considered almost idiotic, who uttered discourses of so elevated a character and in such good French that her hearers said, "The ass of Balaam has a mouth of gold."[9]

George Fox, the leader of the Quakers of the seventeenth century, recognized prophecies and tongues in Quaker prayer sessions, which were known as waiting meetings. While silently waiting on the Lord, members of Fox's meeting often received the outpouring of the Spirit and "our tongues loosed and our mouths opened and we spake with new tongues as the Spirit gave us utterance."

The relatively inconspicuous trickle of the charismatic stream continued on into the eighteenth century. At this time Methodism's founder, John Wesley, made frequent references in his Journal to various phenomena often observable in his services. Wesley actually approved of a period of "uncontrolled laughter" which seized a Bristol congregation. He saw no barrier to the activity of the Holy Spirit in a variety of emotional outbursts in his meetings.[10] When glossolalia was experienced among his converts, Wesley defended the utterances. One of his preachers, Thomas Walsh, entered these words in his diary: "This morning the Lord gave me a language I knew not of, raising my soul to Him in a wondrous manner."

In the early nineteenth century a London pastor of keen intellect and great ability learned of the contemporary operation of the gifts of the Holy Spirit in the British Isles. An honor student at the University of Edinburgh, Edward Irving was an eloquent speaker and commanding in appearance, dramatized by his height of six feet four inches. He drew the most famous people of London to hear him although he never preached for less than two hours. Nonmembers had to secure tickets six weeks in advance in order to hear him. Once when Irving was out of the city preaching in Kirkcaldy, the building was so crowded that one of the galleries collapsed causing the death of eighteen and the serious injury of many others. He conducted open-air services in some cities where as many as 12,000 could distinctly hear his powerful voice. Irving preached before 5:00 A.M. and after 9:00 P.M. in order to reach workingmen during their free time.

For five months Irving and his people had been praying for the return of the gifts of the Spirit. His 6:30 A.M. church prayer meetings drew large crowds of earnest Christians and prayers for the renewal of the gifts were constantly offered. At first they were expressed only in the private services, but one Sunday as Irving was preaching, a quiet woman rose and hurried to the vestry. She closed the door and began speaking in tongues. Many such incidents followed and the London papers were full of jibes at Irving's expense.

Fully convinced that the gifts were the work of the Holy Spirit, Irving permitted tongues, interpretation of tongues, and prophecy at his services. Although he himself never spoke in tongues, he described the utterance as one "with a power, and a strength and fulness, and sometimes rapidity of voice altogether different from that of the person's ordinary utterance in any mood . . . quite supernatural."[11]

Henry Drummond, a member of Parliament for over twelve years, not only believed in the reality of the spiritual manifestations at Edward Irving's services but was himself a participant. During family prayers one day Drummond felt a great anxiety for the souls of men. ". . . I feel a grief of the Spirit which must be experienced to be understood. I am . . . as conscious as I am of my existence, of a power within me, yet distinct from me; not using me as a mere machine, but bending my will and affections to love, to glorify Jesus; giving a peace and joy, and love to God and man, passing all understanding."[12]

Irving's church could not understand. They could not accept the "rantings and the jabbling and the dabbling of what they called hysterical women and the ravings of lunatic men as being that of the work of the Holy Spirit."[13] The church turned upon Irving with holy horror. It did not take long for the Presbytery to summon Irving to answer charges concerning what they considered to be the shocking, untoward conduct he permitted to be displayed in his church. Irving was told he was to be judged by his denomination's rules, without reference to the Bible. He was instructed to renounce his newly adopted doctrines or be defrocked. Despite the fact that he personally had not experienced the glossolalia, he refused to comply with this ultimatum and as a result found the Regent Square Church closed to him and his tongue-speakers. Irving was expelled from the church, despite the custom that once installed in a Scottish pulpit a minister could not be deposed except for some flagrant sin. Mere drunkenness would have been overlooked. The Regents Square Church charged Irving with allowing lay people, including nonmembers and females, to take part in public services and with appointing times for the suspension of the usual order of worship for the exercise of "gifts."

The verdict was severely criticized by the leading lawyers in the country. The Sunday after the trial two hundred new members were to be received into the Church. A large number of people assembled for the early morning prayer meeting but found the doors locked and a notice declaring the church would not be opened again until other arrangements were made.[14]

Edward Irving has mistakenly been called the founder of the Catholic Apostolic Church; indeed, many of its adherents were called Irvingites after his death. Actually, he had no share in the formation of this new sect, and was never a prominent participant, but he was certainly the most celebrated man to enter its communion after his own church had deposed him. Many of his former parishoners eventually identified themselves with the Catholic Apostolic Church after it was established and flourishing.

In a short time the Catholic Apostolic Church had thirty congregations totaling six thousand members.[15] Irving's prestige enabled the new charismatic group to gain serious consideration and investigation. Devout author Thomas Erskine of Linlathen mingled with them for forty days and stated that he believed the work was of God. But he later withdrew blanket support, questioning not the validity of the spiritual gifts but the flagrant abuse of them by the Irvingites.

The Irvingite movement differed from other movements in that its leaders hoped to build a new church order based on charismatic utterances and related gifts, including the apostolic offices. They believed that all the gifts of the Holy Spirit were the permanent possession of the Christian Church, withheld only because of human unfaithfulness on the part of unconcerned Christians.

Unfortunately, the Irvingites placed excessive emphasis upon tongues and prophecies. They also embraced doctrinal deviations such as a dogmatic certainty of Christ's return to earth within their lifetime. The attorney Robert Baxter broke with the movement after unfulfilled, and therefore false, prophecies left him disillusioned. In 1833 he published a refutation of these prophecies. The Catholic Apostolic Church was repudiated by Christians in Britain, most of whom condemned the obvious abuses of the gifts. The Irvingites, even as the earlier Montanists, protested unsuccessfully against church traditionalism and religious forms which to them were void of the presence of God. They longed for the spiritual liberty and power enjoyed by the Christians of the first century. Evidently they were unable to draw the line between liberty and license.

A crushed man, Irving's days were numbered. "The reproaches of my brethren have broken my heart," he said, little realizing that upon his death in 1834 at the age of forty-two the very brethren who deposed him would honor him with a burial within the crypt of the Scottish Glasgow Cathedral. His successor at Regents Square made the following statement in the church:

". . . In each controversy he took what he believed to be the Lord's side; and in every audience spoke clearly out what he believed to be God's truth. . . ."[16] Ironically, within thirty years the gift of tongues was no longer manifested among the Irvingites but was replaced by the ritualism they earlier rejected. The Catholic Apostolic Church has all but disappeared.[17]

Had Edward Irving not died at such an early age, and had he been able to guide the charismatics of his day more cautiously and more firmly for another decade or so, it is possible that the current Pentecostal revival would have been realized a century sooner.

IV

The Rediscovery of
Pentecostal Power

THE TIME HAD ARRIVED. The latter half of the
nineteenth century introduced a climate and mood
which were to cause a breakthrough in the supernatural
gifts of the Holy Spirit. The emergence of what was
known as the Holiness Movement attracted many
Christian believers whose hunger for a deeper relationship with God could not, and apparently would not, be
denied. And it was from these Holiness groups that the
pioneer Pentecostal leaders of the twentieth century
came forth.

Many see in John Wesley, the founder of Methodism
in England, a forerunner of the modern Holiness Movements, for they were outgrowths of his energetic
evangelism. During a lifetime that spanned most of the
eighteenth century, this remarkable man traveled a
quarter of a million miles on horseback to saturate
England with the message of Christ. Yet when Wesley
visited Georgia as a young missionary he confessed, "I
went to America to convert the Indians; but O! who
shall convert me?" His sincere search for salvation was
rewarded in London's Aldersgate Street meeting where
his heart was "strangely warmed" in a crisis experience
of conversion. On the night of May 24, 1738, Wesley
could say, "I felt I did trust in Christ, Christ alone, for
salvation; and an assurance was given me, that he had
taken away my sins, even mine, and saved me from the
law of sin and death."[1]

Within two years this Anglican clergyman with two

degrees from Oxford hammered out his theological ideas, which were to shape not only the Methodist branch of Protestantism but also its Holiness offshoots. Wesley taught that there were two distinct, separate experiences for true believers. The first was a crisis conversion which removed all doubts concerning God's forgiveness and acceptance of the sinner, who was cleansed from his past sins. Following conversion, another experience called sanctification, or Christian perfection, was vital for a life of holiness. By Christian perfection Wesley did not mean "sinless perfection" but a perfection of motives and desires. This second experience could arrive instantaneously after conversion or gradually, but in either case the life-style of holiness could be maintained only by a daily walk of obedience. Such a life of victory over sin required constant vigilance—the methodical discipline of daily devotions, self-examination, and a calculated avoidance of worldliness. Falling once again into sin always remained a distinct possibility.

On this foundation early Methodism thrived. Its converts pioneered the concept of holiness, which was to be embraced by American Methodists and the Holiness Movement. Francis Asbury, the devoted and energetic minister appointed by Wesley to oversee the spread of Methodism in America, once declared during an illness, "I have found by secret search that I have not preached sanctification as I should have done. If I am restored, this shall be my theme more pointedly than ever.[2]

The early Methodists were highly emotional at times. In Wesley's own meetings violent physical displays were common among some of his hearers, especially the poor and ignorant. As E. T. Clark writes of a congregation near Bristol, "They were seized with severe pains and screamed aloud, fell upon the ground in convulsions and shakings, sometimes continuing thus for hours at a time. Sometimes the din was so great that his [Wesley's] voice could scarcely be heard."[3]

In America as in England, the growth of the Methodist revival was not at all deterred by the shouts of joy, trembling seizures, and strong tears of grief often in evidence. Emotions at the religious camp meetings in the midst of American frontier life were completely uninhibited. Strange responses such as falling, jerking, holy laughter, and dancing before the Lord were common. Each major revival also was accompanied by speaking in unknown tongues.

This sort of intensity was nothing new on the American scene. Physical reactions had been visible during the first Great Awakening in America, spread by the revivalist theologian Jonathan Edwards in 1734. They resembled the outbursts which were to accompany the Wesleyan movement. Edwards' famous sermon "Sinners in the Hands of an Angry God," often referred to as an example of his pulpit power, pierced hearts to the extent that many screamed aloud in terror and fell like dead men. Another Great Awakening erupted in the beginning of the nineteenth century, this time in the Middle West. The nervous disorders and physical phenomena accompanying this revival surpassed anything formerly known in the country. It was launched by the Presbyterians in Kentucky and carried on by the Methodists, especially the famous evangelist Peter Cartwright.

The Cane Ridge revival camp meeting in Logan County, Kentucky, was begun in June of 1800 by three Presbyterian ministers and continued for over a year. A clergyman on the scene kept a count of the number of those who were "slain" or fell like dead men, and reported that three thousand—one out of every six present—were thus struck down. In this movement the "holy laugh" appeared, as did a seizure called the "jerks," which was experienced by large numbers. It even overcame irreligious scoffers. During one of

46

Cartwright's revivals, he tells us, a large man "took out his bottle of whiskey and swore he would drink the damned jerks to death, . . . but he could not get the bottle to his mouth, though he tried hard. . . . He became very much enraged, and cursed and swore very profanely, his jerks still increasing. At length he fetched a very violent jerk, snapped his neck, fell and soon expired, with his mouth full of cursing and bitterness."[4]

Within a couple of decades the more frenzied aspects of the western revival which had begun at Cane Ridge subsided, but camp meetings became a regular part of American religious life. Periodic awakenings and revivals continued, and during the latter half of the nineteenth century many Protestant believers, dissatisfied with membership in cold, worldly denominations and convinced that their churches were failing them, were attracted to the Holiness Movement. Indeed, the Protestant denominations were being increasingly staffed by ministers who seriously questioned or flatly denied biblical events and doctrines considered to be fundamental by Christians. Among these were the miracles and revelations found in Scripture, such as the deity, virgin birth, and bodily resurrection of Jesus Christ. The question of divine authorship of the Bible was raised by Protestant preachers who were themselves riddled with doubts. Many of these doubts had been stirred by the criticisms of nineteenth-century German theologians who stripped the miraculous and the supernatural accounts from the Bible. Their confidence shaken, many American ministers were no longer able to trust the Scripture as God's perfect revelation to man and the true guide for faith and practice. The humanistic, rationalistic, naturalistic theology had taken its toll.

In the face of increasing rejection and watering down of the supernatural in Scripture, conservative Christian leaders felt compelled to provide clearly distinguishable guidelines to the historical doctrines of Christianity. The preservation of those biblical truths held to be most sacred and precious was imperative. In this context, thirteen New York Methodist ministers, intent on promoting a deeper Christian faith, issued a welcome to all believers who felt themselves isolated in their stand on holiness. In their attempt to encourage a revival of faith and godly living within the theologically liberal Protestant churches, they organized the National Camp Meeting Association in 1867. The modern Holiness groups stem from these camp meetings, which were to bring about the formation of over one hundred denominations around the world and to give birth to the Pentecostal Movement.[5]

For twenty years the National Camp Meetings were quite successful. The most outstanding meeting was held in 1874 in Round Lake, New York, and was attended by President U. S. Grant, who came for a day of services. Together with twenty thousand worshippers, seven bishops received the exhortation of the presiding bishop in which they were called to stem "the tide of heathenism rolling in upon our shores. Infidelity is making its fiercest onset. We need and must have apostolic power."[6]

Unfortunately, this attempt to unite all serious, dedicated Christians who would advance the teaching of holiness within their denominations failed. Unfortunate, because no less than twenty-three Holiness denominations were created in the few years between 1893 and 1900. Almost half of the four million Methodists of that day were believers in holiness as a second work of grace, but their greater loyalty was to the established church despite its denial of the basic premises of the Holiness Movement. As the controversy continued and was sharply defined, the staunchest defenders of holiness—100,000 of them—made the difficult choice. They left the Methodist Church.[7]

Prominent among the new Holiness groups established in protest against the apostasy they believed existed in the other churches, and particularly the Methodist Church, were the Free Methodists, the Wesleyan Methodists, the Nazarenes, the Christian and Missionary Alliance, and the Pilgrim Holiness Movement. Holiness Movement members all agreed in emphasizing a second, deeper experience subsequent to conversion. The Scriptural phrase "baptism with the Holy Ghost" came into prominence and was applied to a spiritual crisis in the Christian's life after his conversion experience. But beyond this fundamental agreement, unanimity in their approach to perfectionism was a price the Holiness Movement was unwilling to pay. Each splinter group espoused its own definition of sanctification, its own concept of holy Christian living.

Oddly enough, the word "Pentecostal" was commonly used by the Holiness groups. For instance, the Church of the Nazarene, currently a staunch opponent of the Pentecostals, at one time included "Pentecost" in its official name. But at the turn of the century, when the growing number of believers who began speaking in tongues were labeled Pentecostals, the Holiness groups dropped the name to steer clear of any association with the Pentecostal Movement. Pentecostal fire and power were desirable, but the idea of speaking in tongues as a valid experience in the pursuit of sanctification was repudiated.

During the rise of the Holiness Movement, isolated instances of supernatural gifts such as healings and speaking in tongues were noted, but these incidents were dismissed as having no relation to the second work of grace. However, those among the Holiness advocates who were to become pioneers in the Pentecostal ranks later testified that baptism in the Holy Spirit, accompanied by speaking in tongues, was the very experience they sought all the time.

49

Evangelist R. A. Torrey, at one time pastor of Moody Church, is generally credited with introducing the teaching of the baptism in the Holy Spirit as an experience enduing the believer with "power from on high" for witnessing purposes. Famous evangelists such as Dwight L. Moody, Charles Finney, and John Wesley described personal physical manifestations which Torrey equated with the baptismal experience. Finney, formerly a lawyer, described one spiritual experience as great waves of electricity sweeping over him, compelling him to ask God to remove His hand lest he die on the spot. Torrey shared his own experience: "Suddenly it was just as if I had been knocked out of my chair on to the floor, and I lay upon my face, crying, 'Glory to God! Glory to God!' I could not stop. Some power, not my own, had taken possession of my lips and my whole person. . . . I had never shouted before in my life, but I could not stop."[8]

Pentecostal historian Stanley Frodsham, in outlining some of the supernatural events which occurred prior to the twentieth-century Pentecostal outpouring, relates that in 1873 the American evangelist and former shoe salesman D. L. Moody spoke at a YMCA meeting in Great Britain. Connected with the evangelist's visit, an observer wrote of an incident in which "young men were speaking in tongues, and prophesying, . . . after Moody addressed them. . . ." Frodsham also points to a New England revival that same year in which the "talking in tongues, accompanied largely with the gift of healing, was manifested."[9]

In 1896 Shearer Schoolhouse in Cherokee County, North Carolina, became the scene of a revival in which there were many conversions, healings, and manifestations of speaking in tongues. Two Baptist ministers preached in Tennessee meetings where some forty persons received the baptism in the Spirit and spoke in tongues in 1900. Earlier, because of their strong stand on personal holiness, these Baptist preachers had withdrawn from their church.[10]

During this season of deep spiritual searching which immediately preceded the twentieth-century Pentecostal revival, distinct and convincing emphasis on divine healing was proclaimed by such men as Presbyterian A. B. Simpson, founder of the Christian and Missionary Alliance in Nyack, New York, and John Alexander Dowie, a Congregationalist and founder of the Christian Catholic Church in Chicago. In the opinion of Canadian professor Gordon F. Atter, "Dr. Dowie did more to promote the doctrine of divine healing than possibly any other man."

Who was Dowie? Born in Edinburgh, Scotland, John Alexander Dowie attended clinics conducted by the well-known surgeon John Simpson. He listened to lectures and heard the diagnoses of medical doctors. Observing many surgical operations, he heard humble confessions of indecision and conjecture from members of the medical profession. As a result Dowie emerged a severe critic of both medical practice and the doctors of his day. In Chicago he was later to lead a "Holy War against Drugs, Doctors, and Devils."

He pastored in Australia for six years, emphasizing a healing ministry which attracted as many as twenty thousand to some meetings. Dowie then came to the United States determined to introduce and regularly conduct a ministry of divine healing. The year was 1888 and Dowie was forty-one years old and practically unknown. Within a decade, knowledge of his praying for the sick spread throughout the world. People came by the thousands as they saw the signs and wonders following the preaching of the good news. Gordon Lindsay writes of Dowie: "Against overwhelming opposition, a hostile press, bitterly opposed clergymen, antagonistic city officials, unscrupulous lawyers, who, hired by the combined opposition, used every loophole of the law and legal technicality to stop him, he fought for and maintained the right to pray for the sick."[11] Dowie faced a hundred warrants for his arrest in 1895 after a succession of announcements in the Chicago *Tribune* that the State Board of Health was preparing to investigate the preacher for "practicing medicine without a license."

Dowie had leased and furnished several large rooming houses to be used as Healing Homes, conveniently located near the site of his evening services. Although no medical treatment was administered, the press described allegedly "unlawful" features of the homes, calling them "Dowie's Lunatic Asylum" and suggesting that handsome revenues were gained therein for prostitutes. But Dowie could not be discouraged or deterred despite the swearing out of warrants en masse. During one weekend seven warrants were issued to prevent him from preaching at three services. More than once, Dowie was arrested while on his own platform and roughly ushered to the police station. Generally he was acquitted, and whenever he was found guilty, higher courts reversed the sentences. In time, public opinion began to turn against his adversaries.

On one occasion Dowie stated, "I have simply prayed for the sick as a minister of the Gospel of Jesus Christ. If the Lord Jesus Christ should appear in Chicago today laying hands on the sick as He did nineteen centuries ago, He could be indicted and brought before the court and charged with violations of the State Board of Health Act. . . ."[12]

Dowie often prayed for as many as a thousand persons a week and many healings were reported, among them some involving well-known individuals. Sadie Cody, a niece of Buffalo Bill, was miraculously restored when her right leg, three inches shorter than her left, was made whole. A cousin of Abraham Lincoln, Amanda M. Hicks, suffered from a malignant disease. She was carried four hundred miles on a bed and found instant healing when Dowie prayed. Dr. Lillian Yeoman was from a family of physicians, but she found her medical and surgical practice too strenuous and occasionally resorted to morphine to steady her nerves and enable her to get some sleep. She came before Dowie addicted, but left a delivered woman.[13]

In 1896 Dowie founded the Christian Catholic Church and within five short years saw his following multiply into tens of thousands. During Dowie's ministry in Chicago the famous infidel Robert G. Ingersoll delivered a speech in which he charged that "God must perish, because He is useless, and never answers prayer." Dowie assembled testimonies of persons healed of the most serious afflictions, supported by documentary evidence. In his lectures Ingersoll customarily referred to the Scriptural promises related to healing and then announced that they were unfulfilled in the ministry of the contemporary church. When Dowie challenged Ingersoll, the infidel decided to leave town.[14]

On New Year's Eve just hours before the turn of the century, Dowie unveiled a well-guarded secret—his dream city, Zion, was to be built forty miles north of Chicago on Lake Michigan. Covering more than six thousand acres, Zion City would be a bit of heaven on earth—a city where tobacco, liquor, and swine's flesh would be forbidden; where no licenses would be issued for gambling houses, theaters, or dance halls. The land was not to be sold, but 1100-year leases were offered. Within two years nearly ten thousand people were irresistibly drawn to Zion.

Not everyone rejoiced. A few devoted friends were uneasy and disturbed. Zion was to be ruled as a theocracy, not a democracy, and Dowie personally planned it down to the smallest details. Concerned co-worker Anton Darms perceived a crucial turning point in Dowie's ministry before the announcement of the creation of Zion. At a worship service in 1899, Dowie had wept, fearing that he might be set aside for taking some glory for himself when all glory belonged wholly

53

to God. Darms believed this to be a divine warning to Dowie to dismiss his plans for Zion City and devote his time and energies to preaching, especially the Scriptural teaching on divine healing. But Dowie turned his face toward Zion City.

During earlier years in his Chicago ministry Dowie had rebuked a person who claimed to have direct revelation from God that Dowie was the great prophet Elijah returned to earth. Dowie resisted the temptation for years, but in June of 1901 he succumbed to the thousands who almost idolized him and declared that he was indeed Elijah the Restorer, whose return had been spoken of many centuries before by the prophets. The majority of Zion people, though hesitant, accepted Dowie's "Declaration." Other followers of his ministry were sadly convinced he was a victim of paranoic delusion.

Few people can remain humble amidst outstanding success, public adulation, and power. Lindsay believes that Dowie was under a strong delusion, a "fixation" which altered his ego.[15] He looked like a prophet with his white beard, but his preaching deteriorated into denunciations of his enemies. A few years later, while in the pulpit of Zion City's Shiloh Tabernacle at the close of a communion service in 1905, Dowie suffered a stroke which left him paralyzed. It was the beginning of the end. When financial difficulties, which had long been mounting in Zion City because of Dowie's neglect and refusal to face problems, reached a crisis half a year later, a motion to suspend Dowie from his position as General Overseer received the approval of 95 percent of the 3,500 present in Shiloh Tabernacle. Less than a year later Dowie died without fulfilling his goal of creating various Zion cities around the world. Although Zion City faced a debt of six million dollars it survived. Within decades the city laws were changed as the number of new residents exceeded the original Zion inhabitants. Nevertheless, out of Zion several young men of faith emerged to blaze new trails with the message of divine healing. But these would not easily forget the Scriptural warning that "pride goeth before a fall."

Both Simpson and Dowie influenced a Methodist preacher named Charles Fox Parham to expect God's intervention in his own ministry. Once a helpless cripple healed by the power of God, Parham probably would have stressed divine healing even without these inspiring human examples. He was to emerge with a key doctrine for Pentecostals around the world in this century.

Parham attended Southwestern, a Methodist Episcopal College at Winfield, Kansas, and succeeded the founder of Baker University in his first Methodist pastorate in Eudora, Kansas. But because he had a consuming desire to preach to people of all denominations and sects, he left to become an independent evangelical preacher, trusting God to supply all his needs. He preached this way for the remaining thirty-five years of his life, at times to audiences as large as seven thousand, But Parham is best remembered for opening a small Bible school in Topeka, Kansas.

After Parham established a Divine Healing Home in Topeka and regularly published stories of persons healed in answer to prayer, friends pressured him to open a Bible school in the city. He was able to rent a large mansion patterned after an English castle for forty dollars a month. The edifice was known as "Stone's Folly" because the ambitious builder was never able to complete the mansion as originally planned. Its main floor displayed luxurious carved woodwork from cedars of Lebanon, but the upper floor, with its plain pine boards, remained crude in comparison.

By October of 1900 Parham was issuing a challenging invitation to any ministers and Christian laymen who were "willing to forsake all, sell what they had, give it away and enter the school for study and prayer, where all of us together might trust God for food, fuel, rent and clothing."[16] Bethel Bible School, as conceived by Parham, was to prepare men and women to preach the good news of Christ to the ends of the earth. And they came—in horse and buggies, in wagons and on foot with their families. Diapers soon were waving in the backyard of Stone's Mansion.

Bethel taught them to depend upon God to supply their every need, for it existed without tuition, dormitory, or board fees, without a board of trustees or even a group of churches behind the effort. As the students pitched in to wash dishes and milk the cow grazing on the lawn, they prayed for their needs to be supplied on the basis of the philosophy that God was able. Strange events took place. For instance, Mrs. Parham recalled a morning when the rent was due. A gentleman appeared at the front door early that morning with a check for the exact amount required. He had been awakened and made aware of the problem the evening before as Charles Parham prayed for this specific need.[17]

Parham had heard many Holiness groups claim different proofs as evidence of receiving the baptism in the Holy Spirit, the experience foretold in all four gospels by John the Baptist. Determined to research the subject, he assigned the entire student body of some forty persons to discover the biblical evidence of this baptism. The sole textbook at Bethel was the Holy Bible. The students were to trace the disciples' steps in the New Testament Book of Acts, motivated by the desire to "go before the world with something that was indisputable because it tallied absolutely with the Word."[18] While Parham preached for three days in Kansas City, they concentrated on each Scriptural account which described believers in the early church as being filled with the Holy Spirit, looking for any constant factors evident in each experience.

56

Charles Parham returned on New Year's Eve to learn of the unanimity in the students' conclusion—"the indisputable proof on each occasion was, that they spoke with other tongues."[19] They reviewed the experiences on the Day of Pentecost as recorded in the second chapter of Acts, and the events at Samaria, Caesarea, and Ephesus. They accepted by inference that Paul also received the Pentecostal baptism when he was healed of blindness at the hands of a layman named Ananias. Parham pondered, wondering if speaking in tongues was indeed the evidence of this baptism. Weary from his meetings and probably wishing to meditate further on his students' findings, Parham suggested that they all pray for this specific experience the following morning.

New Year's Day 1901 was alive with a special air of expectancy at Bethel Bible School, but nothing unusual happened until seven in the evening. Agnes N. Ozman, who had previously attended A. B. Simpson's Bible School in Nyack, New York, suddenly recalled that hands were laid upon the believers at Samaria, Damascus, and Ephesus before they received the baptism in the Holy Spirit. Boldly, she requested the school's president to pray for her, believing that she would receive the glossolalia as he stretched forth his hands. Parham drew back. "At first I refused, not having the experience myself. I laid my hand upon her head and prayed."[20] At that moment the student "began speaking in the Chinese language, and was unable to speak English for three days. When she tried to write in English to tell us of her experience, she wrote in Chinese. . . ."[21] The writing phenomenon is rare among Pentecostals, but other similar instances have been recorded. Miss Ozman described her spiritual adventure in this manner: "I began to speak in tongues, glorifying God. I talked several languages, and it was clearly manifest when a new dialect was spoken. I had the added

57

joy and glory my heart longed for and a depth of the presence of the Lord within that I had never known before. It was as if rivers of living waters were proceeding from my innermost being."[22]

The heightened air of expectancy at Bethel Bible School may well be imagined. But two whole days passed uneventfully before twelve students, already ministers of different denominations, were filled with the Holy Spirit and spoke in tongues. "Some were sitting, some still kneeling, others standing with hands upraised. There was no violent physical manifestation, though some trembled under the power of the glory that filled them."[23] Unusual singing burst forth as the hymn "Jesus Lover of My Soul" filled the air in a unique manner—it was sung in harmony in six different languages!

President Parham returned from another meeting in time to observe these phenomena. Overwhelmed, he dropped to his knees behind a table unnoticed by the others and soon began worshiping God in the Swedish language, which later changed to other languages. He continued worshiping in this manner until the morning hours.

Reporters from Topeka, Kansas City, St. Louis, and other cities converged upon Stone's Mansion. They were accompanied by professors of linguistics, foreigners, and government interpreters. They agreed that the students were actually speaking foreign languages with proper intonations and accents. One interpreter claimed to have heard twenty Chinese dialects distinctly spoken during one evening. There was no chattering, jabbering, or stuttering. The news media projected the story. "Pentecost, read all about the Pentecost" shouted the newsboys, not knowing a Pentecost from a holocaust.[24]

A Norwegian critic, Nils Bloch-Hoell, wrote about the experiences in the Bethel School this way: "As a proof of the Spirit baptism they expected sensuous experiences, primarily motoric speech, with ecstasy their goal. Bethel College must have been like a hothouse where religious ecstasy could flourish."[25] He overlooked the fact that the program at Bethel placed the students under constant exposure to the hard, real world, as they were required daily to minister and witness in the city of Topeka.

In an obvious attempt to discount the events at Bethel as nothing more than the predictable psychological responses in such given situations, Bloch-Hoell portrayed Agnes Ozman as a person of a nervous constitution and Parham as probably a neurotic.[26] Recounting the Ozman baptism of January 1, 1901, he stated, "Psychologically it is easy to understand that the frenzied prayer passed into motoric speech immediately after the physical feeling of the laying on of hands."[27] But he ignored the fact that twelve students received the same experience without Parham's presence or the imposition of hands.

His lack of understanding is evident as he refers to the experience of speaking in tongues as an abandonment of self-control and the giving of oneself without reservation to one emotional idea. He shows his unfamiliarity with Pentecostal worship in praise and adoration by referring to a Miss Thistlewaite's account of her prayer experience in this gross manner: "Here too we observe the strong terms used to describe the feeling of pleasure, or even lust, connected with the experience of Spirit baptism."[28] Actually, the account of her personal Pentecost was this: "A great joy came into my heart and I began to say, 'I praise thee,' and great floods of laughter came into my heart. Psalm 126:2 I tried to praise the Lord in English but could not. So I just let the praise come as it would in a new language that was given. The floodgates of glory were wide open. The Holy Spirit had come to me, even to me, to speak not of Himself but to magnify Christ. And, Oh, what a wonderful, wonderful Christ He revealed. All around me I heard great rejoicing while others spoke in tongues and magnified God."[29] To Pentecostals this simply suggests the fulness of joy in God's presence while praying in tongues.

Shortly after the introduction of glossolalia at Bethel, a rabbi was present as a young married student read the day's lesson from the Bible. Viewing an English version, the rabbi exclaimed, "No not that one, I want to see the Hebrew Bible. That man read in the Hebrew tongue."[30]

On another occasion Parham spoke in tongues as he was preaching, and then continued with the sermon. At the conclusion a visitor arose, saying, "I am healed of my infidelity. I have heard in my own tongue the Twenty-third Psalm that I learned at my mother's knee."[31]

Unfortunately, before the summer of 1901 was over, Stone's Mansion was no longer available to Bethel Bible School. It had been sold for use as a pleasure resort. Parham warned the buyers that if the building were to be used for ungodly purposes they would not prosper. Although keenly disappointed, he refrained from describing a dream he had in which he viewed the charred remains of Stone's Mansion, burned to the ground. "We were not surprised, but sad, when we received the word from Topeka that the building that had been our Bible school was burned down."[32] Friends shipped them some of the carved woodwork from the doors.

The concept rediscovered at Bethel and impressed upon the hearts and minds of the students there provided a basic tenet for many Pentecostal Bible schools yet unborn.

V

Miracles in the Early
Twentieth Century

PARHAM'S PLANS to share Bethel's biblical discovery
of speaking in tongues as the initial evidence of the baptism in the Holy Spirit were ambitious and optimistic.
He hoped to blanket the United States and Canada
with the full gospel. However, limited acceptance in
the Kansas City and Lawrence, Kansas, meetings, sharp
criticism by the city churches, and an unfavorable press
were to introduce two barren, trying years which
brought the Parhams to the nadir of their ministry,
". . . for weeks and weeks never knowing where our
next meal would come from. . . . When buildings were
closed to us we preached on the street."[1]

An important upturn of events began when Parham
prayed for a woman in El Dorado Springs, Missouri,
in the summer of 1903. The healing of the near blind
eye of Mrs. Mary A. Arthurs set off fires of revival in
her home city of Galena, Kansas. Parham's meetings
had been small and localized but now from the Arthurs'
overcrowded living room the meetings had to be transferred to a tent erected on an adjacent lot. Soon this
was inadequate to accommodate the growing attendance
as word of the Pentecostal revival spread. With cold
weather threatening, an old warehouse was secured and
heated with pot-bellied stoves. It was furnished with
pews made of long planks stretched across barrels. The
meetings continued in Galena for more than three
months and resulted in hundreds of conversions, healings, and baptisms in the Spirit accompanied by the
speaking in tongues.

61

It was in this humble warehouse that two nuns from St. Louis heard an anthem sung in Latin supernaturally by ordinary worshipers. They couldn't get over it because their cathedral choir had tried to learn the difficult anthem for a month and finally abandoned the effort.[2]

In the fall of 1905 Parham opened the first Pentecostal Bible school in Texas. As in Topeka, these Houston classes were of brief duration but among the sixty preachers who attended was one black Holiness pastor. William J. Seymour impressed a visiting Nazarene from California, Neeley Terry, as being a very godly man and she encouraged her church in Los Angeles to invite him to become an associate minister there. His fare raised by Parham, Seymour accepted the call and preached his first sermon from the Nazarene pulpit. The subject? Speaking in tongues! As a result Seymour found the church door closed to him for preaching a "false doctrine."

Sympathetic Baptists invited Seymour to conduct meetings in their home, where both white and black believers worshiped together. Just as Parham's Bethel students had first experienced the glossolalia, even so did seven parishioners speak in tongues on April 9, 1906—three days before Seymour did. Some strange and wonderful events occurred in that little home. Jennie Moore, who later married Seymour, spoke in tongues and then went to the piano and for the first time in her life began to play beautiful music and to sing in an unknown, beautiful language.

As the revival continued there were growing pains. Preaching from the front porch to the crowds who could not squeeze into the house must have annoyed the neighbors. But more urgent, as the exuberance of the overflow attendance reached a peak, the foundation of the frame house on Bonnie Brae Street gave way!

Searching for larger and sturdier quarters, they

located the address known to Pentecostals the world around—312 Azusa Street, Los Angeles, California. With a lumber yard, stable, and tombstone factory as its neighborhood setting, the voluminous praises no longer posed any problems. The framed two-story structure, which long ago had served as a Methodist Church and more recently a stable, had been partially destroyed by fire. Only a single Gothic window above the main entrance of the abandoned boxlike structure gave evidence of its earlier use.

Anxious to meet in the rented quarters without delay, the worshipers cleared just enough space from the debris and rubble and hastily replaced the broken window panes. Reminiscent of Parham's Galena warehouse, here also planks were placed over empty nail kegs, so that thirty persons could be seated in a square, facing each other.[3]

The Azusa Street meetings were held from ten in the morning until after midnight and the crowds came. Seymour served as moderator, teaching at times, but more often seated behind a unique pulpit constructed of two empty wooden shoe cartons, one placed on the other. The humble, one-eyed black leader was frequently hidden from most of the congregation as he prayed with his head inside the pulpit. Prophecies, tongues, and the interpretation of tongues were given with convincing power during the services. The favorite hymns were "Under the Blood" and "The Comforter is Come," and from time to time there came forth singing in tongues which sounded like a heavenly choir, never failing to awe new attendants. People who couldn't carry a tune in a bucket suddenly burst forth in beautiful song. A. G. Osterberg, who attended the Azusa revival, commented, "I am witness to the fact the Holy Spirit can and does make folk sing who cannot otherwise sing." He specifically referred to his untalented father: "I nearly fell off my chair when I heard someone sing like a Caruso close by. Turning my head, I saw it was my father. . . ."[4] Conversions, baptisms, healings, and exorcism were common as the revival continued. Laborers in the area spent their lunch hour at the mission and a Methodist among them became so interested in the meeting that it was 5:00 P.M. before he realized he had not returned to work.

As attendance spiraled, the Azusa building was restored and the congregation found that the main floor, still sprinkled with sawdust, could accommodate six hundred persons. A Catholic donated lumber for an altar. The unpretentious low-ceilinged hall was crowned with an upper prayer chamber, a "tarrying room" where many received the baptism in the Spirit. But many received as they were seated in the services below.

Along with the sincere seekers came the skeptics. The newspapers published critical reports which served to attract the inquisitive. The local ministerial association at one time asked the police department to put a halt to what they termed "unseemly" displays, but the police withdrew after finding no objections from the residents in the area. Indeed, many who came to scoff remained to pray. Sister Hutchinson, the woman who had barred Seymour from returning to the Nazarene Church, was one of these. Not only was she drawn to Azusa, but she received the baptism in the Spirit and later served as a missionary to Africa.

One foreign-born reporter from a Los Angeles newspaper came prepared to lampoon the meetings, but instead came face to face with the supernatural. Unexpectedly, a woman rose and, looking directly at the newsman, spoke in his native tongue, revealing secrets known only to him. He could no longer deny the authenticity of the glossolalia.

News accounts of the Azusa revival spread across the nation and abroad in both the religious and secular press. The visitors who pressed into the building found no segregation as blacks, whites, Mexicans, and Chinese sat together to observe and participate in shouting, dancing, falling into trances, weeping, speaking and singing in tongues, and interpreting these utterances into English. Some of the enthusiastic Holiness churches and missions closed their services in order to attend the Azusa Street Mission. But to many of the Holiness people who rejected the Pentecostal baptism preached there, Seymour was an "instrument of Satan."

The meetings continued at Azusa Street daily for three years. But there were precarious moments when negative forces appeared on the scene to threaten the revival. In his account of the Azusa Street Mission, Frank Bartleman explained that "outside persecution never hurt the work. We had the most to fear from the working of evil spirits within. Even spiritualists and hypnotists came to investigate, and to try their influence. Then all the religious sore-heads and crooks and cranks came, seeking a place in the work. We had the most to fear from these."[5]

Seymour keenly felt his inadequacies in the face of mounting problems of a spiritual nature. He wrote to his teacher in the Pentecostal faith, Charles Parham, for counsel—and to urge him to hurry to Los Angeles to oversee the revival. Parham's wisdom, experience, and leadership might have delivered the Azusa Mission from its grave problems, but what he considered to be a greater need was given priority. Instead of helping Seymour, he answered an urgent call from friends in Zion City to preach to the confused followers of "Elijah" Dowie during the critical period of Dowie's suspension from the leadership of the Christian Catholic Church. Parham was able to give sound scriptural guidance to many, among them several future leaders of the Pentecostal revival.

By the time Parham could reach the Azusa Street Mission he was confronted with some extremists and fanatics who exceeded the bounds of common sense and reason. Parham preached a few times and denounced the "hypnotists" and "spiritualists" who apparently had assumed a growing influence in the meetings. Instead of receiving honor as the teaching pioneer of the Pentecostal message, Parham was informed by two elders, one a hypnotist, that his presence was no longer desired.[6]

Alarmed and humiliated, Parham opened meetings in the local building of the Women's Christian Temperance Union in order to refute the errors he was convinced were being aired at Azusa Street. In a personal confrontation with Seymour, he was unsuccessful in persuading the latter to resign his leadership of the Azusa Mission. Although Seymour was his most famous disciple, Parham may have been chafing at the success and growth of the interracial meetings under black leadership, for he once criticized the Azusa Street meeting because of its "disgusting similarity to 'Southern darkey camp meetings.'"[7]

At any rate, Parham's Los Angeles meetings had but limited success, lasting only several weeks, whereas the Azusa Mission revival continued daily for three years. No doubt the worst of the excesses were remedied as the Azusa Street Mission continued to attract visitors from all parts of the nation and a stream of inquirers from overseas. Hundreds of preachers traveled to Los Angeles to be eyewitnesses of the revival. Most were convinced of the genuineness of the Pentecostal teaching and the manifestations they saw and heard and many received their personal Pentecosts before they returned to their home churches. H. V. Synan declared that, "In later years anyone who was an 'Azusa recipient' was looked on with awe and covered with an aura of respect and 'glory' by their co-religionists."[8]

Parham proved his distaste for leadership by resigning his position as Projector of the Apostolic Faith Move-

66

ment in 1907. He felt that the heritage of truth he had presented was not to be harvested by a single man or movement. He told his brethren, "Let us not become sectarian and seek to have everybody come our way, because others have as much right to demand that we should join them, as that they should join us."[9] In the meantime Parham was the target of smear campaigns against his person as persistent attempts were made to cast a shadow upon the moral character of the man. Mrs. Parham shed some light upon the mood of the times in a dialogue with an individual who had just heard Parham preach a message in a revival meeting in Missouri.

"That was a wonderful sermon, surely Mr. Parham must have got back to God," exclaimed the lady.

"Do you think so? I did not know that he had ever been backslidden," answered Mrs. Parham.

"O yes, had you not heard . . ." And she proceeded to tell Mrs. Parham a long, sad story of how Parham had left his wife and family, and so on. Patiently hearing her out, Mrs. Parham then stated that it was all untrue. "But how do you know?" asked the gossiper. Mrs. Parham smiled and said, "I am his wife." The talebearer hurriedly departed and was never seen again.[10]

Charles Fox Parham died on January 29, 1929, at fifty-six years of age. Picturing him as a wearied warrior, Mrs. Parham said that "he felt he had already spent seventy-five years in the service of the Master, and that he was so tired he wanted to go home."[11]

Evidently much suffering accompanied his weariness, but Parham's belief in divine healing left no room for medical aid so he refused any medications that would ease his pain. Mrs. Patton, an attendant during his illness, mentions a day in which Parham was suffering more than usual. She urged him to receive an injection. "I would certainly give it to him and the world would never know, for I would not destroy the faith he gave

67

his life to establish. . . . I would have cheated to bring relief. . . ." He replied, "Oh, Mrs. Patton, tempt me not. Jesus suffered more than I, and if it is God's will that I drink of this bitter cup, then let it not pass. . . . I must not fail my belief. . . ."[12]

A crowd estimated at 2,500 attended his funeral despite a snowfall. More than a thousand were unable to crowd into Baxter Theater until the casket was open for final viewing. Offerings from all over the United States reached Baxter Springs to help purchase a monument—a pulpit of granite supporting an open Bible.[13] This was all the more remarkable inasmuch as offerings were never taken during Parham's thirty-five years of meetings.

From the beginning of the Pentecostal revival, women have taken active part in blazing a trail for God in the evangelistic and missionary fields. Their great contribution cannot be dismissed or ignored. Lillian Trasher, subject of the film "Nile Mother," is an outstanding example. While engaged to be married she became convinced of God's call to minister overseas. When her fiancé refused to consider a sacrificial life of Christian service on foreign soil, Miss Trasher broke the engagement. She never did marry, but literally thousands of unwanted Egyptian orphans now rise to call her blessed. As an Assemblies of God missionary she placed her life and love selflessly at the disposal of the rejected ones. Lillian Trasher was to mother eight thousand of them over a span of fifty years before she went on to her reward at seventy-four years of age. In the twilight of her life she said, "I have often wished that I had two or three lives to do it over again."

The "Nile Mother" had a constant need for miracles as she attempted to feed, house, and clothe a little army of helpless dependents day in and day out. Surely the supernatural gift of faith was exercised by this courageous woman. When Premier M. Neguib visited the orphanage in Assiout, the impressed leader wrote this in the guest book: "The founder of the institution, the great Miss Trasher, is a precious gift from God. I call upon those who are engaged in social reform to visit this institution and learn from it what they should do if they really wish to achieve."[14]

Many other heroines could be mentioned, such as Florence Steidel, who directed New Hope Town, a colony of love and concern for lepers in Liberia which has been lauded by the Nigerian government; or, Marie Brown whose ministry in New York City's Glad Tidings Tabernacle has motivated members to pour great sums of money into missions, enabling dedicated people to spend their lives in far-flung outposts overseas as the home church labors in the asphalt jungles of "Fun City."

But no early record of the Pentecostal revival would be complete without including the extraordinary exploits of Aimee Semple McPherson. Whatever conclusions one draws from the dramatic episodes of her energetic life and sudden death, here was a woman of great faith and great compassion for the lost and the afflicted.

Born on a small Canadian farm in 1890, Aimee was converted at seventeen, when she began attending a Pentecostal mission where Robert Semple was preaching. The teenager received the baptism in the Spirit while alone in a room. "I shouted and sang and laughed and talked in tongues," she later wrote, "until it seemed that I was too full to hold another bit of blessing lest I should burst with the glory."[15]

Needless to say, Aimee's mother, an officer in the Salvation Army, was terribly upset, fearing that her daughter was being hypnotized. She threatened to discontinue her daughter's education if she continued attending the Pentecostal meetings. Aimee reasoned with her saying, ". . . if the baptism with the evidence of speaking in tongues is not for today, I'll never go to

69

the mission again." The challenge was accepted by the Salvation Army Junior Sergeant-Major, who was certain that such things were only for the apostles' days. "I will look up the Scriptures and prove it to you when you get home tonight." For nine hours she pored over her Bible and was still at the breakfast table when Aimee returned. Convinced of the biblical validity of these phenomena, Aimee's mother admitted, "This is that which was spoken by the prophet Joel, which should come to pass in the last days."[16]

Aimee married the Pentecostal preacher and the Semples soon left for China as missionaries. Death separated the happy pair soon after their second anniversary when Robert came down with malaria. The bereaved wife stood at his grave in Happy Valley, Hong Kong, not yet twenty and pregnant. Aimee remained in Hong Kong to give birth to a daughter. Returning with six-week-old Roberta, the perplexed young widow went through a spiritual low-tide. Longing to make a home for the infant, she remarried the following year. Not, however, before the groom would agree to one stipulation: if at any time in her life God should call her to a ministry or foreign field, she would be obliged to obey God. Mr. McPherson agreed.

After one year her nerves were seriously afflicted. Surgery was tried, but complications set in—heart trouble, stomach hemorrhages, and intense nervousness. Aimee was convinced that God would heal her if she obeyed His call, which she could not dismiss from her mind: "Will you preach the Word?" Finally she submitted, and later stated, "Don't you ever tell me that a woman cannot be called to preach the Gospel." All pain immediately left her and within two weeks she was up and well. Aimee informed her husband, "I have tried to walk your way and have failed. Won't you come now and walk my way. I am sure we will be happy." Rejecting the offer, her husband later admitted that this was in fact her "calling and work in life."

Soon after making this decision Aimee founded a Pentecostal denomination called the International Church of the Foursquare Gospel. Bold and innovative in the ministry, she traveled extensively in an automobile and while in one town, she slipped into a parade of decorated cars to advertise her evening tent services. Later she preached from a plane at an airfield to a large crowd before flying over the city, showering the populace with fifteen thousand handbills announcing the revival meetings. She not only was the first woman to preach a sermon over the radio, but as early as 1924 her church operated radio station KFSG (Kall Four Square Gospel), the third oldest radio station in the Los Angeles area.

She helped the cause of integration while holding services for blacks in Key West, Florida. The white people found it impossible to stay away and they worshiped the same Lord side by side with their black brothers. As early as 1918, the Los Angeles Temple Auditorium, which seated 3,500, was filled long before meeting time. Many agreed that "it outshines even the wonderful days of old Azusa Street . . . such a unity . . . such a laying aside of quibbles and hair-splitting doctrines."[17]

Foreshadowing contemporary ecumenical meetings, Aimee Semple McPherson attracted interdenominational revival services once the pastors were convinced that her work was truly blessed of God. In Washington, D.C., the McKendree Methodist Church people saw her pray for the sick and afflicted at their altar in relays of thirty at a time. During an eight-day revival in the First Baptist Church in San Jose, California, the pastor was baptized with the Holy Spirit and spoke in tongues. "Into one short week was crowded the experiences of a genera-

71

tion," he later reflected.[18] Several deacons and Sunday school teachers also received the Pentecostal experience.

The three-thousand-seat Moolah Masonic Temple was secured for Aimee's three weeks in St. Louis, Missouri. Her only sponsor at the beginning of this revival was a small church with sixty-seven members and a choir of fifteen. They would be lost on a platform stage which seated five hundred. But Aimee's last-minute efforts to advertise the meetings paid some dividends and then miracles started happening. By the beginning of the second week police were needed for protection against crushing crowds. The Board President of Texas Presbyterian University declared, "I . . . have been through the great revivals from Moody and Sankey down, but never did I see multitudes rushing and struggling to hear the Word like this in all my experience."[19]

Before the St. Louis revival concluded they had to move to a twelve-thousand-seat Coliseum where a platform half the length of a football field was filled with ministers of all denominations. They watched the evangelist anoint the sick with oil and, "Numbers rose from their beds, others cast aside crutches, wheelchairs, braces, trusses, casts, supports, ear trumpets, glasses, bandages, declaring to the great throng that they were healed." Several goiters melted instantly before the gaze of the multitude. Mrs. McPherson explained, "The world is hungry to hear the gospel. Not hungering for suppers and concerts and social gatherings. but heart-hungry for a real Jesus who saves and heals and baptizes with the Holy Spirit." One Presbyterian minister said he had preached for fifty years and had never heard the simple gospel of Jesus Christ and Him crucified "more simply, more faithfully, more lovingly preached," than from the lips of Mrs. McPherson.[20]

Her messages were practical. In Alton, Illinois, before

an audience of eight thousand, she told the penitents who came forward to go home and pay their debts. Many bills of long standing were paid voluntarily. In Wichita, the Gas and Electric Company manager discussed some results of the revival saying, "Some magic power has descended upon the city and people who once were inclined to procrastinate are becoming scrupulously prompt in meeting their obligations."[21] During the depression years her Los Angeles church fed and clothed more than a million persons.[22]

Aimee called her mission the Foursquare Gospel to commemorate the four principal articles of her message: uplifting Christ as Savior, the mighty Baptizer with the Holy Spirit, the Great Physician, and the soon coming King. At a time when the Pentecostals were rarely given a fair hearing, she preached her concept of Pentecostal priorities to the multitudes this way: "We don't want anything that is foolish, unscriptural, or impractical, but that which is genuine, biblical . . . with the same methods and results of the Apostles." She firmly believed that the moment a person accepted Christ he was to become a soul-winner, helping to bring the one next to him to Jesus Christ. Evidently a host of followers put this into practice, for the denomination founded by Aimee Semple McPherson and incorporated in 1927 has expanded to 783 churches in the United States and Canada while foreign stations have surpassed 2,500. There are close to 100,000 members in the United States, matched by that number in twenty-five other countries.

In the early 1920s, when Pentecostals were for the most part the objects of scorn and derision, Aimee Semple McPherson had the faith to build a church that would seat more than five thousand. She began construction by hiring eleven mules and scrapers and men to grade the land that was then eight miles outside Los Angeles. When Angelus Temple opened its doors on

January 1, 1923, it featured the largest unsupported dome in North America and was valued at one and a half million dollars. During the first eight months of services more than eight thousand knelt at the altars seeking Christ as Savior. Precision-minded Aimee had communion served to 3,500 persons in fifteen minutes, "without semblance of haste or confusion."[23]

Aimee had many critics during her life of service. Her methods were her own and they were both frowned upon and imitated by many. When Los Angeles was plagued with prostitution, gambling, bootlegging, dope pushers, crime, and political corruption, McPherson was an outspoken crusader for cleaning up the city. For example, she had converted dope addicts testify on her radio program, naming places and persons from whom they had obtained narcotics. Pressure from the vice lords failed to curtail her persistent efforts, including threats of kidnaping which Aimee dismissed as crank notes.

But the kidnaping story made all the headlines. On May 18, 1926, Aimee and her secretary pitched a tent on the sands of Ocean Park beach, where Aimee prepared her sermon and then went for a swim after asking the secretary to check with the Temple by phone for special music and singers needed for the evening service. When her secretary returned, Aimee was missing. Earlier a call had been received at Angelus Temple from desperate parents wishing prayer for their dying child. Advised of Aimee's whereabouts, the couple met her coming out of the water and begged her, still in her wet bathing suit, to accompany them to their car and pray for the child. "The woman had a coat folded over her arm," Aimee later recalled. "This she put around my shoulders with trembling fingers and bade me hurry. She ran on ahead while I followed with the man, and when I came to the car to which she led me, the woman was already inside, sitting on the back seat and holding a bundle which she clasped tightly to her breast. . . . I put my feet on the running board of that car to get inside and pray for the baby which I believed to be in that bundle of blankets. . . . Leaning forward about to touch the babe, there was a push from behind that threw me forward upon the floor of the car. . . ."

When Aimee returned to consciousness the car had already reached the Mexican border village of Agua Prieta, where she learned she was being held for ransom. Meanwhile at the beach an extensive search for her body proved futile and a memorial service was held at Angelus Temple. Negotiations were attempted by her kidnapers, who sent locks of her hair to her mother to prove Aimee was alive. A threatening letter demanded the huge ransom of half a million dollars.

More than a month after her disappearance an exhausted woman escaped across the border from Mexico into Douglas, Arizona. Her return was headlined across the country. A Los Angeles newspaper wrote, "Welcomed home by crowds estimated at more than 50,000 persons, Aimee Semple McPherson, 'dead' to her congregation and to the world for more than a month, last night was safe in Angelus Temple. . . ."

Soon charges of perpetrating a kidnaping hoax were hurled at McPherson and her mother by skeptical critics. Aimee swore before a Grand Jury that she had been kidnaped. "Had I gone away willingly, I would not have come back," she testified. "I would rather never have been born than to have caused this blow to God's work." After weary months of investigation and testimonies in which the "star witness" changed her story so often she was nicknamed "the hoax woman," the whole case was ultimately thrown out by the prosecutor himself without reaching the jury. The "star witness" confessed that she had testified falsely.[24]

Not even Aimee's worst enemies denied her brilliant gifts and the unbelievable energy she possessed right up to her unexpected death. She had preached to ten thousand in Oakland the night before and announced "The Story of My Life" as the theme for the following evening.

McPherson's son Rolf, currently president of the denomination his mother founded, was at her side when she breathed her last shortly before noon on September 27, 1944, in a hotel room. He knew that his mother was suffering from a very serious kidney ailment and that her doctor had prescribed sleeping tablets. There was no doubt in Rolf McPherson's mind that his mother had no thought of taking her life, as had been suggested by the press. She loved life and the opportunity of serving God in evangelism. With eager anticipation she had discussed the coming service with Rolf. He was told by the coroner "the sleeping tablets would not have had the disastrous effect had it not been for the kidney ailment which allowed the compound to go directly to her system." Rolf was convinced it was God's time to take Aimee Semple McPherson.[25]

Almost twenty years after the death of the founder, a famous British Pentecostal author named Donald Gee was the guest speaker at the fortieth anniversary of Angelus Temple. He interviewed the senior member of the Board of Elders who was attracted to the Temple the day it opened and became Mrs. McPherson's principal counselor and friend through all the storm clouds that surrounded her at times. Informed that Aimee was the victim of scurrilous reporting by journalists willing to produce sensational stories at the expense of truth, Gee concluded: "Her undoubted great gifts, her phenomenal success as an evangelist, her glamorous personality, made her an easy target for shafts of venom. Sometimes she was not as wise as she should have been. She knew it."[26]

76

VI

The Global Explosion of Pentecostalism

THE BREAKTHROUGH realized by Parham's Bible
School and Seymour's Azusa Street Mission set the
stage for an unprecedented expansion of the Pentecostal revival. Bethel Bible School discovered the
formula which has been accepted by almost all Pentecostals everywhere: when a Christian receives the "baptism in the Spirit" he begins speaking in other tongues
as the Spirit gives him utterance. The Azusa Mission
provided the interracial and international laboratory
for the successful application of this principle. Visitors
passing through its doors from near and far heard,
believed, and circled the globe with the exciting news.
By 1910 the term "Pentecostal Movement" was applied
to all groups who stressed the need for the baptism in
the Holy Spirit evidenced by speaking in other tongues.
Thus within four years of its founding, the 1906 Los
Angeles Pentecostal outpouring was repeated in many
lives across the United States and Canada, in Europe,
Africa, India, and South America.

Were human personalities the prime movers of this
revival, or was the Spirit Himself initiating these amazing activities? Pentecostals were quick to attribute whatever successes were achieved in their pioneer efforts to
God and they frequently repeated the Old Testament
prophet Zechariah's words that it was "Not by might,
nor by power, but by my Spirit, says the Lord of hosts."[1]

Although Pentecostals are strongly aware of the
person and work of the Holy Spirit in and through their

77

lives, they do not so emphasize the baptism in the Spirit that they forget the Baptizer, Jesus Christ. Most Pentecostals exalt Jesus Christ and gave Him preeminence. His cross, death, burial, resurrection, and ascension are constantly in their teaching and preaching. However, they are convinced that too many Christians too long have ignored the rightful place of the Holy Spirit. When thought of at all He has often been considered an inferior member in the Holy Trinity—"a vague something-or-other with a religious aura." Many fall into the error of looking impersonally upon the Holy Spirit as an influence, an energy, a power, or a force. But Pentecostals believe He is a person coequal with the Father and with the Son—One who is all powerful, everywhere present, and has knowledge of all things. Jesus referred to him in this way: "When the Spirit of truth comes, he will guide you into all truth; for he will not speak on his own authority, but whatever he hears he will speak, and he will declare to you the things that are to come. He will glorify me, for he will take what is mine and declare it to you."[2]

Pentecostals believe the Holy Spirit has been sent by the Son and even today can be to the Christians what Jesus the Master was to the disciples during his earthly ministry. The Spirit is able to endue with power, to teach, guide, and comfort—indeed, He is called by Christ the other Comforter.

But there are those who ignore the Spirit as a person and are caught up in the display of power and miracles alone, as was Simon the sorcerer who said, "Give me also this power, that any one on whom I lay my hands may receive the Holy Spirit."[3] In other words, "How can I get the Holy Spirit and use 'it'?" But when He is properly understood as a person, a Christian will say, "How can the Holy Spirit get hold of me and use me?" Difficulties in forming a clear conception of the Holy Spirit are understandable. He does not speak of Himself, and His administration of the plans and purposes of the Godhead are relatively unseen and internal. But as deity, the Holy Spirit shared in the creation of the world, as indicated in the Book of Genesis, and in Paul's letter to the Romans we learn that the Spirit raised Jesus from the dead![4]

Pentecostals are in the mainstream of historic Christianity in their belief in the Trinity. Although the word "Trinity" does not once appear in the Bible, the doctrine is clearly revealed. In his last discourse to his disciples Jesus said, "If you love me, you will keep my commandments. And I will pray the Father, and he will give you another Counselor, to be with you for ever, even the Spirit of truth."[5] The Trinity is a theological expression that emerged in the second century to describe the Godhead. It is not tritheism, or the belief in three gods, but one God who is a unity of three distinct persons.

During the third century a bishop named Sabellius, desiring to avoid any danger of tritheism, began to teach that the Father, the Son, and the Holy Spirit were three aspects or manifestations of God. Thus the doctrine of Sabellianism introduced three manifestations, but in so doing it denied separate personalities in the Godhead. The teaching upheld the true divinity of Jesus Christ, but denied the distinct personality of the Father and the Holy Spirit. Sabellianism soon met with almost universal rejection, but it was to be on this ancient issue that some American Pentecostals had a head-on collision with the majority of Pentecostals.

As the Pentecostal Movement spread across the United States, several existent Holiness groups, such as the Church of God and the Fire-Baptized Holiness Church, accepted the Pentecostal message and became fully identified as Pentecostal bodies. What was to become the largest Pentecostal group in the country, the Assemblies of God, emerged at a convention in Hot

79

Springs, Arkansas, in 1914. At that time there arose a doctrinal issue that threatened sudden death to the infant Assemblies of God. It was called the "New Issue" teaching and also was known as the "Jesus Only" or "Oneness" doctrine. Its chief proponent was Frank J. Ewart, pastor of a Pentecostal church in Los Angeles. Ewart maintained that there was only one personality in the Godhead—Jesus Christ. The concept of a trinity was erroneous according to Ewart, and the terms "Father" and "Holy Spirit" were simply "titles" employed to designate various aspects of Christ's person.

Ewart began his "oneness" ministry by rebaptizing in the "name of Jesus" instead of the "Father, and the Son, and the Holy Ghost." According to Ewart, anyone who was baptized in the Trinitarian manner was not truly baptized at all! Ewart acted upon his "revelation" and with Glenn A. Cook, another convinced preacher, they rebaptized each other "in the name of Jesus" on April 15, 1914.[6] Ewart heralded the message across the nation, determined to save the Pentecostal movement by introducing an error that was seventeen centuries old!

Many sincere preachers were carried away with the idea and great numbers submitted to rebaptism. Bible teachers such as J. Roswell Flower recognized the rebirth of an old heresy and repudiated Ewart's "revelation." Unfortunately, Ewart's "New Issue" already had gained momentum. The baptism in the Spirit had drawn many Pentecostals closer to their Lord Jesus and they welcomed a doctrine that seemed to further exalt Him. Many water baptisms in the early years of Pentecost had been conducted with the use of either the Trinitarian formula or "in the name of Jesus," but no departure from orthodox Christianity was involved. By 1916 the moment of truth had arrived as every preacher and church was forced to take a stand on the "New Issue." "Charges of 'Sabellianism' and 'onenism'

80

were countered with accusations of 'three-Godism' and 'Popish slavery,'" Synan writes.[7]

At the General Council of the Assemblies of God in 1916 the important decision was made. The trinitarians retained the majority at this climactic meeting and the "New Issue" unitarians left the meeting, taking with them 156 preachers out of 585 and more than one hundred churches. Two "Oneness" denominations later merged, forming what is known today as the United Pentecostal Church, still accounting for about a quarter of the Pentecostals in the United States. Their unitarian beliefs have shut the door to membership in the "Pentecostal Fellowship of North America," a cooperative fellowship of the organized bodies of Pentecostal believers in the United States and Canada. Apparently the United Pentecostal Church is unwilling to subscribe to the second of the eight doctrinal statements, which declares; "We believe that there is one God, eternally existent in three persons: Father, Son and Holy Ghost."[8]

Within the Pentecostal Fellowship of North America are seventeen member organizations, the largest of which is the Assemblies of God—so large, in fact, that it comprises more than 50 percent of the ministers, members, and churches listed in the PFNA. For this reason it is necessary to describe some of their beliefs and practices in order to forward the understanding of Classic Pentecostalism in the United States. Unfortunately, the term "Pentecostal" has become so inclusive in the minds of so many, including some reputable press people, that it is used without any discrimination. "Pentecostalism" has become an enormous umbrella covering sects and practices that no responsible Pentecostal believer or denomination would endorse for a moment. Some of the snake handlers, for instance, are undoubtedly sincere in their actions, but most Pentecostals are convinced they are sincerely wrong.

Like other Pentecostal groups earlier and later, the Assemblies of God organized in 1914 because they became painfully aware of the need for some organization, however minimal, to counteract the evils of independency. As John T. Nichol explains, these evils were made evident in "doctrinal instability, variable standards of ethical behavior, vulnerability of local assemblies to unscrupulous clerical poseurs, and financial inefficiency."[9] They argued for the legitimate protection of all the assemblies subject to such abuses on the grounds that all things should be done decently and in order as recommended in the Bible. They pointed to the sixth chapter of the Book of Acts, where mention is made of nominations, voting, officers, and church records. The exercise of the central church in Jerusalem in overseeing the affairs of other assemblies was noted in the eighth chapter of Acts and the supervisory system of churches over a wide area was employed by the apostles according to Paul's letter to Titus.[10]

Although American Pentecostal denominations have a great deal in common, there are some variations in faith and practice—most of which, to be sure, are not of major importance as was the "New Issue" dispute. Some of these involve the mode of water baptism and the practice of foot washing. While most Pentecostals baptize by immersion, the Pentecostal Holiness Church adopted a liberal approach, permitting the candidate for baptism the choice of immersion, sprinkling, or pouring.[11] The Church of God, Cleveland, maintains foot washing as an ordinance, considering it to be a manifestation of brotherhood and subservience and observing it at least once a year.[12] The Church of God in Christ, the largest body among the black Pentecostals, also practices foot washing. The attraction of Pentecostalism for the black believer was the interracial character of the movement from its beginnings. Because of the prominent part played by Seymour at Azusa Street, many blacks thought of the Pentecostal movement as primarily a Negro phenomenon.[13] Bishop Charles H. Mason, the founder-organizer of the Church of God in Christ, received the Pentecostal baptism while spending five weeks in the Azusa Street meetings. His group, claiming a world constituency of more than two million, has experienced a phenomenal growth at home and abroad, where they had great success in their African and Latin American fields.[14] While the Church of God in Christ has actively participated in the Pentecostal World Conferences, it has not joined the Pentecostal Fellowship of North America. Could it be that the all-white PFNA, in forming the Fellowship in 1948, failed to invite a single black denomination to membership?[15]

Pentecostals differ in their forms of church government as well as in some articles of faith. You will find variations from the completely independent, to a congregational polity, to the more centralized episcopal structure. Those who function under a congregational form of government maintain the sovereignty of the local churches, which possess deeds to church buildings and exercise the final voice in the selection of new pastors. Among these are the Assemblies of God, the United Pentecostal Church, and the Open Bible Standard Church. While guaranteeing the sovereignty of each local affiliated church, the Assemblies of God provide a basis of cooperative fellowship for both ministers and congregations under a General Council and District Councils, which in turn is Presbyterian in form.

Adhering to the episcopal form of church government are the Church of God, the Church of God in Christ, the International Church of the Foursquare Gospel, and the Pentecostal Holiness Church. Most of their highest administrators bear the title of Bishop, whereas churches using the congregational pattern of organization prefer to use the title General Superintendent.

Various attempts have been made to form mergers between Pentecostal denominations, but these somehow never succeeded. The Open Bible Standard Church came within a hair's breadth of joining forces with the Assemblies of God, while the Pentecostal Holiness Church advanced to serious stages of negotiation with the Church of God. If fifteen different non-Pentecostal Protestant denominations can seriously consider a merger into one denomination, as they are doing in the Consultation on Church Union, surely the Pentecostal families need to give it another try. Jesus expressed the longing that all Christians may be one.

The average person does not realize how many churches are Pentecostal because few of the denominational names include the word "Pentecostal" and many of their churches omit the word. It is no wonder that a non-Pentecostal, in trying to describe this branch of American Protestantism, remarked that Pentecostalism "appears not as a single coherent movement but as a congeries of independent, often sharply contrasted, sometimes mutually hostile groups of varying size and strength and of greater or lesser affinity with each other and historic Catholicism or Protestantism."[16]

Despite appearances of disharmony, however, the American Pentecostals have been united by the distinctive doctrine which links speaking in tongues with the baptism in the Holy Spirit, sweeping away the vagueness and ambiguities connected with the experience prior to Parham's discovery in the Bethel Bible School. In England the Elim Pentecostal Alliance, largest Pentecostal body next to the Assemblies of God, endorsed the view that there may be other signs of Spirit-baptism besides speaking in tongues. T. B. Barratt, the founder of Pentecostalism in Norway, supported the view that speaking in tongues was the expected evidence of the baptism in the Holy Spirit but allowed room for exceptions, stating, "The tongues may have been kept back by will-force, from fear, distrust, unwillingness, ignorance, or unbelief."[17]

Pentecostals remind themselves that continued growth does not depend upon organizational structures. It depends on the highest allegiance to their Savior Jesus Christ. It depends upon their baptism in the Spirit, with its empowerment to witness and walk in that fulness daily. It depends upon exemplifying the fruit of Godly living and unselfish concern for others. A Presbyterian minister writing in the Toronto *Daily Star* saw the Pentecostal churches filling the vacuum created by the failure of many larger, older churches. They were able to do this not by means of a highly complicated theology but by concentrating on the "simplicities." He testified, "In a quarter century's acquaintance with Pentecostal pastors I find them men of faith and courage. . . . There have been times . . . that their faith has been awesome in its utter Christlike quality."[18]

A spiritual quality has accompanied the phenomenal statistical success of twentieth-century Pentecostalism. When in the course of time the Pentecostal pioneers stepped aside to make way for new leaders, their younger successors, also Spirit-filled, carried the torch and held it even higher. After an era of ostracism and occasional persecution, the next generation experienced a period of passive toleration. During World War II the toleration began to change to acceptance. In 1943 an invitation was extended to the Pentecostals to become members and to hold offices in the National Association of Evangelicals. The Protestant ministers within this association were in a sense the successors to the American Fundamentalists who had repudiated the Pentecostals in their 1928 Chicago Convention; at that time they described Pentecostalism as "the present wave of fanatical and unscriptural healing which is sweeping over the country today. . . ." They unreservedly opposed "the perpetuation of the miraculous sign-healing of Jesus and His apostles, wherein they claim the only reason the Church cannot perform these miracles is because of unbelief."[19]

Although the National Association of Evangelicals was by no means adopting the Pentecostal doctrines of divine healing and speaking in tongues, they *were* extending the right hand of fellowship to Pentecostals as brethren in Christ. No doubt they had concluded that the Pentecostals "had come to stay, and that fellowship with them was not only possible, but desirable."[20]

Accepting this invitation was a big step for the Pentecostals, who had been isolated from other Christian groups for decades. One Church of God delegate was relieved to discover that "We were not asked to compromise one iota of our distinctive Pentecostal testimony."[21] Now, for the first time in decades, the Pentecostals belonged. Both groups found a common tie in their love for Christ and a common belief in the essentials of the Christian faith. More than one hundred representatives responded from the Assemblies of God.

Both Evangelicals and Pentecostals shared a common fear that modernistic trends within liberal Protestantism had to be met by Bible-believing Christian groups large enough to include entire denominations and missionary organizations. The Assemblies of God and the Church of God were represented on the Board of Administration when they became members. Further respect for the Pentecostals was shown when Thomas F. Zimmerman was chosen to serve a term in the top elective post of the National Association of Evangelicals.

The Evangelicals' fear of the power of religious liberals within the United States was transferred to the World Council of Churches when it came into existence in 1948. At their Amsterdam Assembly the formal basis for fellowship in the World Council of Churches was simply acceptance of the Lord Jesus Christ as God and Savior. This was expanded in their Third Assembly, held in New Delhi, India, in 1961. This time their requirement for members was to confess Christ as God and Savior "according to the Scriptures, and therefore seek to fulfill together their common calling to the glory of the one God, Father, Son and Holy Spirit."[22]

Despite this Trinitarian Basis for fellowship, which actually bars Unitarians and Oneness denominations from membership, the World Council of Churches and its ecumenical movement have been disapproved by most evangelical believers, including Southern Baptists and Pentecostals throughout the United States. In its 1963 General Council the Assemblies of God unanimously ratified a resolution condemning the ecumenical movement and disapproving pastors and churches that participated in any of the modern ecumenical organizations in such a way as to promote it. The Assemblies of God sincerely believes that "the combination of many denominations into a World Super Church will probably culminate in the Scarlet Woman or Religious Babylon of Revelation. . . ."[23]

But will the World Council of Churches, with its scriptural basis for fellowship, actually promote the work of Satan? David J. du Plessis, often called "Mr. Pentecost," did not think so. He reasoned that God would not allow the Protestant world to become Satan's instrument. "Why should Pentecostal unity be of the Lord and Protestant unity be of the devil? Was it not the Lord who was moving us to unity in both movements?" Deeply disturbed about these probing questions, du Plessis prayed earnestly as he sought to learn God's purposes. By 1951, as a result of continued prayer, part of the answer fell into place. "The Lord spoke to me and clearly told me to go and witness to the leaders of the World Council of Churches."[24] Accepting this call, du Plessis stepped forth to become an effective ambassador, not of any Pentecostal denomination, but of Jesus Christ, paving the way for the

87

understanding of the gifts of the Holy Spirit and the unity which may be found under the leadership of God the Holy Spirit.

Doors began to open. Du Plessis was received with open arms and willing ears by ministers anxious to hear what the Spirit would say through this man. In 1952 he was invited to attend the ecumenical convention of the International Missionary Council of the WCC which was held in Willingen, Germany. He was introduced as a Pentecostal to the 210 delegates by Dr. Mackay, the IMC president, and was asked to share his knowledge of why and how the Pentecostals had accomplished so much in so short a time. During his eleven-day stay at the conference du Plessis was requested to meet with more than a hundred of the delegates. In this manner he became known to many leaders and officers of the WCC.

After the convention du Plessis received an invitation from Dr. Visser't Hooft, the WCC secretary, to attend the Second Assembly at Evanston, Illinois, in 1954 in order to witness and chat with as many delegates as possible about his Pentecostal experiences. Du Plessis was afraid that he might be mistaken for a dissident trying to create division in their midst, but the World Council secretary, well aware of du Plessis' ethical standards and winsome ways, had no apprehensions whatever. As a result, "Mr. Pentecost" at times found himself engaged beyond the midnight hour conversing with archbishops, bishops, professors, principals, and presidents of institutions. More doors widely opened to this Pentecostal ambassador-at-large. He has lectured at many institutions, among them Princeton Seminary, Yale Divinity, Union Theological, Colgate's Rochester School of Divinity, and Southern Methodist. After a decade of constant personal contacts, du Plessis was convinced that an entirely new spiritual climate was being enjoyed among churches within the denomina-

88

tions cooperating with the World Council of Churches. He discerned a deep spiritual stir in general, but even more importantly, he found "a sincere recognition of the work of the Holy Spirit among the top echelons of Protestantism." He found divine healing accepted and practiced by most denominations, and even tongues was "receiving more and more favorable attention."[25]

Within the World Council of Churches du Plessis is convinced that there is an open-ended approach to the work of Holy Spirit. He illustrates this by referring to one of the publications drawn up by the Council's Commission on Faith and Order. It appealed to Christians in all churches to join in prayer for Christian unity during a week of prayer and encouraged them to consider their common apostolic tradition.

Regarding miracles, Christians were reminded that all things were possible with God but warned that unwillingness to believe was the greatest spiritual danger. In taking a stand on the healing ministry, the Commission mentioned "Christ's concern for the whole man, spiritual and physical." The prayer bulletin requested specific prayer about the meaning of speaking in tongues and the interpretation of tongues, and called on Christians everywhere to remember "the significance of the unusual and extraordinary in the Christian Church as opposed to the normal and mediocre." Speakers in tongues were described as those "who continually challenge and disturb the Church which all too easily becomes complacent and self-satisfied. . . ." "A Pentecostal could hardly have written a better outline on the ministry gifts," Du Plessis exclaimed.[26]

David du Plessis, who was once called a "World Council of Churches gadfly," has stirred many Protestant clergymen to honestly face their indifference toward the gifts of the Spirit. As a result many men of the cloth have experienced dramatic changes in their ministries. A Reformed Church pastor said this of du Plessis: "Only those of us who serve and fellowship in churches that are members of the National Council and the World Council of Churches can appreciate this man's ministry when we see and feel the strong 'wind of the Spirit' which is bringing a change and spiritual climate into the councils of the historic churches."[27]

His intimacy with the World Council of Churches probably caused some observers to believe that du Plessis was serving as an official representative of the Pentecostals, but this was not the case. Nevertheless, his open espousal of ecumenicism brought him into disfavor with the Pentecostals. But David du Plessis firmly believed the Spirit bade him go and go he did, as a Pentecostal ambassador-at-large representing an experience rather than a movement. The eminent British editor of *Pentecost,* the official organ of the Pentecostal World Conferences, was more impartial than most. He commented that du Plessis "has exercised a striking ministry among leaders of the older denominations where he has been widely accepted, and has done much to create a better understanding of the movement."[28] Nor has it left du Plessis unchanged. When a Pentecostal professor commented that du Plessis had added a new dimension to the Pentecostal experience, the man who had preached in forty-five countries smiled and said, "Yes, when I got out of my Pentecostal shell, I found the Holy Spirit was at work in other churches all over the world with the same blessing and the same manifestations."[29]

Du Plessis was able to make that statement in the early sixties, but half a century earlier many Pentecostals, faced with the intolerance of non-Pentecostal Christians, had been so preoccupied with their own circles of witnessing that a lack of communication separated most of them. As churches multiplied, an increasing number of missionaries were sent to foreign shores to spread the full gospel message of Christ as

Savior, Healer, Baptizer, and soon-coming King. Denominational programs of world evangelism began to appear in the United States, England, Scandinavia, and other countries. Although most of the early Pentecostals were poor economically, culturally, and academically, their zeal to share their spiritual treasures at home and abroad was so intense that nothing seemed to stop them. Some of today's largest Pentecostal areas, such as Brazil, Indonesia, and Soviet Russia, were served by laymen or preachers who answered God's call through prophecy to be missionaries.

The American Assemblies of God has always had an enlarged vision of world missions, and today this single Pentecostal body has almost 1,100 foreign missionaries serving in eighty-seven countries, surpassing in accomplishments the work of other Protestant denominations far larger in size. Support for these missionaries comes in the form of voluntary pledges from the grass-root membership of almost nine thousand Assemblies found in all fifty States. In 1970 they gave more than 18 million dollars to help accomplish the task of world evangelization. Members are continually made conscious of the enormous challenge, and everybody gives. Boys and girls turn in their small, wooden missionary barrels full of pennies, nickels, and dimes each month. Teenagers purchase modern means of transportation to hasten the work of missionaries. Sixty-three percent of the 5,365 students found in the Assemblies of God's nine colleges are theology majors and many of these will in time be added to the missionary force.

In helping churches of each nation to become indigenous—that is, self-supporting, self-governing, and self-propagating—the missionaries concentrate on evangelism and the training of nationals for church leadership. No less than ninety-eight Assemblies of God Foreign Bible Schools have come into existence for this purpose, making this Pentecostal body first in this category among all denominations in the United States. In the light of the rising tide of nationalism, the practice of establishing indigenous churches has proven most effective.

On the world scene Pentecostal adherents possibly have reached twenty million. Their greatest numerical strength is found in the United States, Brazil, Indonesia, Africa, Chile, and Soviet Russia. Radio, television, huge printing presses, modern vehicles, missionary aircraft, and large transmitters for foreign-language broadcasts are all being employed to share the full gospel with those who have not heard the good news.

With relatively few prominent personalities and with no world organization, world Pentecostalism kept growing at an accelerating pace. In 1938 Lewi Pethrus, pastor of the 6,500-member Filadelfia Church in Stockholm, was asked to promote a world Pentecostal conference. Pethrus did not feel the time was ripe for a world conference and instead summoned a European Pentecostal Conference, which turned out to be an important step in the right direction. But it took Swiss pastor Leonard Steiner of Zurich to recognize the value and need for a World Pentecostal Conference right after World War II. During a communion service he was moved to take the initiative in calling a global gathering of glossolalics, one that would assemble Pentecostal national leaders to see the light in each other's eyes.

The year was 1947, a couple of years after Nazi Germany had been brought to its knees in unconditional surrender by the Allied forces. Pleading hands of the destitute left in the wake of Hitler's destruction were stretched forth, hoping for relief and rehabilitation. Many Pentecostals were numbered among those who had endured untold hardship during the holocaust. Already some missionary arms of Pentecostal denominations were busy assisting the needy; others required only direction and some form of cooperation to do the greatest possible good. The need to share mutual problems and spiritual victories, increased speed of travel, and improved financial conditions all helped to bring a response that exceeded all expectations.

The hosts at Zurich expected a compact, semi-private conference of "chief men among the brethren" in the convocation. They were completely unprepared for attendances that reached three thousand. Never were Pentecostals from so many nations afforded such an opportunity to share with each other, and from this opportunity emerged a unity of human spirits under the guidance of the Holy Spirit. Despite differences brought into sharp focus regarding the extent of organization desirable for a worldwide fellowship, a number of the delegates pressed hard for an organization that would speak with authority for all Pentecostals in the world, including the practical arm responsible for coordinated world relief efforts. The Scandinavians avoided organization like the plague, preferring to dwell on the principles that sustained spiritual life and power. Others attended simply for the thrill of being part of a historical first among world Pentecostals. Tactful handling of the delicate question of proportionate representation was needed so that none would feel offended or excluded.

The Zurich Conference focused attention on the obvious truths that united all Pentecostals. The most important symbol of success in a continuing fellowship was the creation of an international quarterly journal called *Pentecost*. Finally, after forty years of confinement to local, national, and denominational magazines which promoted private programs, the Pentecostal Movement had an organ that could broaden horizons and synthesize revival information from scores of countries for its international readership. The unanimous choice for the editor's post was Donald Gee of England, a highly gifted writer who enjoyed the esteem and confidence of Pentecostals everywhere.

93

Editor Gee was commissioned to give news of Pentecostal progress wherever it happened, without fear or favor. Although negative features and problems were included and one need but read a few editorials from Gee's provocative pen to start squirming, positive testimonies dominated each issue. Contributors were reminded to submit news, not views, and reports began to pour in from all parts of the world, as did subscriptions. Readers were most eager to discover little-known facts of the moving of the Spirit in areas curtained off by ignorance or political forces.

Word of revival and revolution slipped out from China. Hundreds of Pentecostal missionaries were still laboring there in the late forties, although they saw the handwriting on the wall. Large indigenous Pentecostal churches existed—an estimated thirty thousand Pentecostal believers were in Shanghai alone. A non-Pentecostal Peiping pastor invited a British missionary to conduct a series of meetings in his church, as a result of which seventy Chinese were baptized in the Spirit and spoke in tongues. As students from the university observed the phenomenon their interest in things spiritual increased. In other meetings geared for Peiping's youth hundreds of Chinese stepped forward to receive Christ as their personal Savior while three thousand in the crowded arena watched. This was the fruit of training native workers in the Pentecostal Truth Bible Institute.[30]

A missionary walked more than 1,200 miles in six months in the area of Ka Do Land, baptizing 1,100 converts in water. During this time he found the local Communists tolerant, even friendly. Later, when in Hong Kong, he learned that some of the nationals he trained had baptized another four hundred within a two-month period.[31] But already arrests and false accusations were mounting. Earlier reports indicated some atrocities. In 1948 Mrs. Beruldsen of the British

Assemblies of God reported, "In one city captured by the Communists five of the Christians were taken, terribly ill-treated, and then nailed to five crosses, where they died a slow, agonizing death."[32]

Some missionaries who overprotected the converts were fearful of Chinese failures under the fires of persecution. But the grace of God was proving to be sufficient. A veteran Pentecostal missionary made this incisive remark before being compelled to leave China: "The Chinese Church belongs to China and not to any group of churches in the West, and the secret by which this development can be speeded up is, first, for the missionary to get out of sight, and secondly, let him get further out of sight, and thirdly, let him get entirely out of sight."[33] Forced to leave China, the foreign missionaries were indeed no longer to be seen, yet the Chinese believers faithfully carried on. And the voices of Pentecostal teachers could still be heard by means of the Far East Broadcasting Company located in Manila in the Philippines.

Far from the scenes of the persecution at the hands of Chinese atheists, and perhaps more difficult to understand, was the persecution of Pentecostals in the religious land of Italy. Umberto Gioretti related their plight before the 1952 Pentecostal World Conference in London. He presented a documented charge revealing the denial of constitutionally guaranteed religious liberties to the Pentecostals. Pastors were arrested and churches closed under acts based upon the 1935 Fascist law which forbade Pentecostals the rights of organization and freedom of assembly.[34]

Harassment was the order of the day. In Rome pastor Roberto Bracco saw the Chief of Police and six constables enter his church during an evening service. They had come to seal the church doors, but he prevailed upon them to take no action because American guests were present. Denied tax exemption, one church was assessed $2,700 a year. In southern Italy a Pentecostal congregation was intimidated as the police recorded their names. This was done after a member who was in prayer was whipped several times. The flock was menaced by a tommy-gun and its pastor was jailed overnight.[35]

Years passed before the injustice dealt to the Italian Pentecostals reached the country's Supreme Court. The highest court of the land ruled that police decrees restricting freedom of worship were "automatically abrogated" by the adoption of Italy's 1948 Constitution which guaranteed religious freedom. It was 1954 and everything looked fine. But it took five long years before the decree was officially registered in the office of the Ministry of the Interior. At long last the five hundred Pentecostal churches could legally hold property and enjoy tax exemption. Pastors were able to conduct services without securing police permission for each meeting. And the 100,000 members, largest of all Protestant groups in Italy, rejoiced to know that their pastors could legally perform weddings and bury the dead. Governmental hostility and bureaucratic obstructions were now but bad dreams of the past. Since 1960 the Pentecostal movement in Italy has enjoyed juridical recognition.[36]

The Italian Pentecostals wasted no time implementing cherished plans of evangelistic expansion. Within two years they built a five-story Bible school with accommodations for one hundred students within walking distance of the Vatican. The Italian Pentecostals invited missionary evangelist Hal Herman for a citywide effort in Rome's Brancaccio Theater. They utilized paid newspaper ads, posters, handbills, and a sound car with loudspeakers which toured the city streets. As the meetings progressed hundreds came forward to publicly confess Christ as Savior and prayer was offered for the sick. Newsmen filmed the services and the scenes were viewed in theaters all over Italy.[37]

96

Attempts at harassment were not entirely over, however. A high-salaried executive, John McTernan, had
left California in obedience to the call of God to minister in Italy. Only seven years later, in 1966, he was
ready to dedicate the 1,500-seat Marconi Theater as
the International Evangelical Center in Rome. Suddenly an official from the passport office informed the
American Pentecostal he must leave, never to return.
McTernan challenged him with a direct presentation of
the gospel of Jesus Christ. The official later testified
publicly: "I came to put this man out of the country,
but he led me to Christ."[38]

Like Italy, Mexico did not always welcome Pentecostals with warm embraces. In 1948 near Toluca,
seven Pentecostals were clubbed to death when a band
of fanatics entered their homes during the night. At
Atlixco, nine were slashed with machetes, shot, stoned,
and tortured for nothing more than the testimonies they
boldly proclaimed. Today the Pentecostals are the
largest group among the Evangelicals in Mexico and the
common people hear them gladly.[39] Further south,
Colombia was a hotbed of persecution for all evangelical believers, especially Pentecostals, who displayed an
aggressive, jubilant, apostolic type of Christianity
which generated either favor or fear in the hearts of
those they met. From 1948 to 1956 more than two
hundred Protestant church schools were closed by the
government and forty-six church buildings were destroyed by fire or dynamited. The largest Protestant
church closed by the authorities was the Pentecostal
Church of the Foursquare Gospel in Barrancabermeja.
Ignoring widespread persecution, the Pentecostals in
Colombia multiplied from 415 in 1952 to 8,174 members in 1962.[40] The persecuted Pentecostal church
seems to lack no ingredient for continued growth.

In 1949 Pentecostals from thirty countries converged upon Paris for the second world conference.
Much had happened since the first convocation in

Zurich two years earlier. Pentecostal leaders in Great Britain, Germany, and India had formed national fellowships in response to recommendations at Zurich and the Pentecostal Fellowship of North America took in both American and Canadian believers. On the national level representatives of the various Pentecostal denominations meet annually for studies and exchange of views in the fields of home missions, foreign missions, and youth programs.

Pentecostal unity was severely strained at the Paris Conference when some impatient delegates suggested that the Conference proceed to organize without the Scandinavian Pentecostals, who were noted for their entirely negative attitude toward centralization. Delegates from Sweden didn't even care to elect a World Conference Secretary or a five-member Advisory Council that would serve between conferences. The Scandinavians were determined at all costs to preserve the principle of freedom in church government. The deadlock was broken when all agreed that the structure for the world fellowship "become as free and simple as possible." David du Plessis was unanimously elected as Secretary and five Advisers from different parts of the world were chosen to assist him. Absolutely no authority over Pentecostal churches or movements rested in their hands. At last the Scandinavian brethren were content and at ease. A bright future was promised for continued global gatherings—a future that would emphasize and encourage spiritual fellowship. Pentecostal unity was cherished more than outward organization and the delegates were to discover much enrichment in sharing beliefs and practices, in probing common problems, and in tentatively touching on the possibilities of cooperation in world evangelism.[41]

Discussion on the comity problem, the avoidance of proselytizing members of each other's denomination on the mission field, seemed to be taboo. The British complained about the scant time and attention given to the missionary programs of the participating groups. Although missionary secretaries of many Pentecostal bodies were present in Paris, not a single session was called so that these important leaders might share reflections on their common interests.

Subsequent Pentecostal world conferences were held every three years. After Zurich and Paris they gathered in London, Stockholm, Toronto, Jerusalem, Helsinki, and Rio de Janeiro. At the Ninth World Conference representatives of forty nations met in the United States for the first time, in Dallas. Never before had delegates from Soviet Russia attended, and they marveled as they saw the response of hundreds of young people coming forward to dedicate their lives to Christ as Dave Wilkerson preached before the packed Memorial Auditorium.

The Sixth Conference held in Jerusalem was a unique experience for the 2,589 registered delegates from thirty countries. The Nations Building was donated freely by the Israeli Government, which did all in its power to accommodate the Pentecostals at the conference. Hotels were taxed to the limit so that some delegates had to be housed in distant Tel Aviv. It was most fitting to hear an utterance of tongues and its interpretation on Pentecost Sunday in Jerusalem exhorting the throng to praise God for Christ, the greatest of His gifts. That afternoon D. L. Williams, the black Bishop of the Church of God in Christ, preached on "First-Century Pentecost." The Swedish interpreter tried his best to keep up with the flow of the American's growing torrent of words and volumes of praise filled the auditorium as the Bishop concluded. The more conservative delegates learned to understand those of their Pentecostal brethren who enjoyed more exuberant worship. Before they left Jerusalem the Pentecostals donated more than two thousand dollars to plant trees in Israel, a lasting tribute of gratitude from believers who loved the land and its people.[42]

The Eighth Pentecostal World Conference held in Rio de Janeiro was easily the largest gathering of Pentecostals ever held anywhere. Services averaged from ten thousand during the day to as many as forty thousand at night in Maracanazinho Stadium and the crowning Sunday afternoon rally necessitated the use of the world's largest stadium. In spite of threatening weather, more than 120,000 attended the closing service, graced by a two-thousand-voice choir and a three-hundred-piece band. For periods of ten to fifteen minutes everyone praised the Lord with uplifted hands and the sound of their voices was as the sound of mighty waters. Many delegates received a new vision of the impact of missions upon a nation and the world. As the Elim evangelist Alexander Tee of England preached on the second coming of Christ, the entire service was reaching the nation via Radio Tupy, Brazil's most powerful radio station.

This was a soul-winning conference, as "altar calls were given with fervor in all the meetings three times a day." Sinners always responded, sometimes by the scores. Every effort was designed to fulfill the conference theme, "O Espirito Santo Glorificando a Cristo," meaning the Holy Spirit Glorifying Christ. Daily radio and television coverage introduced Christ to many more than the thousands who attended.[43]

Pentecostalism has led the way in Latin American church growth. J. Philip Hogan, foreign missions director of the American Assemblies of God, called Brazil the ripest mission field in the world, a land where the greatest national revival of the twentieth century is now in force. Pentecostals in that one nation are increasing too fast for accurate statistics, but they already have passed the three million mark and there is no slowing down. Each church has a number of preaching points, which may be nothing more than a rented room, a home, or a street corner. Before long the preaching point becomes a congregation and then a church with its own preaching outstations. When zealous believers work at it, as do the Spirit-filled Pentecostals in a free country such as Brazil, advances resemble a multiplication table. And the explosion started with a few pioneers who came to Brazil as a result of prophecy uttered back in the States. In 1910 two Swedish Americans, Gunnar Vingren and Dan Berg, decided to leave Chicago for Belem to tell Brazilians about Christ, and the result is that today the Assemblies of God they founded among the Portuguese-speaking populace numbers 1,700,000 active adult members. The Brazilian Assemblies in turn sent a Pentecostal missionary to Portugal to establish the first Assembly in that land of religious restrictions.[44]

Louis Franciscon, an Italian-American, also was directed by prophecy to South America in 1910. Preferring not to use the name "Pentecostal," he became the founder of the Christian Congregation. Taking with him the divisive attitudes that had been prevalent among the Italian-American Pentecostals in Chicago, he trained the denomination not to mingle with other groups, even Pentecostals. With more than half a million members they had no official organ to carry news of the Christian Congregations. Among these members in Brazil are 250,000 Italian Pentecostals—more than in Italy. In 1962 they began building a church in São Paulo to seat 25,000, thought to be the largest in the world. A non-Pentecostal missionary trying to explain the phenomenal growth in Brazil said it was because ". . . instead of repressing and ignoring emotionalism, [Pentecostalism] has recognized it and harnessed it to the program and to the discipline of the church."[45]

In Chile, where there are mostly Methodist Pentecostals among more than 750,000 Spirit-filled believers now under a Marxian government, the *British Weekly* had this to say about their worship: "Three cheers for God? Embarrassing? Probably. The joy of the Lord is apt to be sectarian nowadays and we are no longer sects. We are denominations. But, maybe, renewal of life and three cheers please God immensely, especially among 'the most ignorant classes' to whom our frigid politeness about 'Christian principles' has notoriously no appeal. Jesus appealed to them also and they followed Him about."[46] Meanwhile, the official Methodist church, from which the Methodist Pentecostal Church separated in 1909, remains approximately the same size today as it was then—four thousand members.[47] What made the difference? Emotional release? A style of worship?

At the Second Evangelical Conference in Latin America, David du Plessis was disturbed to find that many non-Pentecostals thought the secret of the instant success of the Pentecostals was a special technique and that this could be applied by training their people. He knew they were wrong and was happy to inform them that the secret was "the power of the Holy Spirit in the ministry of the Word and in the lives of converts." Inquirers among the two hundred delegates from twenty-two countries representing Protestant denominations from Episcopalians to Pentecostals learned that the only name for this "technique" was the "Baptism into the Holy Spirit, by the Lord Jesus Christ, the mighty Baptizer."[48]

Equally Pentecostal but quite reserved in comparison with the Latin Americans are the Swedes. Although all Scandinavian Pentecostal churches are independent and self-governing, without any superintendents or bishops overseeing them, they are highly disciplined and work closely together. With almost 100,000 members in a nation of less than eight million, Sweden is a country with a high ratio of Pentecostals. Its 560 churches have scattered six hundred missionaries in forty countries, more than twice the missionary force of Sweden's State Church.

The acknowledged national Pentecostal leader, by virtue of his spiritual status, has been Lewi Pethrus. Outwardly gentle, but inwardly a man of steel, this former Baptist was led into Pentecost by T. B. Barratt, the Pentecostal Apostle of Northern Europe. From a nucleus of nineteen members, Pethrus pastored the little flock to what is believed to be the largest Protestant church on the continent of Europe. Filadelfia has an adult voting membership of over six thousand. This huge congregation receives the attention and spiritual care of forty-five elders who assist the pastors. On the first Friday of each month a prayer meeting is held in 150 homes in Stockholm.

Pethrus has been criticized for being too conservative by those who favor the exercise of the more spectacular spiritual gifts. Wildfire, fanaticism, and extremes have found no room in the Filadelfia church. During a span of forty-seven years as pastor, the gifted administrator has edited *Dagen,* the country's only Christian daily newspaper. Sold on stands throughout Sweden, it has a circulation of thirty thousand. A prolific writer, Filadelfia's pastor also authored some fifty books.

Pethrus believes that Christians should control their own economic welfare as well as church life. For this reason he led in establishing a savings and credit bank which in turn helps to finance sound church projects. Its profits are disbursed annually to meet the greatest needs in the Pentecostal work. Faced with the restrictions of a noncommercial State radio, Pethrus launched a short-wave station from Tangier, North Africa. IBRA, the International Broadcasting Radio Association, carried only Full Gospel programs in as many as twenty-three languages, including broadcasts in Russian, Ukrainian, Hungarian, Polish, and Estonian.

The Filadelfia parishioners clearly appreciate such a gifted administrator. When he tried to step aside at sixty-five, they would not accept his resignation and he continued to minister to the people at Filadelfia for nine more years. The Swedish Annual Pentecostal conferences, which attract many thousands, found the Wednesday night message of octogenarian Pethrus the highlight of the week.[49]

Vast differences in culture, customs, and climate are leveled before the sweep of Pentecostalism. Far removed from Scandinavia and Brazil is a pastor sometimes called "Africa's Billy Graham." He is Nicholas Bhengu, a Zulu Pentecostal preacher, the son of a Lutheran pastor who studied at Taylor University and speaks English, Afrikaans, and four African languages. A communist before his conversion, Bhengu was catapulted into prominence in 1951 by the results of his meetings in East London, South Africa. The Manchester *Guardian* described his success in these words: "An African evangelist who persuades his audiences to hand in their knives, blackjacks and knuckle-dusters, and to forswear crime is moving through Southern Africa."[50]

Indeed, many converts had been drunkards and thieves who voluntarily surrendered more than two van loads of merchandise stolen from the whites. Their former philosophy maintained that only stealing from fellow blacks was a sin. Dangerous weapons were turned over to the police with the startling announcement that these converts were prepared to pay for their sins. Because of the substantial decrease of crime in the city, the local city council submitted a choice building site valued at twelve thousand dollars to Bhengu as an outright gift. The Africans themselves constructed a church seating four thousand at a cost of $75,000.[51]

On one Sunday a massive ceremony took place in a little creek. Nicholas Bhengu, waving his hand toward a long line waiting to be baptized by immersion, stated that not one of them was unemployed. "They are now happy in their jobs, and most important, they are now right with God." He then proceeded to baptize 1,300![52]

Bhengu's platform technique is subdued. Testifying before a group of Full Gospel Business Men in New York City, he shared his impression of the Pentecostal meetings he had observed in the United States. He was always amazed that it was necessary to ask people forward to be baptized in the Spirit. Recounting his experiences in Africa he described this scene: "In most cases we do not call people to come out for salvation, they start crying and wailing before we call them. As for the baptism in the Holy Spirit—He just comes, comes on the whole crowd; you will find people lying down, you will find them speaking in other tongues, you are not sure who is baptized and who is not when this happens to thousands at the same time. That is what God is doing in our country."[53]

In 1962, when Bhengu was recognized as the chairman of the African section of the Assemblies of God of South Africa, with an all-African executive body, some criticism arose that Nicholas Bhengu was anti-white and anti-missionary. David Newington, director of Emmanuel Press in South Africa, was convinced that nothing could be farther from the truth. Nicholas Bhengu was, he said, without a doubt "the man of God's appointment for this time of crisis in emergent Africa." His standing with the leaders and governments, both black and white, of many African countries has been without parallel. Bhengu's appreciation and evaluation of the wider implications of Christian missionary policy and development in Africa is "far beyond that of any other African leader."[54]

Bhengu endorses the principle of an indigenous church for his people but refutes the argument that missionaries are no longer needed. He realizes their value in training young Africans for the ministry, assist-

ing in Sunday School methods, publishing gospel literature, and conducting radio evangelism. The Zulu
evangelist once stated, "I thank God for the missionaries. I am the product of missions. The African people
from their earliest years have been taught to hate white
people, but the missionaries have brought a Gospel that
has taught us to love the white men. The Gospel of
Christ is the answer to Africa's problems."[55] Coming
from a former communist, these words have added
significance in today's ideological warfare.

The story of T. L. Osborn's missionary evangelism
in scores of foreign cities reads like fiction. He has
managed to achieve spectacular results by being in the
right place at the right time too often to permit any
doubts but that a higher intelligence has been active in
preparing the way. A member of the Pentecostal Church
of God of America before becoming an independent
interdenominational missionary evangelist. Osborn has
his headquarters a few miles from Oral Roberts University in Tulsa. Like his neighbor, Osborn has communicated the healing Christ to the multitudes, but unlike
Roberts, he has ministered almost exclusively overseas
for the greatest part of the past twenty years.

The apostolic results of his foreign crusades are too
numerous to detail, but a few examples may serve to
depict the man and his method in the ministry. Excitement and elements of danger seem to go hand in hand in
some of the countries Osborn and his wife, Daisy, have
visited. Take, for example, the revolution and revival
that broke out simultaneously in Guatemala. Even
while thousands were mobbing the Government Palace
downtown, in another part of Guatemala City Christ
was being proclaimed in power "and hundreds were
accepting Him and being healed." The morning papers
reported the damage and deaths but the Pentecostal
meetings continued. As news of the revolution diminished, the power of Christ became the talk of the town

106

and the crusade audience increased to more than twenty thousand during the five weeks of services.[56]

Not to be recommended as standard procedure unless one has the complete assurance that the supernatural gift of faith is functioning, was the challenge Osborn flung out to an audience of ten thousand Moslems in Java, Indonesia. Standing before a sea of Islamic faces, the fearless missionary reminded them that they believed Jesus Christ was a good man—even a prophet— and that He healed the sick everywhere. "Your Koran tells you that. Now I have come to tell you what this Bible tells us about Him," continued the evangelist. "He is more than a prophet—that He is the Son of God, born of a virgin, and that after He was killed in Jerusalem, God raised Him from the dead, and that He is the only Savior today, and that His blood is the only remission for sins." Letting the words sink in, Osborn then dramatized Christ's offer to forgive sins and to heal the sick with, "If He is dead, He cannot heal. If He is alive, He should be the same as before. Do you believe that?" The large crowd agreed.

Osborn then called for anyone in the audience totally deaf in one ear to come forward. A number walked toward the platform and nine persons were permitted to stand before the Christian evangelist. The first man to face him was a Moslem priest! Osborn realized his predicament. The credence of ten thousand non-Christians hinged on whether or not this Moslem would be healed. Taking the priest by the hand, Osborn turned to the throng and said, "If I pray in Jesus' Name and his ear receives hearing, it will be a miracle wrought by Jesus Christ who is risen from the dead, because I cannot cure anything. My hands are like yours. I am just a man. But if he hears, after I pray in Jesus' Name, then it will prove that Christ is alive. Will you believe then that He is God's Son, risen from the dead and the only Savior?" The audience again responded affirma-

107

tively. Osborn then placed his finger in the Moslem's ear and prayed, asking for divine confirmation. And it came—the priest's ear was perfect! The people gasped and fifty ministers seated on the platform sighed with relief. When the multitude quieted down, Osborn repeated Christ's offer and authority to forgive their sins and he called for open decisions. Thousands raised their hands in ready response.[57]

After several others on the platform were instantly healed of deafness, Osborn directed the people to pray for each other on the assumption that Christ could heal a thousand as easily as He could heal one. He instructed them to lay hands on loved ones who were deaf, including the children. "I will now pray for all the deaf at once and He will heal them if you will only believe," Osborn declared. Many in the crowd moved toward friends and relatives in need. As soon as they reached them, the crowd became silent and reverent. Osborn slowly prayed and paused long enough for his interpreter Espinoza to repeat the prayer. It all seemed dry and empty to the evangelist, but when he asked the people to examine their loved ones they did so with great expectation. When he requested those healed to make their cures known, he was staggered by the response. Imagining that they must have misunderstood, he asked his interpreter to repeat and explain what he meant. A greater number of hands went up. Those healed were invited to give testimonies and this lasted for more than two hours! The military field in Java became an open cathedral for four weeks as Osborn continued to minister with signs following the proclamation of the gospel.[58]

In Santiago, Chile, Osborn preached in a stadium for a month before fifteen thousand and received a standing invitation from the government to return each summer.[59] Among the forty thousand who witnessed Osborn's prayer for the sick en masse in Lagos, Nigeria, was the Christian King of Ibadan. As "cripples were healed everywhere," the crowd began surging forward. The steps leading to the platform were so jammed the police could not control the crowd and the meeting had to be dismissed.[60]

The thirtieth country Osborn visited was Holland. For ten days under the open skies in The Hague, an estimated seventy thousand heard the Pentecostal full gospel message. One night thousands remained for hours in the pouring rain accompanied by thunder and lightning in order to hear and see the Gospel in action. Some Dutch Reformed ministers participated in the crusade committee while others actively opposed the meetings.[61] The services so captivated the attention of the nation that mail simply addressed "Brother Osborn, Somewhere in Holland" reached him without delay. More than a hundred ministers came to a conference to further examine the vital questions raised by the Pentecostal testimony. Some remained violently opposed.[62]

A few years later, Donald Gee visited Holland and found a revival atmosphere everywhere he preached. The impact of the Osborn meetings was obvious. Editor Gee declared, "It would be ridiculous not to recognize that this impressive new revival spirit in Holland stems from the immense campaign conducted by T. L. Osborn in the summer of 1958. It stirred the whole country." But behind the scenes for eight years groups had been praying for revival, preparing the hearts of the people before the arrival of the American preacher. Pentecostals are convinced that "true revivals always have their spiritual roots in prayer and praying groups."[63]

The Osborn Foundation introduced a Native Evangelism program designed to accelerate world evangelism. Tapes and films of his sermons and crusades translated into fifty languages were placed in the hands of missionaries and nationals. Native preachers were subsi-

109

dized for twelve months, by which time Osborn hoped their new churches would be able to assume their full support. As the number of financially assisted nationals reached into the thousands in far-flung countries, along came the problems of missionary-native relationships in some areas and the "rice-Christian" opportunism of natives in other regions. Osborn ceaselessly works to iron out these wrinkles as he continues to supply mobile evangelism units to hasten the establishment of more churches, none of which bears the Osborn Foundation name. Through the years some hundred Missionary Church organizations have requested his tools for evangelism.[64]

Another Pentecostal evangelist sought by multitudes was William Branham. An unusual man even among Pentecostals, his ministry included the exercise of the supernatural gifts of the word of knowledge, discernment of spirits, faith, gifts of healing, and miracles. One missionary, who had observed the lame leap and walk, the deaf hear clearly, and demons exorcised under Branham's hand, said that as "Branham declared by revelation the nature of the person's complaint, never once being even partly wrong, faith rose and the people were healed. . . ." One black man who had been crippled for many years decided to test his limbs and ". . . ran through the streets and was chased by a policeman who demanded an explanation."[65]

In Branham's Johannesburg meeting, the daughter of Stephen Jeffreys, perhaps Britain's most famous Pentecostal evangelist, said, "It was marvelous. The healings were not greater than I have seen in my dear father's campaign but Brother Branham's ministry is different. He diagnoses everybody's disease, tells them what is wrong with them, . . . He sees all this by vision." Branham's type of ministry—which is today being repeated by Katherine Kuhlman—is characterized by this typical declaration before a large audience. "There

110

is a lady out there in a pink dress, wearing a white hat.
. . . You had hernia trouble, didn't you? You are healed.
There is a man behind you in a blue suit. Stand up!
You had kidney trouble, didn't you?" When he
responded, Branham said authoritatively, "You too
are healed."[66]

Did these healings last, or were the people simply
carried away with a display of psychic phenomena?
Branham was so appreciated by the natives who were
healed that one Swiss missionary in South Africa
received four thousand letters from recipients of healing who made the effort to express their thanks.[67] In
meetings unprecedented at Durban's Greyville race
track, fifty thousand Europeans, natives, and Indians
were attracted by both the favorable newspaper publicity and the antagonistic criticism and denunciations
from some ministers of the established churches. An
editor of *The Standard Bearer* conveyed some sense
of Branham's compassion when he wrote, "His supernatural ministry held us breathless, but when he prayed
for the masses at the close of the service, many of us
felt we had never heard such impassioned interces-
sion."[68]

Remarkable healings occurred during the mass
prayers voiced by this humble preacher who possessed
only a fourth-grade education. In Capetown, as was his
custom, he requested everyone to be reverent. Suddenly
the silence was broken by the crying of a child. A missionary seated behind the mother asked her what was
wrong. When she learned that the child had been born
blind, she realized that the cry of pain was caused by
the sudden burst of light that met the child's eyes
which had opened miraculously during the evangelist's
prayer.[69]

Attacks by the Communist press against Branham
only served to boost the attendance in sophisticated
Finland. One hundred State Church clergymen were

among the seven thousand who filled an auditorium to witness demonstrations of God's power and to see a thousand Finns accepting Christ as Lord. This spectacle awakened a keen hunger in many of these Lutheran ministers, who longed to have a ministry of divine power in healing and in other supernatural manifestations. During Branham's last two nights under a tent in Kupois, the amazed Finns saw "piles of crutches and canes" left at the altar. One little girl removed the brace "she had worn on her leg for years and ran all over the church while the people shouted and wept for joy."[70]

I attended one of Branham's services in New York City's Manhattan Center in the early 1950s. The man in his ministry so portrayed the love of God for needy humanity that I was deeply moved. As the service progressed and people were being healed, the soft-spoken evangelist would say to the thousands gathered, "If you care to stand for a few moments and praise the Lord and give Him glory, go right ahead." I did just that. I had never spoken in tongues and my words seemed entirely inadequate to express what I felt in my heart. And then it happened. Out of my inner being flowed a river of praise in a tongue I had never before uttered or heard. Never did I feel Christ closer.

VII

Oral Roberts, Evangelist Extraordinaire

FOR A QUARTER of a century evangelist Oral Roberts has been preaching the Gospel and praying for the sick and afflicted. In a staggering worldwide ministry this Pentecostal Holiness evangelist has brought the good news to auditoriums and the Cathedral Tent in hundreds of cities across America and to more than fifty countries of the world.

For two decades many Pentecostal preachers were proud to have as a champion the tall Oklahoman, Oral Roberts. His crusades were drawing as many as 25,000 persons in single stateside services, while his television ministry during the late 1950s brought the Pentecostal ministry right into the homes of millions who knew nothing about the power of God. For almost a decade, the unrehearsed prayer lines of Roberts' crusade services opened hearts in America to the promise that God was still healing the sick.

What kind of a person is Oral Roberts? Why is he so innovative? What makes him "tick"? How could so unpromising a youth—who came from a preacher's household so poor that even poor people called them poor; who stuttered and stammered so badly at times that he couldn't complete a sentence; who lay wasting upon a deathbed for 163 days, cursing the day he was born—how could such a person emerge from this background to become a world-famous evangelist and university president?

At sixteen, in a day when the expression "generation

113

gap" was unknown, Oral Roberts ran away from home. Mama Roberts had asked God to give her a blue-eyed preacher before Oral was born. When the fifth of her one-eighth Indian children was delivered, he was the only one with blue eyes, and Claudius and Ellis Roberts joyfully dedicated him to the Lord's service. Now this son had willfully left home, but his mother reminded him that he would never be able to go beyond their prayers. She was confident that he would return and become a minister of the Gospel.

In less than a year he was carried home. While playing in the final game of an Oklahoma Seven basketball tournament, Oral collapsed and was carried off the court. Blood was flowing from his mouth and he was coughing with every breath. Herman Hamilton, his coach, placed him in the back seat of his car and drove him home. The dread diagnosis was tuberculosis in both lungs. To make matters worse, family records indicated that his mother's father and sister both had died of tuberculosis. Five long months dragged on as Oral dropped in weight from 160 to 120 pounds on his more than six-foot frame. Many well-meaning visitors served as Job's miserable comforters of old, stating that God had put this affliction upon him. But Oral's mother assured the teenager that, far from trying to destroy life, God instead would heal him.

Thus the seed of faith was planted. It was watered within a week as his sister Jewel came for a visit and shared the conviction that God was going to heal Oral. He said nothing, but hope leaped in his heart. Soon after, an evangelist brought his large tent to Ada, eighteen miles from the Roberts' parsonage in Stratford. Oral's oldest brother, Elmer, attended and was amazed at the miracles he observed in the services as God answered the prayer of faith. His thoughts turned to his brother Oral as his own faith was quickened. He borrowed a car and with his last thirty-five cents purchased gas, feeling strongly that if he could bring

Oral to the tent for the preacher's prayer, "the Lord will heal his body."[1]

Oral readily agreed and was carried to the car. On the way to the meeting, while lying on a mattress in the back seat of the borrowed vehicle, Oral Roberts received in his heart both a confirmation that he was to be healed and a call from God. The words were, "Son, I am going to heal you, and you are to take My healing power to your generation." He was all anticipation. When they reached the tent Oral was placed in a rocking chair propped with pillows. The evangelist preached for more than an hour and then give the altar call for the unsaved in the audience to receive Christ as Savior. Finally he started to pray for the sick. At about 11:00 P.M. the last to be prayed for was the tall, skinny teenager. The prayer was brief; "Thou cursed disease, I command you in the name of Jesus Christ to come out of this boy's lungs, loose him, and let him go."

Something struck his lungs and Oral leaped across the platform with upraised hands, shouting, "I am healed! I am healed!" A thousand people in the audience rose to their feet, among them many who knew the family, and they spontaneously shouted and praised God in unison. The evangelist placed a microphone before Oral and said, "Son, tell the people what the Lord has done for you." The lifetime stutterer, ever fearful of crowds, realized that his tongue was now free in a double healing as words poured forth from his lips describing how Jesus Christ enabled him to breathe all the way down without pain, coughing, and hemorrhaging.[2] Elmer's thirty-five cents had been well invested.

His intimate acquaintance with poverty and pain during his youth may be two good reasons why Oral Roberts believes that God does not desire Christians or the Christian Church to have less than the best and that God does not delight in the acceptance of affliction as His will. "God is a good God," and "Something good is going to happen to you," are more than clichés to Oral Roberts. They represent his way of life, his life principle and philosophy.

Two scripture verses often quoted by the evangelist are, "Beloved, I wish above all things that thou mayest prosper and be in health, even as thy soul prospereth," (III John 2) and "My God shall supply all your need according to His riches in glory by Christ Jesus," (Philippians 4:19). He constantly exemplifies these concepts in his daily approach to life's opportunities and problems. Chronologically past the half-century mark, Oral Roberts is the picture of vibrant health, with a demeanor suggesting inner peace and a positive concern for meeting the needs of mankind.

He began to preach two months after his healing, but it was to be twelve years before God's call to heal the sick would become a driving force that demanded an extended, expanding ministry.

His mother recalls an incident when, as a teenage evangelist, Oral Roberts had to walk along the highways from place to place in order to preach the gospel. A post on a corner in Sulphur, Oklahoma, "gave Oral the support he needed one day when he could walk no further." The post became a landmark for his family, reminding them each time they passed that corner of Oral's determination to fulfill God's call. "I believe Oral felt God's call so strong until he would have crawled if need be to preach and win souls to Jesus."[3]

During the long years of a quiet, maturing ministry, there were occasional healings wrought through faith by the prayers of young Roberts. When Oral was pastoring the Pentecostal Holiness Church in Toccoa, Georgia, one of his deacons accidentally dropped a heavy motor on his foot. Oral Roberts raced to answer the urgent call and found Clyde Lawson screaming with pain as he pointed to his crushed foot. A sudden compassion washed through the young pastor. He knelt down,

116

touched the shoe, and prayed earnestly and briefly. As he arose, the deacon stopped screaming. When he found he could move his toes he jumped up and asked, "Brother Roberts, what did you do to me?"

"Clyde, I didn't do a thing," replied Roberts.

"Yes, you did. The pain is gone. My foot is healed."[4]

Such instances of healing caused Roberts to open his mind to the possibilities of hastening world revival through divine healing. The idea began germinating. Soon after, he left Georgia and returned to Oklahoma where he was able to squeeze in several semesters at Oklahoma Baptist University and Phillips University. It was while attending classes at Phillips and pastoring in Enid that the call of God he received twelve years before while riding in the backseat of a borrowed car returned in compelling force. He recognized the lack of God's power in his life and ministry and the dissatisfaction that remained despite a healthy growth in his church. Divine discontent led to desperation and Oral Roberts began to seek God both day and night. He decided to study diligently the life of Jesus Christ and the apostles by turning to the four gospels and the Book of Acts. This time he would approach them with fresh eyes, as though he had never read them before. As he read alone in his room, most of the time upon his knees, he made discoveries which were to lead him into a global deliverance ministry. From this searching experience came four concepts which were to form the basis of many sermons that have blessed multitudes and released positive faith in the lives of many.

First, God wished his people to prosper and be in health, even as their souls prospered. Roberts had heard many Christians state the belief that God had placed sickness upon them in order to keep them subdued and saintly—that is, in order to make better Christians of them. But he saw in John's Third Epistle that, " . . . God wants man to be happy, normal, healthy,

117

strong, and prosperous. I saw that mankind can be delivered in soul, mind, and body."

Second, he observed that "Jesus was anointed with the Holy Spirit and with power and healed all who were oppressed of the devil." He went about doing good, for God was with him. Roberts concluded that sickness was not the gift of God, nor the blessing of heaven, but the oppression of the devil.[5]

Third, Roberts discovered that "the Son of Man is not come to destroy men's lives but to save them."[6] Christ came to save men's lives—their souls, minds, and bodies. Sickness was a destroyer and the oppression of the enemy.

Fourth, Jesus said, "The thief cometh not but for to steal and to kill and to destroy. I am come that they might have life and that they might have it more abundantly"[7] Roberts concluded, "This showed me that God was a good God and the devil was a bad devil. There is no badness in God and no goodness in the devil."

Oral Roberts was satisfied that he had a foundation for his faith and that instead of praying with a begging, whining voice, he could take authority over the torments of mankind in the name of Jesus Chirst of Nazareth and cast them out. He had come to the crossroads and it was time to launch out in answer to God's call, "you are to take My healing power to your generation."

When Oral Roberts was ready to leave the pastorate he shared his plan with a leading minister in whom he had great confidence. This was the man who had dedicated Oral to God when he was a month-old infant and the person who ordained Roberts to the ministry. "What do you think about this call I feel in my heart?" asked Oral. "I believe you are in God's will—the high will of God for you," were the encouraging words to the young preacher, then almost thirty years of age.[8]

It soon seemed evident that Oral Roberts was indeed in the center of God's will for his life and ministry.

The numbers responding at the conclusion of his messages took a decided upturn. People eagerly walked forward to receive Christ as Savior and to openly confess their new inward faith. His meetings then continued with prayers offered for the sick and afflicted by the laying on of hands. Healings became more numerous and there were outstanding cases of supernatural intervention.

An early turning point came in Tulsa, where nightly evangelistic meetings continued for nine consecutive weeks as people converged upon his services from far and near. It was this successful effort in 1947 that helped Oral Roberts decide to make the city of Tulsa his home base. His monthly magazine, started in the living room of the Roberts' home in North Tulsa, grew rapidly until first the living room and then the garage were inadequate for handling the constantly increasing mail. Today, four buildings later, hundreds of helpers are needed to keep up with the many phases of the ministry—editorial, correspondence, literature, outreach, radio and television schedules.

The months and years that followed the Tulsa breakthrough are full of unbelievable acts of faith of a man set on fire to present Jesus Christ and the gifts of the Holy Spirit as eminently relevant to needy men and their hurts. Oral Roberts has likened himself to a private in an army who unquestionably obeys the orders of his general. When absolutely confident that he has heard from God, Oral Roberts knows no better than to carry out such orders.

Along with the phenomenal growth and blessings has come the inevitable publicity. The press has often been unable to understand the man or his ministry. As a result, mistakes and misrepresentations have protruded in a number of articles. An example of this is the term "faith healer." Oral Roberts dislikes this phrase because it implies that he is doing the healing, rather than God. He insists he can heal no one. In the Garden City, Long Island, crusade a young reporter from the New York *Post* sought an interview with Mr. Roberts. I carefully explained the inaccurate connotation of the term "faith healer," and with sympathetic understanding he promised not to repeat the error. The following afternoon my eyes lighted upon his article: "Faith Healer Comes to Town."

In a major magazine article Oral Roberts was described as the "biggest practitioner of faith healing in the country." The conclusion stated, "Oral Roberts is enormously popular. He is equally controversial. He has helped to sharpen the whole discussion of healing by faith—a discussion which should involve a glory of belief and a tenderness in the uproar of the spectaculars that Ringmaster Roberts runs under his crowded and hysteria-filled tent." The *Tulsa Tribune* was quick to oppose the unfriendly spread of this article. Oral Roberts issued no defense; he has never replied in kind to his critics. He was too busy helping people to waste time becoming involved in negative reports and argumentations. The *Tribune* suggested that the authors of the article "would prefer apparently, silent prayer or little healing seances in hushed rooms." The Tulsa editorial continued; "the fact is that the tension-packed excitement of a crowded tent may be a very important device for getting timid, frightened, or introspective people to throw off complexes that may have been poisoning them. When mass enthusiasm becomes 'hysteria' we'll leave that to the *Life* writers, but Roberts' tent exists because in a tent he gets the best results. And he does get results. Again, we don't know whether this comes about through the power of the Lord or through the peculiar magnetism of the man. There is that magnetism. You can't talk to Oral Roberts for thirty seconds without sensing a most unusual personality. When we first began hearing about Brother

Oral Roberts we were skeptical. There are plenty of religious racketeers. But we gradually changed our opinion. . . . He needs no apology. We are proud to have him in Tulsa."[9]

I have often wondered how our contemporary news media would write up the events related to Christ's ministry of healing among the vast crowds who pushed their way to get his attention and touch.

Through years of misunderstanding and criticism, the parents of Oral Roberts assumed a wonderful, positive attitude which helped both Oral and his wife, Evelyn. Mama Roberts knew that "while some are persecuting Oral, others are praying for him." One day she visited Evelyn and the children and noticed that her daughter-in-law was disturbed about a smear article.

"Granny, why does Oral have to go through all of this? He's out trying to help people. . . . Why do they print all of these lies?" asked Evelyn.

The answer that came back was a surprise. "In spite of all the bad things they said about him," Granny pointed out, "they had to admit some good. Did you read all of those *good* things they said about him?" She pointed out that the article had mentioned that he was "brilliant" and "good-looking" and "half-Indian." Evelyn started laughing.[10]

His father, Reverend E. M. Roberts, was asked if he worried about the lies told about his son. With characteristic patience and wisdom he replied, "I don't need to worry. They are the ones who tell the lies. They are the ones who should worry."

Prudencia Damboriena, who included a chapter on divine healing in his book, *Tongues As of Fire,* claimed that "No faith healer . . . surpasses the popularity and wide influence of Oral Roberts." He selected Roberts as his prime example to describe the techniques "of these professional healers." This writer is convinced that the preparation of the people before the arrival

121

of the "the healer" is an important part of the technique. Handled by experts, its purpose is twofold. First, the audience is keyed up to the desired psychological state by extensive use of the press and radio. Then the individuals desiring healing are "revved up" by attending services to hear sermons and to see people healed before receiving personal prayer. Damboriena sees the healing service itself as one requiring "an excited, almost hysterical, audience." This is produced, he feels, by congregational singing, to "prepare their patients to expect healing." He then adds that a "careful screening of the individuals who will be admitted for healing" is conducted and that they "are well-known to the organizers, while others are excluded or postponed."[11] Speaking for Oral Roberts' crusades, I can unhesitatingly exclaim, "Nonsense!" For more than a year I served as crusade coordinator and had the privilege of working with the sponsoring ministers, assisting them and the committees many weeks before each crusade. I then joined them in the crusades held across the United States, Canada, and abroad. With thousands attending each service it was necessary to expedite matters in an orderly and impartial way. For the benefit of the sick and afflicted, this was effected by the distribution of prayer cards during the afternoon services. These cards were alphabetized and numbered so that those who first received them would be the first called to the prayer line. Relatives of the infirm and those incapacitated were able to receive dated cards which indicated the date they could bring the afflicted member of the family, with the assurance that he would receive personal prayer that evening. Depending upon facilities in the city auditorium or the invalid tent to be used, about fifty to a hundred helpless persons were accommodated each night. These were in addition to the hundreds able to stand in the prayer line. Occasional misunderstandings arose when people tried to enter the prayer line without a card. Far from screening the sick, the principle employed was first come, first served, regardless of race, color, or creed.

Unless one has actually attended a crusade service, it would be difficult to understand how the positive faith of the vast majority in the audience helps provide the climate of expectancy in which the supernatural seems to come naturally. God is sovereign and He can heal no matter what the climate. For finite creatures of dust, however, an atmosphere of "all things are possible" may help individuals to tap the inexhaustible supply of God's healing power. Great faith accepts the promises of God as though they were already fulfilled. But how many persons believe so strongly? God has given a measure of faith to everyone, and confidence in God is increased by hearing the Word of God. To witness the healing power of God after hearing a sermon strengthens the desire to release one's own trust to God, Who is the source of spiritual healing.

I have attended scores of crusade services conducted by Oral Roberts and his associate of many years, Robert DeWeese. I have seen with my eyes and heard with my ears many supernatural phenomena and have interviewed and listened carefully to a number of people in the crusades who testified to being healed. At one of the crusades in New York I spoke to a woman who recalled having been healed in a meeting six years earlier. She said, "The Lord healed me of arthritis in my leg and arm while seated in the audience. When I arose, I no longer dragged my leg. When I see my doctor in the neighborhood, I say, 'Hello, Stranger!' and he laughs along with me. He recalls that for four years I was under his care, always in pain and never smiled." Beaming, she added, "I hadn't been to church for thirty years, but now I never miss." I thought to myself—here was a person marvelously touched by God years before in a crusade in which I served as the local chairman with fifty-seven sponsoring pastors, and I was completely unaware of this healing. Who is to estimate how many other lives have been revolutionized while attending such services?

Another gentleman who looked sixtyish told me that he was healed of cancer three years before. "After an exploratory operation," he explained, "the doctors told my wife that I had from six months to one year to live. We determined to attend the crusade and on the closing Sunday I was prayed for." It was the practice for any not yet prayed for to be included in the closing crusade services, when one to two thousand persons from the vastly larger audiences received prayer with the laying on of hands. At such times lengthy lines would sometimes form at the peripheral edges of the larger auditoriums. A moment's prayer accompanied by a light touch on the forehead or shoulder by the evangelist was carried on in reverence as the service continued for another hour or two. A few seemed disappointed that Oral Roberts could spend no more time with them when he reached them, as if spiritual healing required lengthy prayers. So I asked the man if his hopes had faded while standing and waiting. "No," he answered, "I was in earnest. . . . After prayer, I felt like a new person; there was no pain. Over twenty dollars' worth of pills were left on the shelf and I've been back to work."

I remember the heavy-set man who had neuritis of the optic nerve for a year and a half in the right eye and for one year in the left. He was able to walk off the platform without assistance and seemed anxious to test his ability to read. His wife, overcome with joy, threw her arms about his neck as he calmly, slowly, and intently began to read. I leaned over to listen and heard him improve as he verbalized sentence after sentence. "I couldn't read this before tonight," he exclaimed as his wife wept and said repeatedly, "Oh, I'm so thankful—thank God, thank God!"

At the Roanoke Crusade a beautiful college sopho-more was flown in by her Baptist parents. Just a month before, she had seen Oral Roberts pray for the sick on television for the first time. Having undergone brain surgery several times, she hadn't walked for months. "She's had it," said her mother. As she stood before the evangelist and ten thousand people under the Cathedral Tent, she remarked, "I believe God's going to heal me tonight."

A volume of prayer accompanied Roberts' release of faith as he stretched forth his hands. Then slowly, with calm confidence, she walked—alone! The sight caused many to weep unashamedly, as did Evelyn Roberts. After the young lady walked to the end of the long aisle, I asked her father if he had anticipated this. "No, I really didn't expect it. I can't believe it. It's too good to be true. I believed in miracles and healings for Bible days but doubted them for today." The next day I was told by several waitresses at the motel restaurant: "You know the girl in the wheelchair . . . she came walking in by herself this morning!"

In the invalid room at the Jacksonville Crusade, Oral Roberts showed his empathy for the afflicted as he stated, "I know it's discouraging. I know how difficult it is. I was the last one prayed for. It looked like I'd been forgotten. I know what it is to come in a prayer line when you're so sick you can hardly hold your head up. . . . If crying would have healed me, I would have been healed. But as I believed, He reached down His hand and touched me that night." He then began pray-ing quietly as he moved among the people. I saw two leave their wheelchairs and two others get out of hospi-tal beds to march in a cadence of victory. One lady kept repeating, "Thank you, Jesus." Her daughter reported to me that cancer had so affected her mother's back that she couldn't turn. But here she was doing calisthen-ics without any trace of pain.

125

Across the prayer ramp through the years have come people of all ages and from many walks of life—infants, schoolchildren, housewives, businessmen, farmers, ministers, nurses, attorneys, scientists, school teachers, service men, Protestants, Catholics, Orthodox, and Jews. In succession at a Portland Crusade, Roberts prayed for a Nazarene, a Catholic, a Pentecostal, and a Methodist—"and they all shout alike," he noted.

It hasn't been easy for Oral Roberts to bear this message to the burdened and beaten of this world. He has come away bone-weary after laying hands on literally thousands in a single service. He has prayed for lepers, putting his hands upon their sores. He has prayed for people with tuberculosis who blew their breath in his face and he kept on praying. Once he was asked how he could stand it, praying for the crippled, the dying, and those who had lost their minds. Oral answered, "That's the very crowd that Jesus laid His hands on!"

As important as the laying on of hands has been in the ministry of Oral Roberts, he has consistently emphasized the greatest of all miracles—the salvation of a lost soul. Invitations for the unsaved, or those who have not committed their lives to the Savior Jesus Christ, take priority immediately after his sermons. Jesus once said, "Follow me and I'll make you fishers of men." After the message has been delivered, Roberts puts out the net for a catch. He has been one of the Lord's best fishermen. Overseas he has preached to throngs at times reaching thirty and even sixty thousand, and it has been impossible to accurately calculate the number who have responded to and accepted Christ. In a single service held in South Africa approximately five thousand were brought to Jesus Christ.

At one American afternoon service conducted by Robert F. DeWeese, Roberts' associate minister for twenty years, hundreds of earnest seekers were standing in front of the platform, encouraged to reverently worship the Lord. Meanwhile, the evangelist himself was praying in tongues for an extended period of time. A man in the audience turned to staff member Jim Nash and inquired, "What is this? . . . He is speaking Latin. In fact, that's Latin as spoken by a scholar and with perfect enunciation. I thought it was the Pope's voice, although this man is speaking lots faster."

Jim cleared up the man's perplexity by explaining the phenomenon of speaking in tongues as recorded in the second chapter of the Book of Acts. The man could scarcely believe Jim's explanation, for he had studied the langugae at Duke University. At this moment DeWeese could be heard praying in English. "He *must* know Latin. Now he's translating into English, telling the people exactly what he said in Latin. Come on, level with me. He must know Latin!"

"No, he doesn't. What you've just heard is a miracle given by God," answered Jim. Earlier in the service DeWeese stated, "When you speak in tongues it is inspired utterances. . . . I wouldn't be surprised when we speak in tongues, we speak in a known language."[12]

DeWeese is ever grateful to God for the deliverance of his wife, Charlotte, who was suffering with acute leukemia. While under the care of two physicians for three discouraging, difficult months, the constancy of their faith in the contemporary healing power of Jesus Christ was severely tested. Bob DeWeese had prayed by her bedside a hundred times without any results. But somehow Bob and Charlotte each knew that God was going to heal her. One day DeWeese received the sudden assurance, "Now is the time." He walked to her bedside and authoritatively declared, "Now is the time!" Charlotte was instantly healed of the dreaded blood cancer. And her cure has lasted. Bob and Charlotte travel 65,000 miles across America conducting 150 meetings a year with the partners of the Oral Roberts' ministry.

Over thirty years have passed since her dramatic healing!

In the fall of 1970, as Oral Roberts was introduced by Pat Boone as a guest on the Mike Douglas television show, Boone declared that there have been "few men more the object of controversy" than Roberts. He confessed that his former negative opinion of the evangelist was due to his lack of knowledge, but now he enthusiastically promoted the man and his ministry to the television viewers.

Host Douglas suggested that many healings were of the mind and Boone interjected the thought that Christ as the Great Physician also reaches the cause of psychosomatic illness. Roberts explained his own function as a point of contact, a catalyst, an instrument, but he carefully explained that it must be God who intervenes if any are to receive real release, for He alone is the source of healing.[13]

That same year Dick Cavett interviewed Oral Roberts on his program and, true to form, posed some subtle but provocative questions. He asked Roberts if he at times in his ministry heard words he "thought came from God"? The evangelist responded, "Yes, they were words to me. Inside of me I felt God was speaking to me. Whether it was audible, I'll never know. It was real to me."

Cavett probed further. He referred to the *Life* article written years before, stating that people presumably were "cured" by the evangelist. Roberts replied, "I think some were helped. Some great changes occurred. God heals in many ways . . . through medical science, love, and climate. He also heals through the power of prayer."

Oral Roberts has always held the highest regard for medical science and medical doctors. This is proven in his own home, which has never been without a family physician. A great number of early, Classic Pentecostals firmly believed and preached that the only approach to illness and affliction was through prayer and that Pentecostals who turned to medicine and medical aid for anything other than child deliveries and the setting of broken bones were failing God and compromising their faith. This has never been a problem in the Roberts' household. Oral's parents taught him a blessed balance in this aspect of faith even though some early advocates of divine healing, such as John Alexander Dowie, were militant against doctors.

Cavett understood that the evangelist had abandoned the ministry of prayer for the sick, or, as he put it, "faith healing." Roberts promptly corrected the false notion. "No. I continue to pray for people. I no longer have crusades in a big tent cathedral," he continued, explaining his concept of God's healing power for the whole man and his telecast messages. When asked what baffled him about God, Roberts candidly shared a mystery still puzzling to him. Incomprehensible were the apparent failures after he prayed with great confidence and the supernatural healings which occurred following his barren prayers. He thought he had all the answers twenty years ago, but lingering mysteries remain to this day.[14]

Oral Roberts illustrated further bewilderment by recalling the time he prayed for two blind persons in the same prayer line on the same evening. He prayed for both with equal intensity and released the same positive faith to God, yet one received sight while the other did not. Roberts does not wish to attribute all apparent failures to the lack of faith in those prayed for. He refuses to accept ultimate defeat for the one who does not receive divine healing. He disagrees with a fatalistic acceptance that this "is God's will." Somewhere, sometime, perhaps after certain spiritual lessons have been learned, there is divine healing for each in answer to someone's prayer. The exception allowed by Roberts is the sickness unto death. The appointment of death must be met by every man.[15] He has prayed for several people whom he felt were healed of their afflictions, but he discerned that it was their appointed time to die.

Sharing his feelings about prayer for the sick with hundreds of key Pentecostal pastors at a global conference, Oral Roberts explained that compassion is not sympathy. He feels a violence toward sickness and an irresistible urge to touch the sick. When the dying child of Carl Hamilton, Dean of Academics at Oral Roberts University, was fighting for her life in an oxygen tent, Roberts came to pray. One toe protruded from a corner opening of the tent and the evangelist stretched forth his hand and touched it as he prayed. The child recovered that very hour.

When asked by a delegate from Lebanon if he believed it was God's will to heal all the sick, Roberts answered, "Yes, the same as it is God's will to save all. But a very small minority are saved."[16]

He went on to advise the ministers from fifty nations of the world that it was very foolish to speak against medicine. "Medical doctors are trying to heal the sick; many preachers are not." Considering the vast amount of persons for whom he has prayed, Oral Roberts candidly admits that more people had been prayed for by him who were not healed than by any man in the world. While Oral Roberts' most severe critic has often been Roberts himself, multiplied thousands are thankful that this man has dared to obey orders from above.

VIII

University President and
Charismatic Methodist

MANY FOREIGN audiences already knew from personal observation of Oral Roberts' successful campaign against human misery. They had attended some of the massive meetings where the American evangelist ministered and prayed for the sick in more than fifty countries. He had conducted crusades from Finland to South Africa, from Japan to Australia, from Chile to Indonesia, from Canada to the Caribbean, and from Wales to Vietnam. His message had been the same in India as in Poland, to the gypsies in France as to the Maories in New Zealand.

During these years of international travel Oral Roberts' dream was to see this ministry of deliverance for the whole man multiplied through the lives of young people. But how was this to be accomplished? As first he envisioned a boot camp made up of young potential ministers from different countries. If they were fired with faith, filled with the Bible message and method, and energized with evangelical zeal, would they return to their own people and minister effectively? Would their own people accept them readily after study abroad? These and other problems on the mission field led Roberts to look for a different approach. The answer came sooner than he planned. The means to his global goal would be through training young people in a top-notch university.

But did Roberts really wish to found a university? Would the creation of yet another American liberal arts

131

institution be worth the evangelist's time and energy? Would it make an impact on the world for evangelism? Could it make some unique contribution within a fast-changing world in which collegians insisted on practicing a philosophy of situation ethics—often accompanied by declining moral standards—which exalted man alone as the measure of all things and captain of his soul? Could his dream of a university program designed to educate the whole man evolve from a ministry of healing?

Oral Roberts University was not to be a glorified Bible school. To Roberts the secular and spiritual were to be as one, a unified whole helping to form whole persons who would become part of the answer rather than part of the problem in their careers. Spiritual power would overflow from Christ-centered lives capable of using the gifts of the Spirit to meet the complexities of human need.

Roberts realized that each professor at such a university would need more than expertise in his academic discipline. Each had to be a committed Christian, open to the leading of the Holy Spirit—the only One who could transmit through them the compassion of Jesus which reaches out to touch humanity. These men and women would face the enormous challenge of applying the wisdom and power of the Holy Spirit in an educational milieu. One great difficulty Roberts would face would be to attract men and women who would not be ashamed to stand before the academic community and say that Oral Roberts University was connected with the ministry of evangelism.

I recall the time Oral Roberts visited my apartment in Queens before catching a trans-Atlantic flight from Kennedy Airport to the Helsinki, Finland, crusade. Our conversation touched upon his newest concept, the launching of a Christian liberal arts university. Sensing the magnitude of the project and the astronomical costs involved, I asked him whether he believed he could raise sufficient funds for such an enormous project, which would be greater than the many former accomplishments. His answer was revealing: "When I am confident that a new step is in the will of God and I know that it is God's time, I do not doubt that God will provide the needed funds." Some of this attitude has rubbed off on me. I have tried using this sort of spiritual screening test to challenge students who tell me they wish to accompany me to the U.S.S.R. I put a couple of questions before them—first, "Is it God's will for you to go to Soviet Russia?" and second, "Is this God's time for you to go?" If the answer to both questions is affirmative, then I encourage them to pray and work so that the need will be met without going into debt. It works!

Fully aware that his major decisions affected the lives of others, Oral Roberts weighed the consequences of founding a university. His own team members at first misunderstood and reacted negatively, feeling that he was abandoning world evangelization for higher education. They clung to the traditional idea that the power of the Holy Spirit and higher education were incompatible. But as usual, Oral Roberts had to obey God when he was assured that the move was in God's will and in God's time. Humanly speaking, it seemed an impossible dream, but his partners began to respond joyfully. They seemed to sense their indispensable role in this venture of faith and they began to send in financial support along with words of encouragement and prayers.

For many years Oral Roberts held his vision of educating young people intellectually, spiritually, and physically. His concept of education embraced the whole man. He even prayed for God to hold a beautiful site in Tulsa which he drove by many times. One day, while conducting a crusade on the west coast, Roberts received the supernatural gift of the word of knowledge regarding the property. He called his office and instructed his men to see the owners the very next morning in order to purchase the hundreds of acres of farmland in question. The men remonstrated, convinced that the owners, who had refused many offers, would not sell. Nevertheless, Roberts' aides would oblige. The following morning, as the owners opened the door and learned the purpose of the call, they exclaimed, "Just last night we decided to sell."

On one occasion a carload of high school seniors drove to the farm soon to be a campus, scrambled out of the car, and dropped to the ground, kissing it. "At last somebody thought of us!" they exclaimed. Several seminars were held each year for high school juniors and seniors during the preparatory stages before opening in May 1965. Many of these high school students have returned to spend four years at Oral Roberts University. Meanwhile the University also has sponsored seminars for ministers and laymen through the years, and tens of thousands have received inspiration and instruction on a campus that is an ongoing miracle.

No tangible assets were on hand to start the major building on the 500-acre campus of Oral Roberts University. When the first three buildings were completed, President Roberts reminded himself that God had allowed him to start with the same ingredients He used when He made the earth—nothing. From every side his steady diet was, "Oral, you can't do it." To the faculty he recently explained, "I've never done anything of a major nature until God spoke to me. . . . I don't take any steps . . . unless I hear God. Every time I've allowed somebody to overly persuade me and take his private dream and put it here on campus, I've failed. . . . When God spoke to my heart, I felt *that* was the important thing, not raising the money. You don't sit down and say, how can we raise the money to build this building? . . . You determine, does God want it built? You start from there."

134

Roberts' beliefs about having one's needs met are clearly articulated in his recent book entitled *Miracle of Seed-Faith,* which has been secured by one million persons. The book revolves about three key principles of "Seed-Faith" discovered in the Bible. The first is to recognize God as one's Source: human beings and jobs are the means and instruments, not the source. "My God shall supply all your need according to his riches by Christ Jesus."

The second key is to "Give that it may be given to you." One must follow the life-style of Jesus, who gave Himself for others. It is the law of sowing and reaping. If a person gives nothing of his time, talents, money, and love to God and man, then he will receive nothing. It is more productive to give than to receive.

The last key is to "Expect a Miracle." When a person looks to God as the Source and gives to God as Seed, then he should expect a miracle from God. Some people objected that this approach was a form of indulgence, a sort of bribe—give in order to get. Roberts acknowledges the danger of this misunderstanding, but he sees nothing wrong with giving of one's time, talents, money, and love to God and man for the purpose of receiving God's best. He recommends the giving as a way of establishing a point of contact with God; it is "something you do, and when you do it, it helps you to believe."[1]

Today this man is the President of Oral Roberts University, a four-year liberal arts institution with a futuristic complex of buildings valued at forty million dollars. It already has nearly two thousand eager students from every state of the union and from dozens of denominations. It also has a competent faculty of close to a hundred, all striving to become more like the only whole man, Jesus Christ.

At the heart of the five-hundred-acre campus is an unusual prayer tower, its twenty-story glass and steel height peaked with a tongue of flame, suggesting a Pentecostal witness. Against a sunset the building reminds me of a modern cross and its prickly appendages point in all directions from the prayer rooms, suggesting a crown of thorns and Christ's undying love for all of the earth's afflicted. It symbolizes the importance of prayer and the validity of supernatural answers to the prayers of mortals today.

Around the clock, every hour of every day of the year, trained staff members in the tower extend the ministry of Oral Roberts as they receive phone calls from troubled people across America and from foreign lands. Almost twenty thousand reach out for help every month, including several would-be suicides.

This telephone ministry was initiated in 1958. Frequently, requests come in on behalf of people undergoing surgery. Medical treatment is recommended as an ally in the battle against disease, for the workers counsel that God takes over where doctors leave off. One desperate caller sobbed, "My child has just pulled a bucket of boiling water off the stove," as the youngster could be heard screaming in the background. "We'll pray. You call the doctor," directed the prayer counselor. Later in the day the mother again called, reporting that the child was resting easily. Occasionally, a caller expresses no specific need. One little boy phoned to say, "I'm not sick. I don't want nothin'. I just want to hear you pray." The counselor obliged and the lad hung up with a "thank you kindly."

Oral Roberts reminded the twenty thousand people gathered on the Oral Roberts University lawn at the formal dedication of the university on April 2, 1967, that it was no accident that the Prayer Tower was at the center of the campus or that it was taller than any other building. The assembled crowd, including Billy Graham, the honored guest speaker, listened to Roberts' explanation: "It portrays our dependence on prayer while the eternal flame on top symbolizes our charismatic walk in the power of the Holy Spirit. Yet our spiritual emphasis cannot be a substitute for academic excellence in our quest for knowledge." His confidence was rewarded on March 31, 1971, when full regional accreditation was granted by the North Central Association of Colleges and Secondary Schools to Oral Roberts University, the second private school in the nation ever to receive this honor so soon after its opening.

Why was the school named after Oral Roberts? The Board of Regents recognized that the name of the institution was more than that of a person. It was symbolic of a ministry of deliverance for suffering humanity. When people hurt, and human help is inadequate, many think of and turn to this ministry. The identification is inescapable.

Roberts is pleased that the faculty and students have established an honor code whereby negative forms of behavior have no place in their lives. "This is a clean place to live, study, play, worship, grow, and emerge as whole men and women," he beams. All students must sign an agreement to abide by the principles and specifics of the code. The few who remain uncooperative are reminded that attending ORU is a privilege and not a right. Very few have been expelled and all but the defiant have the option to return to campus after a semester's absence.

Once I was in President Roberts' office as he held a final counseling session with a young man who was about to be dismissed from the school. Oral Roberts illustrated his faith in young people as he laid hands upon the student and prayed a prayer which encouraged the youth to follow God's plan for his life. I wasn't prepared for what happened next. Roberts asked the student being expelled to pray for him. The young man looked surprised, but he prayed. In some strange way,

137

perhaps more positive results may be forthcoming because of such spiritual confidence placed in those who err. After several years this student returned, a highly motivated person.

As president of a university, Oral Roberts has never vacillated or shirked his duties to level with the entire student body whenever straight talk is necessary. Usually his hardest-hitting messages are given after the expulsion of a few students who have been guilty of violating the most serious regulations of the Code of Honor.

Some students arrive on campus expecting a utopia, but they discover that ORU is composed of ordinary people at a university trying to serve God. The president is not a sentimental softy. He believes that "there is no such thing as divine forgiveness without repentance and repentance is a change. It's not something you did because you were caught. God will not forgive those who do not truly repent, neither can we." The prayer and desire of Oral Roberts is that no student will come to the University without feeling that God has directed him there.

Do the majority of students want to enter the ministry? Far from it. About 90 percent of them are involved in the twenty-two majors other than theology. They are constantly learning to wed the secular with the sacred whatever their life's pursuit may be. The faculty members have been carefully selected for both academic and spiritual qualifications. A number of them had never dreamed of teaching at Oral Roberts University. But with his amazing sense of God's timing in launching new projects, Oral Roberts opened the doors of the university in the fall of 1965 when a number of professors had just received the baptism in the Holy Spirit. Because of this Pentecostal experience they were open to the exciting venture unfolding at Oral Roberts University, where they could share their academic disciplines in a charismatic Christ-centered institution. Most of them felt the distinct call of God to Oral Roberts University and were challenged by the opportunity to participate in a bold experiment in education.

My own background was somewhat different before I joined the faculty. During the early sixties I found the challenges and blessings of working with evangelist Oral Roberts as crusade coordinator very satisfying. In a number of cities I worked closely with the sponsoring pastors, planning the many necessary details of the evangelistic efforts many weeks before each crusade began. While the meetings were in progress I labored with these faithful pastors and their trained laity who served as personal workers helping the hundreds who accepted Christ as Savior after hearing Oral Roberts preach the Gospel. Each crusade served thousands in need of spiritual, mental, and physical renewal. The last thing I wanted was a change. But one day Oral Roberts asked me if I had given any thought to schooling beyond the master's degree to earn a doctorate. Frankly I hadn't. He expressed his concern that the university yet to be born be staffed with men and women who shared his vision for making Christ and His power known to the world. I was flattered but didn't answer at the time and he didn't press me. About a month later he faced me with the same question. I had given the matter serious thought and prayer in the meantime, and my wife, Nadja, had displayed the same confidence in me that the evangelist did. They were both sure I could succeed, but I had sincere doubts inasmuch as I hadn't attended a university for a decade. Now, in retrospect, I am confident that this was God's will for my life. Oral reminds me from time to time of former fears, adding with a smile, "There wasn't the slightest doubt in my mind." Oral Roberts somehow has this ability to bring out of a person far more than the individual thinks is resident within his being.

The Great Commission issued by Christ to His disciples involved going into all the world and preaching the gospel to every creature. To Roberts this means that the Christian is to go into every man's world. With an eye singled to Americans who do not attend church and whose Bible is the sports page, the evangelist determined to gain their attention by developing a basketball team able to compete on a national level. The team, called the Titans, already has attained top national ranking among major colleges and was honored to compete in the National Invitation Tournament at Madison Square Garden. ORU athletes now play in a new Special Events Center which seats more than any other arena in the State of Oklahoma—over 10,500. (By filling the playing court area with portable seats Oral Roberts will be able to conduct crusade-type meetings for 12,500.) It is equipped for national live-color telecasting because the lad who loved basketball so much that he collapsed on the court visualizes the popular sport as a means of projecting a clear witness before the world. Recently the national magazine *Sports Illustrated* gave the Oral Roberts University team a most favorable write-up stressing the charismatic philosophy of the school's founder.[2] Thanks in part to this exciting sports attraction, the city of Tulsa is responding as never before. Several civic organizations, proud to have ORU a part of the community, have made contributions. The faith of this man is contagious.

An unexpected move that dumbfounded many American Pentecostals came with the transferral of Oral Roberts' ordination from the Pentecostal Holiness Church to the United Methodist Church in 1968. While a few Pentecostal leaders possibly envious of Roberts' fame may have been relieved by the surprise move, thousands of pastors were disappointed and upset at the loss of the world's best-known Pentecostal minister. Oral Roberts personified the Pentecostal evangelist par excellence. His preaching was inspiring and effective in winning people to Christ; his prayers for the sick and afflicted were accompanied by many healings; no extended plea for funds ever marred the crusade services—on the contrary, the brevity of the offerings pleased everyone. And budgets were easily met. Now the champion of thousands of Pentecostal pastors and laymen appeared to have abandoned them for membership in the huge United Methodist Church.

Many pastors and laymen who actively participated in his crusades had learned to work in close harmony with members of Pentecostal denominations other than their own. Often these area-wide crusades resulted in the formation of Pentecostal fellowships on a grass roots level. Oral Roberts was a cohesive factor in these united efforts to advance the full Gospel. The joy and camaraderie of working together to serve the needs of many people displaced the narrow, distant denominational attitudes which prevailed in some areas.

Why, then, did this most famous son of Classic Pentecostalism accept a transfer of his ordination to the United Methodist Church? Had he betrayed his Pentecostal heritage? Had he changed his theological position and become a liberal? Or was Oral Roberts University, then only three years in existence, in some financial plight so serious that a major denomination alone would save it from a dreadful demise?

Opinions varied greatly. A few even consigned him to fiery judgment! When I visited Soviet Russia I was asked by a Pentecostal preacher there, "Is Oral Roberts still Pentecostal in his belief?" A *New York Times* writer suggested that his move to the Methodist Church "was apparently part of an attempt to improve his image."

The guesses were completely wrong. Oral Roberts is still the same person with the same beliefs he had before he joined the United Methodist Church. Once again

141

Oral Roberts was convinced that he was obeying God. Oklahoma's Bishop Angie Smith had asked him to seriously consider joining the Methodist ministry just as he was. The Bishop made it clear that no change in his views was expected; the church needed what he had. Only after much prayer and thought was the decisive step taken.

Recently in *Abundant Life Magazine,* the organ of his association, Oral Roberts wrote, ". . . being filled with the Spirit should deliver us from exclusiveness, and enable us to genuinely include any Christian as our authentic brother. One's membership in any denomination should not be equated with being a child of God, or held above one's personal relationship with Christ and others who know Christ as personal Savior."[3]

A striking statement in the *Scottish Journal of Theology* claimed: "The fact that the well known Pentecostal evangelist Oral Roberts joined the Methodist Church in 1968 is a significant indicator of the new direction of Pentecostalism, and may mark a turning point for the whole movement, old and new."[4]

Since this change in affiliation many invitations to minister to Methodist clergymen and laymen have reached Roberts. Recently at a Methodist camp meeting in North Carolina Oral Roberts addressed 2,500 Methodist laymen. As he preached and poured out his heart he suddenly became aware that some of these people might not know Christ. As he later described it, at the end of the sermon "I asked everyone in that audience who was not saved, who had not accepted Christ, to raise his hand and I was startled. Over 1,000 of these laymen stood up—I mean not saved! So I led them in the sinner's prayer I prayed fifteen years ago: 'Lord, be merciful to me, a sinner.' "[5]

Another commotion was caused among Pentecostals when Oral Roberts returned to nationwide television with a new format and the World Action Singers, all students of Oral Roberts University. Roberts makes no apologies for changes in method; he is married to principles alone. But to Pentecostals the choreography of the collegians had nothing in common with the customary evangelistic outreach. *Christianity Today*, a non-Pentecostal evangelical magazine read mostly by clergymen, maintained that the hour-long television specials were "certain to prompt some secular rave notices, along with some frowns from members of the evangelical old guard who might view it all as a bit too avant-garde, too hip. But so smart is the execution of the programs—amid much mediocrity in religious broadcasting—that they can't help receiving notice in this month's primetime premiers."[6]

Why did Oral Roberts drop the format used earlier when the services in the cathedral tent were filmed? For years the gospel had been preached from a platform with a backdrop of pastors, followed by prayers for the sick. Countless adults and children were helped and many were healed by the power of God as a result of viewing the prayer lines filmed during the services. There is no denying that this technique accomplished the goals set forth. But the youth were not being reached—certainly not in masses. The time for change had arrived—change in method, that is. The quarterly television specials successfully entered the homes of millions who rarely or never see the insides of the institutional churches. Young people don't switch to another channel because the appeal of modern song and choreography and the illustrious guest stars from the entertainment and sports world hold them. Young Richard Roberts, his wife, Patti, and the World Action Singers relate with many youth who are saying, "Jesus, yes. The Church, no." Oral Roberts confines his message to about eleven minutes before his closing prayer. The extent of audience response is indicated by the fact that mail is at an all time high and the peak television years in the fifties and early sixties are being surpassed fivefold. More than a half million letters were received following the Expo '70 Special, filmed in Japan.

By multiplied thousands young people are writing to Roberts, pouring out their hearts as they seek supernatural help. Enrollment at Oral Roberts University has shown a marked increase as the generation gap has been closed. The message is getting through.

IX

Pentecostal Merchants
on the March

THERE IS AN ARMY of Pentecostal businessmen who give joyfully of their time, talents, and money to promote Jesus Christ. Not a church, denomination, or a movement. Just Jesus. In addition to the many individual Pentecostals who practice the presence of God in the mundane affairs of life, there is a host of men who join hands and hearts in the Full Gospel Business Men's Fellowship International (FGBMFI).

The Fellowship started in the heart of a Downey, California, dairyman who was sold on the idea that successful business leaders from all walks of life could also be dynamic Christians, men who would introduce the living Jesus to other businessmen. Demos Shakarian, the founder and president of the FGBMFI, had seen too many Christian businessmen pursue success in secular society, only to forget God in the process.

The Shakarian family originally had come to the United States in direct response to prophetic warnings to flee from Armenia. This miraculous warning came about because an illiterate Russian boy of twelve who lived in Armenia wrote for seven days and nights while under the power of God, drawing pictures, maps, and charts. The message foretold the massacre of the townspeople by the Turks unless they emigrated to America, where they would prosper and be free from religious persecution. Thirty-seven uneventful years passed before the Russian lad, now middle-aged, had another prophetic message to share with the Pentecostal Christians in the town. The Shakarians were told that the time was at hand for the predicted destruction. Unbelievers mocked, but the Shakarians left Armenia in 1905 and the exodus of other Christians continued until 1912, when the last Pentecostal family departed. Then World War I erupted and Turkey overran Armenia. Every soul in the village was slaughtered.[1]

Soon after the Shakarians landed in New York they journeyed on to California and settled in Los Angeles. They arrived in time to witness the outpouring of the Spirit in the Azusa Street Mission in 1906. As the Americans praised God in other tongues, the Armenians could say, "This is that which God gave to us in Armenia many years ago." The pattern was identical, for when they were baptized in the Spirit they spoke in tongues as the Spirit gave them utterance.

Faith in God, good judgment, and hard work multiplied three milk cows to three thousand by 1943, thirty-four years after Demos' father, Isaac, had made his initial purchase. Young Demos, while yet in high school, was given a two-thousand-dollar nest egg by his dad and the teenager invested this in the dairy business with a friend. The youngsters built it up to a herd of sixty milk cows and were earning more than their high school teacher. But reverses during the depression scaled Demos down to his original nest egg money and caused him to drop the venture. After marrying Rose Gabriel he experienced six years of business failure before he awakened to the conviction that he was laboring without God.

Demos was well acquainted with God's power in his life. Baptized in the Spirit at thirteen, he spoke in tongues for four hours and when he arrived home the power of God came upon him so strongly he was unable to rise. He could never deny the reality of that power and the assurance of God's love. Now in this time of testing, Demos and Rose reconsecrated themselves to

146

serve God with greater determination. Since then the Shakarian dairy farms have been among the world's largest.

Although he himself was never called to preach the gospel, Demos decided in 1940 to sponsor Pentecostal evangelists in their meetings by accepting the financial responsibilities involved. His first joint venture of evangelist and sponsoring businessman was launched in a tent seating three hundred persons. The effort was amply rewarded as sixty-seven persons received the baptism in the Spirit. Ten years of consecrated effort behind aggressive evangelism came to a climax when Demos served as chairman of an Oral Roberts crusade in Los Angeles. More than 200,000 attended the services, thousands of whom were sick and afflicted. Many were healed and four thousand penitents stepped forward to acknowledge their need and acceptance of Christ.[2]

It was during this crusade that Demos Shakarian shared with evangelist Roberts his idea for the creation of a Full Gospel Business Men's Fellowship. Demos reasoned that if one businessman could invest his money and efforts to cause many to become interested in the gospel, how much more could a united, nationwide force of businessmen accomplish! Oral Roberts urged him to form such a group of laymen and assured Shakarian of his continued interest. With this word of encouragement, Demos wrote the first page of the thrilling accounts of the FGBMFI by calling the initial meeting of Pentecostal laymen to the upper room of Clifton's Cafeteria. Some two hundred persons attended to hear the dairyman's concept of a men's fellowship.

Shortly after this meeting, Shakarian and Roberts met with another group of businessmen during the evangelist's Fresno Crusade. With about 150 Pentecostals present, Roberts again challenged the men to

147

action. This time Demos' dream took on tangible form as five directors were appointed—Demos Shakarian as president; Lee Braxton, George Gardner, and Miner Arganbright as vice-presidents; and Earl Draper as secretary-treasurer.

A year later the Articles of Incorporation were signed in the upper room of Clifton's Cafeteria amidst praises of God from the hearts of rejoicing businessmen yearning to do business for God. Lee Braxton predicted: "There will be many opportunities for our organization to render valuable service. It might be in foreign missions fields, it might be educational or financial, but I'm sure an open door awaits us to do our part in the upbuilding of God's Kingdom and the spread of the Full Gospel."[3] Eleven years later Braxton was elected the first Chairman of the Board of Regents of Oral Roberts University in Tulsa.

For almost a full year the businessmen met, planned, prayed, and spent a small fortune to promote the organization, but somehow the FGBMFI was getting nowhere. Then came the crucial night when Shakarian prayed and wept before the Lord. He received a vision in which God showed him that "before He could begin to work, he had to get *man* completely out of the way." He saw thousands of men all over the world standing "immobile, frozen, waiting for *something* to release them for service." At that moment Shakarian surrendered himself unconditionally to God, willing to die completely to self. Then the vision changed. "The glory of God came down, and I beheld that vast army of men raise their hands to God in praise and thanksgiving." The dairyman was convinced that progress in the work of God depended neither on man's might nor on his money. It had to be the Spirit of God empowering humble men to achieve the impossible.

The breakthrough was evident at the Saturday breakfast meeting. God had also been working in the hearts

148

of other members. The entire atmosphere was different—supernatural faith was at work. One man drove three hundred miles to the meeting because God "told him there must be a magazine established that would carry this message around the world."[4] The *Voice* was given birth that year with an issue of five thousand copies. Today a much larger edition reaches more than a quarter of a million homes and offices. A Baptist pastor wrote, "We look forward to each issue with anticipation. Probably not until Eternity will you realize something of the extent to which our blessed Lord Jesus is using your little magazine to bless souls. . . ."[5]

During the *Voice's* first year of publication, Shakarian prayed that FGBMFI chapters would be established throughout America and around the world. These secular pioneers believed that men would gather together from all walks of life and denominations so that God could pour out his blessings and bring about "a world-shaking, soul-stirring movement such as the world has never seen."[6] Much of this prayer has been answered but even greater blessings are constantly anticipated.

The FGBMFI has grown from a single Los Angeles chapter in 1953 to more than six hundred active chapters, five hundred of them within the continental United States.[7] The local chapters promote cooperative efforts in spreading the Full Gospel, those that feature Jesus Christ as Savior, Healer, Baptizer in the Spirit, and soon-returning King of kings. Evangelism is the heartbeat among these businessmen who encourage one another to take Christ into the marketplace, the factories, and the offices.

A Chicago editor, referring to the FGBMFI stated, "It is sweeping into its wake hundreds of clergymen of many denominations. More significantly, perhaps, it is enlisting the enthusiasm and devotion of hundreds of thousands of laymen—sophisticated, educated, and wise in the ways of big business." The FGBMFI has been referred to as the "noisiest—and most often—promoters of the 'second baptism' among non-Pentecostals."

On one occasion David J. du Plessis affirmed before several thousand persons from twenty-two denominations that the "Full Gospel Business Men's Fellowship has been bridging the gap between Pentecostals and 'mainliners.' "[8] Tracing the rise of Neo-Pentecostalism, faculty members of the Southern Baptist Theological Seminary readily admit that it had "no small boost from the FGBMFI."

According to Catholic author Kevin Ranaghan, "The greatest Protestant Pentecostal contribution to the charismatic renewal in the Catholic Church has come through the agency of the Full Gospel Business Men's Fellowship International."[9] When FGBMFI president Shakarian was asked if the movement received opposition from the churches, a reporter received an unexpected reply. The opposition "comes mainly from those we believe should support us. None from liberal Christians."[10]

The relaxed atmosphere of an informal, unhurried FGBMFI meeting in a downtown restaurant, motel dining room, or banquet setting in a prestigious hotel attracts many people who might never step inside a Pentecostal church. The FGBMFI, with no denominational axe to grind, has played a decisive role in introducing the charismatic options to many laymen, ministers and educators from the historic Protestant, Catholic and Orthodox churches. In some of America's major cities as many as 80 percent of those attending these meetings are non-Pentecostal.

The FGBMFI is well designed to supply the needs for spiritual fellowship among new charismatic believers. Without leaving their churches, such groups can meet together for a time of unique fellowship and enjoy the graces and gifts of God. Most of them are dependable church members who find in the FGBMFI a breath of supernatural air and evangelism not often found in the institutional church.

The hundreds of FGBMFI local chapters are attended by people who come not out of a sense of obligation but because they want to be there, to enjoy the ecumenical fellowship, and, more importantly, to receive something directly from God. The flexible programs, which sometimes last for three hours, seem never to be hurried. At an Oakland-San Francisco Saturday breakfast in a downtown restaurant room the entire gathering was moved as people wept and cried out to God. "Hands were raised high and tears streamed down faces of men and women alike. A Catholic photographer at the scene laid his camera down, raised his hands and began to commune with God as tears flowed. . . ."[11]

Summing up the benefits of the meetings, a *Voice* editor declared, "Unsaved people are saved, saved people receive the Baptism of the Holy Spirit, Spirit-filled people are refilled and drawn closer to God, sick bodies are healed, and there is a refreshing of spirit, soul, and body that only the very Presence of God can bring."[12]

Today the Fellowship attracts women and young people as well as businessmen. More recently, seminars have been added to the sessions, with systematic Bible teachings on the gifts of the Spirit. College students have been attracted to them, but the seminars do not terminate when critical minds are satisfied. Instead, the invitation is given to experience the truths which have been presented by Spirit-filled professors and ministers. As a result many collegians have received the Pentecostal baptism.

One reporter asked Shakarian why he restricted the Fellowship's name to "businessmen" and why he stressed the financial success experienced by so many FGBMFI members. Demos answered with his customary deep conviction that spiritual dynamics are often nonexistent in the lives of laymen in positions of secular leadership, men who have a great capacity for getting things done. In order that they may become better stewards of their possessions, power, and popularity, Shakarian urges all laymen to surrender first place in their lives to God. Successful Pentecostal commercial leaders have learned this lesson well. In giving more of themselves to God's work, they discovered that they could not outgive God.

The late Nick Timko was among the pioneer officers of the FGBMFI who believed that anyone living a godly life seven days a week didn't have to lie, cheat, or bribe a purchasing agent, buyer, or salesman to get business. A Detroit manufacturer of auto body dies, Timko even believed that God would, as his business "Partner," direct him in quoting the prices on contracts he desired. At one time when he sorely needed the business, eleven firms were bidding for a contract to produce dies for automobile doors and only three of the bids would be selected. "Lord, I need that business" prayed Nick. The next morning he received a call from the general manager of the company awarding him the entire contract. Timko kept praying, giving more to God's work, and God continued blessing. The business kept expanding until a second plant was necessary. With an investment of more than four million dollars and a payroll of three hundred persons, Nick helped other businessmen pay more attention to his "Partner."[13]

One real estate developer maintained that those who claimed they could not live according to the Bible and also enjoy prosperity were those who had "never truly lived according to God's word." A certain Velmer Gardner *was* living according to God's word, and even preached it to the multitudes in large salvation-healing meetings throughout the world, yet he had no faith for finances. When complete physical exhaustion made it necessary for him to leave the full-time ministry, he returned to the business world and shortly after the formation of the FGBMFI met Demos Shakarian. The

Armenian advised Velmer that "the same faith you use in praying for the sick, I use in business. It will work!" The idea witnessed to his heart and he decided to try it.

A few days later, Gardner was driving past a four-acre piece of property and was suddenly convinced it was God's will for him to purchase it. He consulted leading businessmen and was told that the ground was useless. No one would join him in the venture. But he promised God he would buy it, so he sold his home to raise the necessary money. "God," he said, "told me this piece of ground would be the best motel site in the city, so I bought it. I put $5,000.00 down. . . ." Two weeks later he returned to close the deal. "I walked into the lawyer's office and was offered $50,000.00 profit! I turned it down." Within six months he was offered $100,000.00 profit and still wouldn't sell. They had opened a freeway right in front of the property! Major hotel chains were calling him long distance and the offers kept going up. When Gardner felt the time to sign a contract had arrived, he called the president of Ramada Inn and leased the land that only a short time before had been called useless. They built a motel costing more than a million dollars and Gardner's investment is netting him, in rentals and percentages, one million dollars! He now owns interest in other major motels, and lives from the earnings of one of them. Remembering God's supernatural guidance, the Gardners have dedicated everything else to advance the Gospel, saying, "It's going one hundred percent to support the work of God."[14]

The owner and operator of L. P. Safford Rambler City of Silver Springs, Maryland, would "rather get a soul saved than sell a new automobile." An unusual weekly ad appears in the *Sunday Star,* a Washington, D.C., newspaper. Instead of "A Super-Special of the Week," Safford writes "A Thought for the Week," a comment that turns the reader's attention to the offer of free salvation and eternal life through Christ. These ads have played a significant part, he feels, in the growth of the automobile agency, which employs sixty persons who sell and service new and used cars and does a business running into the millions of dollars each year. Buying up every opportunity to witness about Christ comes natural, like breathing, and Safford finds the FGBMFI a wonderful vehicle for accelerating the Gospel.[15]

Don Locke operates a chain of wholesale plumbing and heating supplies stores, but insists that he possesses only ordinary business ability. He is sure that without God as his business partner he would have folded up long ago. In 1955, the same year he accepted Christ, he recalls, "God put me into business." Starting on a shoestring in Oklahoma City, he became the owner of eight outlets within eleven years. He has given many tens of thousands of dollars to advance God's program, stating simply, "I feel God calls men to make money to support certain phases of His work."[16]

Henry Krause of Kansas was afraid he was making too much money! His business was expanding and he found himself resenting its growth. His early training had taught him to fear prosperity as something dangerous and deadly for a Christian. But when he realized that many people never gave anything to God, he felt assured that he would be given the ability to make money by dealing with these people. He was no longer afraid to prosper, for he knew this money would be used to build churches and promote the work of God. At the time farmers were using an ordinary tractor to pull a plow that would cut a ten-foot furrow and plow a maximum of thirty acres a day. "The Lord gave me a plan for a plow that would cut a fifteen-foot furrow and would plow a hundred acres a day," Krause explained. He consulted with the engineers at the Agricultural College and elsewhere to obtain the proper materials. They informed him that it would be absolutely impossible to put his plan into operation. "So I went home and built that plow. It went together and fitted perfectly." The Kansan went on to produce plows enabling one man to plow as many as five hundred acres a day. "Krause" plows were sought after everywhere wheat was grown and it took him ten years to finally catch up with the overflow of orders. Over the years he has donated systematically to his church and other churches, missionaries, and evangelists as he continues to maintain a close walk with God.[17]

Most of the busy FGBMFI directors and chapter presidents have learned that time given to God's work has not hindered their business pursuits, but in some mysterious manner has enhanced their secular efforts. Al Malachuk, a manufacturer's representative in the graphic arts, works on a commission basis. If he doesn't produce, he earns nothing. Because of the time required to serve as both director and chapter president, it looked like his business would suffer. "But as a result of my surrender to the Lord Jesus Christ and putting Him first," said Al, "my business has doubled." Another director said, "It's worth it and I love it."[18]

Other International Directors of the FGBMFI have held positions as varied as corporation presidents, attorneys, distributors, surgeons, real estate developers, building contractors, owners of insurance agencies, and retailers; the list also includes a geologist, dentist, mayor, diplomat, and advertising executive—all of whom have learned the secret of seeking first the Kingdom of God.

Actually, organization within the FGBMFI is kept to a minimum. The executive officers exercise authority in a few necessary matters and act upon applications for affiliation. Only when it is absolutely imperative do they disfellowship a local chapter. FGBMFI's California headquarters has the power neither to try nor to expel individual members, for this authority is vested in the individual chapters.

The FGBMFI is not intended to be a substitute for, or in competition with, the Church. It does not duplicate the work of local church men's fellowships. Indeed, as a rule, its members are members of local churches. Its doctrinal safeguard is the acceptance of a ten-point outline as a condition of membership; rejection of this Pentecostal position would hinder the very purposes for which the FGBMFI exists. Nevertheless, a great stress is placed upon love as the true basis of unity, rather than doctrinal agreement.

Early in its history well-known Pentecostal evangelists have been featured in the popular annual national conventions. Men such as Oral Roberts, Jack Coe, R. T. Richey, Gordon Lindsay, William Branham, and Tommy Hicks have participated in fanning the flames of evangelism among the receptive laymen. Mass meetings, radio broadcasts, telecasts, and healing services have produced results which are staggering in their cumulative effects.

By the end of the FGBMFI's first year of activity Oral Roberts commented on the rapid progress of the new organization and saw in it the promise of a world-changing movement. He urged all Pentecostals to support the FGBMFI in every way possible. New chapters began springing up in major cities across the United States.

Shakarian's faith continued to grow. He even tried to secure President Eisenhower to speak at the 1954 FGBMFI meeting in Washington, D.C. The aggressive Shakarian did succeed in getting then Vice-President Richard M. Nixon to address the convention at a breakfast session in the Shoreham Hotel in the nation's capital. In his brief address on "The Minds and Hearts and Souls of Men" Nixon referred to the organization's belief in God as a symbol of one of the greatest advantages Americans had over the appeal the Communists were projecting. He encouraged the Pentecostal businessmen

156

to continue spreading their influence all over America. Oral Roberts spoke to the thousand people who attended the closing banquet. At the conclusion of his inspiring message all the men present joined hands and marched to the cadence of "Onward Christian Soldiers." Shakarian beamed as he thought of the twenty-three businessmen marching in like fashion two short years before. "What will the next two years bring forth?" he wondered.

David du Plessis, one of the early architects of the Pentecostal World Conferences, thoroughly enjoyed the Washington Convention because of the complete absence of denominational barriers and the total freedom in the Spirit. This experience served to change the course of his life and ministry, causing him to thrust into the field of evangelism with greater faith. He went on to present the claims of Pentecost in seminaries and ivy league colleges, opening minds to the divine wind of the Holy Spirit.

One of the charter officers of the FGBMFI was a Binghamton, New York, Oldsmobile dealer named George Gardner. The local FGBMFI director tells of an incident in which Gardner was used by God to pray for the Garbett family. Mr. Garbett and his four sons were looking at Gardner's display of new cars one day. In order to communicate with Mr. Garbett, Gardner had to write his words, for the whole family had been born deaf and dumb. Inviting them up to his office, Gardner became a salesman for God, sharing the promise found in the fourteenth chapter of John's gospel which declared, "Greater works than these shall you do. . . . And whatsoever you shall ask the Father in my Name that shall He do." As the presence of God seemed to fill the room, the businessman placed both hands on the man's shoulders and prayed, "asking Satan to loose his hold on the man." Then he "commanded the deaf and dumb spirit to come out, and immediately the man could

157

hear. . . ." Gardner then turned to one son who had followed his dad into the office, and repeated the prayer. Immediately the boy could hear. The next day the family of six attended Faith Tabernacle and received prayer. "God opened all of their ears and loosed their vocal cords. . . ."[19]

In 1954 a short, middle-aged evangelist, at one time in the construction business, became the first American to hold mass meetings in the Argentine Republic. Tommy Hicks was a staunch supporter of the FGBMFI from its inception, and little did the businessmen know how mightily their prayers on his behalf would be answered. From a Foreign Letter report written in Argentina the Journal of the American Medical Association printed the following: "An American evangelist, Tommy Hicks, from Lancaster, California, has been speaking to groups of 10,000 to 40,000 persons assembled on football fields. He claims that faith in God can completely cure most diseases. Many people of Buenos Aires, having become conditioned to the authority of radio addresses, are readily impressed by anything broadcast over a loud speaker. The number of persons announcing 'the cure of cancer, hypertension, etc. without any demonstrable evidence has greatly increased.' "[20]

A religion editor of the Los Angeles *Times* wrote of the phenomenal buildup of attendance from five thousand in the first April meeting to a May throng of 200,000 reported by a Buenos Aires newspaper.[21] Divine healing was heavily emphasized in the meetings which, to the surprise of many, were permitted by the president of Argentina. Hicks had boldly sought out and presented Juan Domingo Perón a Bible and several copies of the FGBMFI *Voice*. Perón's unheard of special permission paved the way for the full Gospel to be presented in mass meetings, over the radio, and in the press throughout the Catholic country. Money alone could not have accomplished this feat—and anyway Hicks was down to forty-seven dollars. It was God's time.

Tommy Hicks used an expert interpreter, Paul Sorenson, who effectively translated both messages and gestures. At a meeting in the Temuco Country of Argentina, held in Plaza Recabarren, Hicks reported, "Multitudes were so great that it was impossible to lay hands on all the sick. . . ." Struggling evangelical churches, which after long years of labor averaged but forty in their congregations, were suddenly overwhelmed as their attendance skyrocketed twentyfold. Every Scripture warehouse in Argentina was emptied and thousands of Bibles had to be flown in.

People walked for miles to reach the meetings. One woman who hadn't walked in five years was brought twenty-five miles in an oxcart. After Hicks prayed for the throng in an authoritative voice the woman fell asleep. During the long journey home all efforts to awaken her were futile. The following afternoon as they neared her village the woman awoke and began shouting, "I am healed! I am healed! I am healed!" She got out and ran to tell everyone the good news.

An amazed Hicks shared the accounts in FGBMFI meetings across the United States. Nothing before or since in his ministry could come close to matching the Argentinian revival. Experienced ministers and missionaries claimed they had never seen anything like it. When asked to explain the reason for the size of the crowds, Hicks summed it all up by saying, "I brought to them the word of Jesus Christ. They were hungry for it."[22] Another hidden clue came from Edward Muller, who had already planted the Gospel seed in Argentina for eight years and watered the seed with much prayer. During one six-month period he interceded in prayer for revival eight hours a day.[23]

When Hicks returned to Argentina the second time, his meetings were banned after a few services and the preacher was arrested. Had the same faithful investment of prayer time been made, or had success been taken for granted?

And speaking of prayer, the members of the FGBMFI usually enjoy nothing more than the privilege of praying with others to be healed and to receive the baptism in the Holy Spirit evidenced by the speaking in tongues. That's what makes them Full Gospel Business Men. A Baptist minister who resented the term "Full Gospel" stated, "It infers that the rest of us Christians who are not Pentecostal are not believers in the full gospel." His resentment vanished two years later when he felt a void in his own ministry and hungered for more of God after reading an account of evangelist William Branham's meetings in the *Voice.* He sought out a Full Gospel believer and asked, "Tell me how to receive the baptism. . . ." Within a few minutes he experienced what the FGBMFI men radiate and are so eager to share with everybody.[24]

At times the Pentecostal businessmen become hilarious givers. During an International Convention breakfast in Denver, Velmer Gardner challenged the men to support the evangelistic outreach of the Fellowship in a magnanimous manner. They did just that. Within minutes sums of from one hundred to one thousand dollars were placed before the evangelist. The voluntary gifts totaled $33,000. The following morning Raymond T. Richey repeated the challenge to give liberally. Within a few minutes $22,000 was placed upon the platform.[25]

That church members should thus give beyond the offering plates of their home churches may irk some pastors but the joyful spirit of giving will tend to benefit the home church as well. Through the added enthusiasm, increased dedication, and deeper spirituality Full Gospel Business Men can be better disciples and more active members of their individual churches. They witness about Christ more readily to those who are in their circle of daily activities in a world of industry and commerce. They confront many people their pastors may never meet or who would tend to politely receive and then disregard the pastors' words as coming from men of the cloth whose duty and profession it is to speak to men about their souls. But these are laymen speaking to laymen in laymen's language. The president of the Hong Kong Chapter, Bulson Chang, declared, "The peoples of Asia do not trust the motives of professional Christian missionaries or ordained clergymen but they respond readily to evangelism by laymen who 'pay their own way.' "[26]

Bulson Chang's words of 1957 seem prophetic today as China's trade doors open to the world once again. Chang, a former counselor of the deposed Chinese government, felt that the answer to China's problem was Christianization. "But I mean Christianization in the Apostolic sense, when Jesus called fishermen, merchants, lawyers, and tax collectors to follow Him, not as professional teachers of dogma, but as self-supporting individuals, under the guidance of God, igniting men's hearts by the fire of their own example."[27]

A decade after the federation's founding, FGBMFI "Airlifts" were dropping these dedicated businessmen into many nations for a witness. Paying their own expenses, hundreds have participated in airlifts to the Near East, the Far East, Scandinavia, Europe, Great Britain, South America, and the South Pacific. In 1969 a group of 150 members and friends visited Rome and witnessed to men on the street, in homes, and in churches. One Director of FGBMFI gave an inspired witness while in Cossenza, Sicily. He didn't know that a man crazed by his wife's insistence on attending services against his wishes stood against the back wall purposing to kill the pastor. But when he saw men and women kneel at the altar and the sick prayed for, he came under tremendous conviction. He joined his wife at the altar

161

confessing, "I want to be saved right now!"[28]

Five consecutive annual airlifts to Scandinavia have brought FGBMFI representatives all over Northern Europe, ready to do business for God. In Sweden doors opened in Baptist, Methodist, and State churches (Lutheran) because Swedish businessmen banded together and arranged some forty meetings in twelve days. The venerable Lewi Pethrus remarked, "I do not believe Christianity should be promoted by 'professionals' but by 'amateurs,' as in the beginning. *All* believers should be 'priests' and every person should have the opportunity to give a testimony." For this reason he praised the FGBMFI as an instrument for opening the churches to the "Charismatic Renewal."[29]

Nor are the Pentecostal businessmen inhibited outside church doors. Most are aggressive and adventuresome in their commitment to evangelizing others, be it at home or abroad. Demos Shakarian leads the way at times with his bold and unorthodox approaches to sharing the Gospel message. When the Armenian Anastas Mikoyan, Deputy Premier of the Soviet Union, visited the United States in the late 1950s, Shakarian sent a 285-word telegram to him requesting permission for a religious crusade in Soviet Russia with evangelist Oral Roberts. The Soviet Embassy in Washington declined to comment.[30]

When Demos Shakarian and others visited Havana, Cuba, to help establish a new FGBMFI chapter in 1959, he met Fidel Castro, the victorious rebel leader. Surrounded by armed soldiers, the young revolutionary entered the Havana Hilton dining room as Shakarian was leaving. Demos extended his right hand, saying, "Mr. Castro, I'm from California." Castro firmly clasped his hand. He later was able to sit with Castro and share news about the FGBMFI. The bearded leader wanted to know who sponsored the work and was surprised to learn that the businessmen paid their own way and that

162

some had traveled around the world to help establish new chapters. Castro appeared impressed and as he again shook Demos' hand he remarked, "I like what you men are doing!"[31]

On another occasion, in response to eighty thousand pounds of food sent to his country by the FGBMFI, Haiti's Senator Arthur Bonhomme read a letter from President Duvalier before a Regional Convention. The Pentecostal businessmen were invited to come and freely evangelize the country and also to consider further aid and investments in Haiti. Shakarian responded at once. Taking along evangelist Morris Cerullo and a dozen businessmen, he flew to Haiti and found an official welcome party at the airport. Before they left the island thousands had accepted Christ in response to the preaching and the praying for the sick. The laymen gave forceful testimonies as the crowds swelled to many thousands. Senator Bonhomme reported a 90 percent drop in the practice of witchcraft in Port au Prince during the meetings.[32]

During a Miami Beach Convention in 1961 Demos Shakarian explained why FGBMFI members were so friendly to the members of the Teamsters Union when both organizations converged upon the Americana Hotel. The FGBMFI had been placed in a strategic position to present the challenging claims of Jesus Christ. As the Spirit-filled men eagerly witnessed on every hand, the Teamsters scoffed, then became curious and concerned. Night after night when both sessions were over, the teamsters posed questions and probed into matters of eternal importance. Throughout the week many of them attended the Full Gospel conferences and three accepted Christ as personal Savior. They were baptized in the hotel swimming pool by a Mennonite preacher attending the sessions. A thriving industrialist from Philadelphia then witnessed to the crowd that had gathered. The FGBMFI knows what spiritual power could be released if the rank and file of all unions would receive Christ as Savior and Baptizer. The Teamsters in Miami Beach were convinced that the happy faces of the FGBMFI delegates communicated genuine love.[33]

When a group of FGBMFI flew to the Holy Land to attend the Pentecostal World Conference, they participated in what was the most dramatic event of the session. A crippled Hebrew Christian, Rachanim Raskin, expected to be healed if he could gain entrance to the Nations Building where thousands of Pentecostal delegates had gathered. But the guards refused him entry. A Christian worker led him to Shakarian, hoping he could use his influence to get the man past the guards. Instead Demos turned to the lame man and said, "If you really believe that the Lord Jesus can heal you, you can be healed right here and now!" Laying hands on the surprised Hebrew, Shakarian boldly commanded the spirit of affliction to release the man in the name of Jesus Christ. The cripple straightened up instantly. "Hallelujah, the pain is all gone," he cried. He pushed his crutch aside, decisively proclaiming, "I do not need it any more!" Hours later, during the evening service, James Brown, the guest Presbyterian speaker, announced the healing to the large Pentecostal audience. When the shouts of praise subsided he said, "The power of Pentecost is yours today! Claim it! Accept it! Use it for the spreading of God's Kingdom. . . ."[34] If it seems paradoxical for a Presbyterian to be admonishing Classic Pentecostals in Jerusalem, the site of the first Pentecost, Mr. Brown did not see it that way. In fact, he said, "Don't be less Pentecostal. . . . Be more Pentecostal."[35]

The FGBMFI wants to be just that as it continues to grow. Have these men reached their goals? Demos Shakarian's response is an emphatic "No—we have just gotten through 'boot camp'!" He clearly recalls the prophecy that Charles Price shared with him before this man of great faith passed off the earthly scene. It had been revealed to him that in the last days God would "raise up a ministry among laymen, witnessing like they did in the Early Church, and then the Lord will come."[36] Earlier Price had correctly predicted the rise of the deliverance ministry when thousands would be saved and healed, after which a laymen's movement enlisting multitudes of men would carry out God's plan. Could the FGBMFI be the fulfillment of this prophecy? Shakarian is convinced the greatest move of the Holy Spirit ever seen is just ahead.[37]

Twenty years of exciting history and growth of the FGBMFI is past. Not wishing to be satisfied with past accomplishments, Shakarian urges each businessman to reevaluate the priorities in his life. He will be satisfied only when all conflicts of interest are resolved and the men go forward with a singleness of heart. Successful Pentecostal businessmen will then march as an invincible army doing mighty exploits in the marketplaces of the world.

X

Protestant Neo-Pentecostals

"IF IT'S A CHOICE between the uncouth life of the Pentecostals and the esthetic death of the older churches, I for one choose the uncouth life," declared a past president of Princeton Theological Seminary.[1]

An unknown but large and growing number of historical Protestants are choosing the charismatic life of the Pentecostals, though they cool most of the ardent emotionalism still engaged in by some Classic Pentecostals. These Protestants would rather not be called Pentecostal. They prefer the "Charismatic" label, which derives from the Greek word *charisma*, meaning gift. The term was used by early Christians to signify a spiritual gift from God flowing through a Christian. Inasmuch as the Pentecostal experience includes speaking in tongues, which is a charismatic manifestation of the Holy Spirit, then Pentecostals may be called charismatic and charismatic Christians who speak in tongues can just as well be called Pentecostal.

The retired president of Union Theological Seminary made this startling statement: "The Pentecostal movement is nothing less than a revolution comparable in importance to the establishment of the original apostolic church and to the Protestant Reformation."[2] That's saying a great deal, but the Pentecostal movement at its best may well play a most significant role in the critical years ahead. And while most historic Protestants still avoid Pentecostalism like the plague, an ever-increasing number of serious, dedicated ministers

166

and lay people in this branch of Christendom are quietly becoming part of the late twentieth-century Neo-Pentecostal movement.

Some years ago the Anglican Archbishop of York referred to Pentecostalism while preaching in London's St. Paul's Cathedral: ". . . To neglect what is one of the most extraordinary features of religious life in the twentieth century is to show lack of responsibility or an unreadiness to face evidence." He reminded the congregation that in Latin America four out of five non-Roman Catholics are Pentecostals.[3]

Back in 1949, a pastor in Los Angeles acknowledged the potency of the Pentecostals in his magazine *The Methodist Challenge* when he wrote: "We high-brow Methodist preachers with our university degrees and new gospel of a Christ-directed social order are apt to make a deadly mistake concerning some of our more lowly brethren, of whom we often speak with condescension and sometimes with disdain. The Church of England and her ministers made the same mistakes in their estimate of the early Methodists."

Referring to the Pentecostals, he continued: "They butcher the English language. They are emotional and excitable. They are noisy. In fact, they are very much like we Methodists used to be. But, my brethren, they are reaching the masses, and the people are hearing them.

"I am far from being a Pentecostal. I shrink from any boisterous show of fanaticism. I believe in doing things decently and in order. But I am not so dense that I cannot see the trend of these times."[4]

Shuler was more perceptive than some Protestant leaders. The decade of the fifties was a period of phenomenal growth among the Pentecostals in the United States as massive meetings emphasizing salvation and divine healing were conducted across the land, especially by Oral Roberts, who brought these truths sharply

167

into focus on the television screens in millions of American living rooms. The Full Gospel Business Men's Fellowship began publishing the *Voice* in 1953 and an increasing number of Protestants from the old-line, historic churches were being irresistibly drawn to the demonstration of the supernatural power of God inherent in the Pentecostal proclamation of the Gospel of Jesus Christ.

David du Plessis, one of the Pentecostal leaders present at the mid-century Seventh Conference of the National Association of Evangelicals, stated, "I was astounded to see with what love and consideration my Pentecostal brethren were received and treated by the leading evangelicals of America. . . . Frequently . . . speaking in tongues among the Pentecostals was mentioned without any ridicule or apology, and no offense was taken. Personally I . . . never felt that anyone cooled towards me when I introduced myself as a Pentecostal worker. On the contrary several expressed their admiration for the glorious work that was being done through the efforts of those who share in this wonderful outpouring of the Holy Spirit. . . . I felt convinced that something wonderful is taking place, and that revival is on the way."[5]

As Pentecostalism continued to find open hearts a minister by the name of Dennis Bennett came to serve the parish at St. Mark's Protestant Episcopal Church in Van Nuys, California. He had received his seminary degree from the University of Chicago's Theological Seminary, where one of the most respected professors began all of his semesters' classes in the psychology of religion with the statement, "I want you to understand that I am an atheist."

In his suburban church of Los Angeles, Father Bennett demonstrated great leadership, guiding the expansion of the flock from five hundred members in 1953 to 2,600 members seven years later. Little did he realize, however, that his personal probing into the Pentecostal experience

would bring the Van Nuys church national notoriety and
that the Bishop of the Diocese of California, James A.
Pike, would label the charismatic results "heresy in
embryo."

It all started when a neighboring Anglican priest told
Bennett about a couple in his church who had received
the baptism in the Spirit and spoke in tongues. They
became so enthusiastic about God and Jesus Christ that
Bennett and his wife found their attitude contagious.
"I don't know what these people have, but I want it!"
Mrs. Bennett told her husband.[6]

Dennis Bennett met often with the couple. The presence of God he felt in them attracted him to seek the
cause of their abundant life. The rector poured over his
Bible anew and discovered that their experience tallied
with Scripture. After observing John and Joan for three
months he was ready to act. "I was like a starving man
circling a table on which a delicious-looking feast is
spread . . . trying to make up his mind whether it is
really safe."

Finally he said to the couple, "I want this nearness
to God you have, that's all; I'm not interested in speaking in tongues!"

Their reply was disarming. "Well, all we can tell you
about *that* is that it came with the package!"

For about twenty minutes they prayed calmly and
quietly. Bennett was about to give up when a very
strange feeling came over him. "My tongue tripped,
just as it might when you are trying to recite a tongue
twister, and I began to speak in a new language!" He
was convinced that he was not the object of some psychological trick or compulsion. "I was allowing these
new words to come to my lips and was speaking them
out of my own volition, without in any way being
forced to do it. . . . It was a real language, not some
kind of 'baby talk.' It had grammar and syntax; it had
inflection and expression. . . ."[7]

Four days later he visited John and Joan again and

169

during prayer he again spoke in tongues. "I still felt nothing out of the ordinary, no great spiritual inspiration, no special inner warmth of God's presence. It was interesting, though, and somehow refreshing. . . ." The glossolalia continued for a half hour as the elated priest spoke "with fluency and eloquence that I had never dreamed possible."

As a pastor, Dennis Bennett discovered that his counseling changed completely. Now he often terminated the session by praying for the person "to accept Jesus and to be filled with the Holy Spirit." He was puzzled to note that one by one those who received the Pentecostal experience would stop smoking, though many had far worse habits and problems. Then lives began to change more profoundly. Healings, rare in the past, occurred more frequently. "Could it be," reasoned the Neo-Pentecostal pastor, "that this 'Baptism in the Holy Spirit' had something to do with the release of that kind of power. It seemed so."[8]

After sixty of his parishioners had received this baptism, Bennett took a census and learned that these few were supporting 10 percent of the budget of the 2,600-member church. They included the junior warden of the parish, the directress of the Altar Guild, the president of the most active Women's Guild, and the church librarian. The wife of a well-known neurosurgeon in the San Fernando Valley was one of the recipients of this spiritual baptism. Expecting unfavorable reaction from the doctor, Bennett was surprised instead to hear him recommend the phenomenon of speaking in tongues. "You see," remarked the neurosurgeon, "the speech centers dominate the brain. If they were yielded to God, then every other area would be affected, too. Besides, I think about God sometimes, and I run out of words. I don't see why He shouldn't give me some additional words to use."[9]

One of the rector's three assistants reacted against

170

this penetration of Pentecost at Van Nuys. With the
benefit of hindsight, Dennis Bennett now admits to
making a wrong move in confining the Pentecostal invasion at St. Mark's to quiet, unofficial, house prayer
meetings. He had practiced the compromise of silence
for several months, allowing the dissidents opportunity
to sow "seeds of discontent." The Episcopal minister
learned that, "You can't keep Pentecost under wraps—it
burns through!"

Not many Neo-Pentecostals have openly acknowledged, as did Dennis Bennett, a respect for and debt to
the Pentecostals. He knew from his research that "these
were the Christians who had preserved the understanding of the Baptism in the Holy Spirit, sometimes in the
face of real persecution, and I owed them gratitude for
the blessing that had come into my life."[10] He recalled
the first time he spoke to a group of Pentecostal ministers and the wise counsel he received. Instead of suggesting that he join the Pentecostal ranks, they urged
him to remain in the Episcopal denomination and share
the Pentecostal experience, "for they will listen to you
where they would not listen to us."[11]

The crucial day arrived. Dennis Bennett selected
Sunday, April 3, 1960, as the time to set aside the
scheduled preaching theme and publicly declare his
charismatic involvement, hoping to dismiss the rumors
and misunderstandings which had spread in the five
months since his initial Pentecostal experience. It was
necessary to repeat this statement at each of the three
morning services at St. Mark's. The reaction of the early
worshipers was "open and tender." However, the bomb
burst at the end of the second service. Bennett's second
assistant "snatched off his vestments, threw them on
the altar, and stalked out of the church crying: 'I can
no longer work with this man' "[12]

The rector was appalled. One of his vestrymen handed Bennett another blow, saying, "You should resign!"

171

An Episcopal rector who is guilty of no moral or canonical offense need not resign; nor could he be forced to do so. Moreover, the opposition group was a minuscule faction acting from prejudice and hearsay. But Bennett, who detested the thought of a court battle and bad publicity for his beloved church, stood up at the last morning service and announced his resignation. So it was that the members had heard their pastor openly declare: "The Holy Spirit did take my lips and tongue and form a new and powerful language of praise and prayer that I myself could not understand."[13] Bennett's confession became a milestone that helped many Neo-Pentecostal pastors and laymen come out from positions of embarrassing compromise and take an open stand. The outbreak revealed a Pentecostal movement within the Episcopal church that was gaining momentum. National publicity only added to the momentum. Glossolalia spread so rapidly that leaders in the Episcopal, Methodist, and Lutheran churches established commissions to investigate the matter.

Bishop James A. Pike was quite upset by those who talked to God in tongues. He desired to introduce a system of disciplines whereby the glossolalics would be seen but not heard. He issued a pastoral letter which was read to 125 congregations, informing Episcopal laymen to avoid the practice of speaking in tongues and directing the clergy not to propagate glossolalia. Tongues were banned from confirmation services and both clergy and church members were advised to desist from speaking in tongues in "churches or in homes or elsewhere." Not even the militant Soviet atheists have been able to succeed in so difficult a proscription. An Episcopal commission found at least twelve clergymen of the diocese "actively involved" and concluded that glossolalia "may be either an unhealthy element within the personality or a creative influence." They decided to study the movement further.

In the early sixties the Neo-Pentecostal movement came in for a number of caustic comments from various church dignitaries. Seattle area Methodist Bishop Everett W. Palmer called speaking in tongues "a perversion." To Palmer, glossolalia ranged "from incoherent babbling, unintelligible monologue, and ecstatic ejaculation, to [the] trances of a medium." Evidently embarrassed by those Methodists who were involved, the Bishop stated, "It tends to make the Church look ridiculous."[14]

In 1960 California's Methodist Bishop Gerald Kennedy tried to dismiss the movement, saying, "In the past there have been movements of this sort, but they never did the Church any good."[15] Although many did not favor the Neo-Pentecostals, it was no longer possible to ignore the facts of their growth. Donald S. Metz, a Nazarene professor, authored *Speaking in Tongues* in 1964 after observing the dramatic spread of Pentecostalism within the historic denominations. He admitted, "The problem appears to be of such magnitude that no group can evade the issue." Metz acknowledged the fact that six hundred members of the First Presbyterian Church of Hollywood, the world's largest Presbyterian Church, professed to have the gift of tongues.[16]

The American Lutheran Church Commission on Evangelism met in Minneapolis on October 24, 1962, yielding "A Report on Glossolalia." It went on record with a cautious endorsement of speaking in tongues, stating that it was "one of several gifts of the Spirit described in Scripture."[17]

By 1963 the Protestant Episcopal Church actually sent official representatives to the Pentecostal's largest denominational headquarters, the Assemblies of God, to discuss the doctrine and manifestation of the Holy Spirit. The Pentecostal penetration of the historical churches had indeed continued and, although one might have expected this situation to produce a fair amount of resentment, in fact there emerged from this meeting a deep sense of Christian understanding and mutual trust. A joint statement declared, "We found ourselves a fellowship, open to the leading of the Holy Spirit to a degree which we hardly dared to expect."

A Lutheran author who was opposed to tongues admitted that within the historic churches those deeply interested in the phenomenon claimed to have found in the tongues movement a "special manifestation of the Holy Spirit." He noted within Neo-Pentecostalism a more intellectual and sophisticated atmosphere and a more "rational theology of speaking in tongues" than was to be found in Classic Pentecostalism. Even the term "glossolalia" had a more sophisticated ring than "speaking in tongues."[18]

Dennis Bennett wasn't alone. During the same year he resigned from St. Mark's, the Episcopal publication *Living Church* editorialized: "Speaking in tongues . . . is in our midst, and it is being practiced by clergy and laity who have stature and good reputation in the Church. . . . Its widespread introduction would jar against our esthetic sense and some of our more strongly entrenched preconceptions. But we know that we are members of a Church which definitely needs jarring. . . . If God has chosen this time to dynamite what Bishop Sterling of Montana has called 'Episcopalian respectabilianism,' we know no more terrifyingly effective explosive."[19]

What about Father Dennis Bennett? Did he throw in the towel and quit the ministry? Not at all. Calls flooded in from ministers and lay people of many denominations because of the national publicity given to the Van Nuys church. As a result many began to receive the baptism in the Holy Spirit. Bennett was one of the first ministers of the historical denominations to stick his neck out to publicly share the experience of Pentecostal power. His background and academic training qualified him to present the work of the Holy Spirit in such a manner that clergymen and intellectuals sat up and took notice. And his easygoing manner proved most winsome.

When the Episcopal Bishop in Olympia, Washington, heard Bennett's story, he remarked, "Look, Dennis, what about coming up to this diocese? Bring the fire with you!" The offer was both challenging and discouraging. The Ballard district of Seattle included a sixty-year-old mission called St. Luke's Episcopal Church. "I've got to do something or close it up," pleaded the Bishop. It meant a cut of four thousand dollars in Bennett's salary, and the mission's operating budget was in the red. But the Spirit-filled ex-rector felt the tug on his heart and mind. He was eager to see what would happen when the baptism in the Spirit was openly accepted and taught in a local parish. His answer came as he spoke to five hundred men at an annual Men's Fellowship retreat of the Assemblies of God. During the service tongues were exercised. The interpretation was, "If you will go with Me and not deny the work of My Holy Spirit, I will prosper your ministry!" That did it. His decision confirmed, Bennett left for Seattle.

Ten years elapsed and Seattle's St. Luke's was now regarded by the Bishop and other chief ministers as "one of the churches that is 'going upstream against the current, in a day when many churches are shrinking and dying.'" In one decade the budget had increased fourteen fold, from $12,000 to $170,000 a year in the absence of any financial drives or "every-member canvass." Five services were held each Sunday, and during the week various other meetings drew large numbers of visitors from numerous denominations for prayer and instruction, bringing the total weekly at-

175

tendance past the two thousand mark. The Sunday mornings still retain a conservative atmosphere, but on Tuesday nights several hundreds "share in enthusiastic gospel singing, praise, prayer, testimony, and teaching. . . ."[20]

Buried in a tiny mission church, Bennett attributes the dramatic growth at St. Luke's to no man. The blessing of God falls whether Pastor Bennett is present or not—and the understanding congregation has gladly agreed to share their pastor with the world, so Bennett is gone one third of the time. Yet the Friday "informal meeting" has so much of the fire of Pentecost that it has drawn multitudes over the past ten years and an estimated eight thousand have received the Pentecostal experience at these meetings! The membership of this church is less than a thousand only because the Spirit-filled leaders at St. Luke's have always insisted that the visitors "return to their own churches to share. . . ." Bennett is passing on the words of wisdom he received years earlier from the Pentecostals: remain in your denomination to share the baptism in the Spirit, "for they will listen to you where they would not listen to us."

In a sermon delivered to ministers in the Sacramento, California, Crusade, Billy Graham went to bat for the Pentecostals by issuing this challenge: "I wonder if one of the secrets of Pentecostalism cannot be learned by our mainstream churches with the great emphasis on the Holy Spirit. I am sure that my Pentecostal brethren that are here today would agree with me that there have been extremes and excesses that have embarrassed many of them at times, but I want to tell you I believe the time has come to give the Holy Spirit His rightful place in our preaching, in our teaching, and in our churches. We need to go back and study again what Paul meant when he said, 'Be filled with the Spirit.' We need to learn once again what it means to be baptized with the Holy Spirit. I know that we can rationalize and immediately ten thousand theological questions arise and we try to figure it all out; but, brethren, I want to tell you that we need to accept, we need to get something. Give it any terminology you want, but we do not have the same enthusiasm, the same dynamics, and the same power the Early Church had."[21]

The Catholic Director of the Institute for Ecumenical and Cultural Research believes that because Pentecostalism is not a denomination or a doctrine, but a spiritual experience, "a way of life, which has a scriptural basis, it can fit into a Roman Catholic, a Lutheran, a Presbyterian context. Its central concern . . . is fulness of life in the Holy Spirit and the exercise of all the gifts. A decisive moment in this fulness of life is the baptism in the Holy Spirit."[22] Some hope that the return of the Pentecostal experience within older traditions will result in "a new Christian presence which is both truer to the over-all balance of the New Testament and more suited and adaptable to our fast changing world."[23]

Some strange adaptations have occurred throughout the 1960s and undoubtedly will continue to spread even further during the seventies. By 1963 only one Lutheran pastor in the state of Montana had not received the Pentecostal baptism. Unexpected areas such as Fuller Seminary, Wheaton College, Westmont College, the Navigators, and the Wycliffe Bible Translators—all evangelical institutions with their defenses up—have felt the penetration of Pentecost.[24] Some Protestant churches insist upon repeating the rigid stand taken against the Pentecostals early in the century, but increasing numbers of churches are applying caution and forebearance. And more pastors are coming to the realization that charismatics are serious Bible believers who desire to be used in the local church and neighborhood to advance the kingdom of God. One minister

177

bragged that his "glossolalia flock" constituted a church-within-a-church. By that he meant that the tongues-speaking people were those he could depend upon "to tithe and pray and work with a special fervor." What this pastor had been seeking to effect through the years of preaching and persuading, he realized "instantly by the Holy Spirit through the 'baptism' and its attendant gifts."[25]

No Pentecostal, be he Classic, Neo-Pentecostal, or Catholic, should look upon the baptism in the Spirit as an end in itself. Unless the result is the exaltation of Christ and a greater concern for carrying out His Great Commission, believers are not realizing the full significance of the Pentecostal experience. For instance, until John L. Peters spoke in tongues, he found his life somewhat empty even though he was a theologically trained Harvard graduate and a member of a Methodist church. He claims that no other single event in his life produced the power he found in his personal Pentecost. And, as president of World Neighbors, a people-to-people project designed to help the unfortunates in underdeveloped nations to help themselves, he needs all the aid he can get. His life proves his premise that the Pentecostal experience inspires men to deeper Christian action.[26]

Not at all new to the Episcopalian Church is the practice of laying hands on the sick in prayer for divine healing. Probably the most prominent among the parishes engaging in this practice is Philadelphia's St. Stephen's Protestant Episcopal Church. The historic doors of this famous church were ready to be closed in 1942, when Alfred W. Price arrived as its rector, hoping he could be its man of the hour. While yet in seminary he had been alerted to the great challenge of spiritual healing by a medical doctor who stated, "Ministers, if they really knew how to pray, could probably be doing seventy-five percent of the healing work of physicians."[27]

Rediscovering the place of healing in the ministry of
Jesus Christ and its support in the New Testament,
Price made an important decision. Weekly services for
the sick would be offered each Thursday at 12:30 and
5:30 P.M. Fewer than twenty attended at the very beginning, but the work grew. A group formed a chain of
intercessory prayer linked twenty-one hours a day, each
person praying for half an hour. Their task was to bring
to Christ those who were in need—all kinds. By the mid-
1950s St. Stephen's was in the forefront of a rapidly
spreading movement in the United States, reinstating
healing to the important place it deserved. The yearly
attendance of almost twenty thousand proved the
point.

The people who came were informed that such
prayers were not to be considered a substitute for medical treatment. "We believe that all healing is from God,"
taught Price, "whether through medicine or prayer or
both. Which gets the credit is unimportant. But this is
important: Just as doctors work hard at becoming experts in medical treatment, so more Christians should
work harder at becoming expert in prayer. . . ."[28] One
of the members of the fellowship, a medical doctor,
said, "I have seen too much of the power of prayer in
healing to doubt that what are sometimes called 'miracles' do happen. Prayer and the Prayer Fellowship are
an indispensable part of my practice."[29]

Earnest seekers filled the altar rail at St. Stephen's
in response to Price's matter-of-fact invitation: "Come
in confidence, knowing that the Lord is not on the side
of sickness, but of health; that he desires for you, beginning now, a wholeness of soul, mind, and body." As
he placed hands on each, the rector prayed, "May the
mercy of God and the love of our Lord Jesus Christ and
the power of the Holy Spirit, which are here now, enter
your soul, your mind, and your body, for healing."[30]
According to Martin E. Marty, about 40 percent of the

179

3,800 people who sought prayers during a single year "were convinced that they were helped. Many people report little physical gain, but immense spiritual growth."[31]

In 1947 the International Order of St. Luke the Physician was founded. Consisting of medical doctors, ministers, and laymen, the Order promoted the ministry of spiritual healing under the order and discipline of the church. By 1965 it had over four thousand members in chapters located in the United States, Canada, Great Britain, Scotland, Ireland, South Africa, Ceylon, New Zealand, France, and Australia. Clair King, a member of the Order, reflected, "At first I was skeptical of spiritual healing, as are almost all doctors, but the more I studied it, the more I was convinced that it has a major place in healing today."[32] Dr. King tells of Frank F. Fluno, a patient who was told by two specialists in Pittsburgh that he was developing cataracts in both eyes, that his vision would grow worse, and that an operation would be necessary in a few years. He quit driving his car but he faithfully attended the divine healing services held weekly in the Trinity Presbyterian Church in East Liverpool, Ohio. One day while in King's office for a routine eye examination, five years after the diagnosis of the specialists, Fluno was found to have normal sight in one eye and almost 20/20 in the other eye with correcting lenses. "Being an eye specialist," King commented, "I could understand how cancer could be cured by spiritual healing, but never a cataract until I saw it myself."[33]

Within the last decade several large denominations have officially recognized spiritual healing and it is optionally included in the churches' outreach. In May 1960 the General Assembly of the United Presbyterian Church adopted a report on "The Relation of Christian Faith and Health." In February 1961 the Evangelical and Reformed Church prepared for its membership "A

Report on Spiritual Healing." And in January 1962 the United Lutheran Church national convention heard a "Report of the Committee on Anointing and Healing." Each of the three reports cautiously pointed out their church's responsibility regarding a Christian healing ministry.[34]

George F. MacLeod, leader of the Iona Community in Scotland, addressed himself to the question of whether there is a valid place in the local church for any kind of healing ministry. Basing his remarks upon ten years of experience with a weekly service of prayer for the healing of the sick, he declared, "Healing is the central obligation of the Church. Christ came neither to save souls nor to save bodies. He came to save me. Thus our whole ministry is one of healing."[35] In agreement with most ministers involved in praying for the sick, MacLeod maintains that all healing is of God, explaining that, "The Church's recovery of her healing ministry is in cooperation with, and not in defiance of, the medical profession."[36]

Iona's weekly prayer service for the sick was launched through sheer necessity. It happened during a week-night service when the congregation was asked for the names of any for whom they were anxious. Thirty-five bits of paper came in listing needs, some of them desperate ones. Ever since this eye-opener occurred, the loving congregation has shared the burden with its pastor as members nearest him join him in laying hands on the sick.

Spiritual healing is to many a subject of dispute. The American Medical Association takes the position that all reported cures are the result of suggestion, spontaneous remission, or improper diagnosis. While this is questioned by some of the AMA's own professional members, strangely enough many clergymen readily support the view. Presbyterian minister Carroll R. Stegall, Jr., who attended many healing services, flatly stated that "Those that are apparently successful are the result of careful advance screening. The 'healers' restrict their choices to those suffering from functional ailments—arthritis, rheumatism, migraine, for example. They smoothly sidestep those suffering from organic illness."[37] No doubt many would be inclined to agree with Stegall. However, if the question concerns *divine* healing, then such a view places a limitation upon an omnipotent God.

William Standish Reed, a surgeon who served on the Administrative Council of the Order of St. Luke the Physician, maintains that the patient with an "incurable illness" has every right to turn to the Christian church expecting positive help. He gives Jesus Christ the credit for all healing and stresses the imperative need for the "prayer of faith" in all illnesses believed incurable. He and many physicians hope "that the Church will continue in its meditation, research, and labor in this powerful working of God's wonderful Holy Spirit in the realm of His healing power. . . ."[38]

In order to demonstrate, analyze, and sum up the status of spiritual healing, a group of prominent business and professional men belonging to the Laymen's Movement for a Christian World decided to make an independent study of spiritual healing. They invited clergymen, medical doctors, and persons who had successfully prayed for the sick to attend a series of seminars over a five-year period, meeting under the auspices of the Wainwright House in Rye, New York. The intention was to find a medically certifiable case where the healing of a fatal or serious organic ailment was wrought by purely spiritual means.

They had the time and money to follow through on only sixty cases, and among these they found six which had "many convincing, authenticated elements." An example of the problems of documentation may be better understood by viewing the case of an engineer scheduled for a lung cancer operation. All the major tests were positive. The evening before the scheduled surgery, while the afflicted was resting in bed at home, his church congregation met and offered prayers for his healing. He was aware of a tingling sensation at the same hour. The following morning he entered the hospital and was given a few additional routine tests, which, to the surprise of the doctors, were returned marked negative. A rerun of the entire schedule of tests, including x-rays, bronchoscopic examination, biopsy, and blood counts, was then ordered by his doctor. These also were returned marked negative and the engineer was discharged from the hospital. "Wrong diagnosis" was the comment of the physicians![39]

The study also indicated that the documentary researcher in the field is hampered by human faults such as "forgetfulness, self-delusion, and a convenient sense of drama." Repeatedly, the Wainwright House researchers in their pursuit of evidence discovered that "some well-meaning person had cheerfully supplied the missing link in an important chain of evidence simply by inventing it."[40]

When their five-year study was complete, the Wainwright House investigators cautiously concluded that: "A healing power exists. It seems to manifest itself through both individual healers and intercessory prayer. . . . A sense of friendship, of knowing that someone cares, is of great importance in achieving spiritual healing. In this sense it is akin to modern psychiatry." The element of mystery continues for many. A worker at the clinic associated with New York's Marble Collegiate Church observed that as all doctors recognize the importance of the "will to live" in critical cases, so "transference or identification with a divine power often brings about a quickening of the healing process to an extent not yet understood by the medical profession."[41]

183

On the other hand, many have endeavored to expose spiritual healing as nothing but a hoax and delusion. Emily Gardiner Neal tried it as a professional journalist. But instead of having her doubts confirmed, she was converted and became a strong proponent of divine healing. In another instance during a crusade in Winston-Salem, Tom Holt planned to expose Oral Roberts as a fraud. He received a prayer card and was advancing in the line, prepared to execute a dramatic exposé before the audience of ten thousand. The second person ahead of him happened to be a woman with a large goiter, and when Holt saw it melt away before his very eyes, he confessed his scheme openly before the multitude and asked for forgiveness.

Among the prominent Neo-Pentecostal evangelists is a woman who has been called by *Time* magazine "one of the most remarkable charismatics in the United States, . . . in fact, a veritable one-woman Shrine of Lourdes." Baptist Kathryn Kuhlman baffles many thousands during the weekly meetings at her home base in Pittsburgh and the monthly services in Los Angeles' seven-thousand-seat Shrine Mosque. You name the disease, the affliction, and it probably has disappeared during her ministration. Since her personal baptism in the Spirit in 1946, she has viewed her ministry as a return to the supernatural experienced in the early church. "Everything that happened in the early church we have a right to expect today. This is exactly what we're going to get back again."[42]

Kathryn Kuhlman's father served as mayor for several years in the small town of Concordia, Missouri, where the evangelist was born. Her mother was a Methodist and her father a Baptist, "but he never worked too hard at it," she recalls. Four years after an early marriage, Kathryn Kuhlman was faced with a difficult decision. Her husband had pressed her to cease preaching and finally forced the issue. Despite her love for him, she

184

simply could not disobey God's call upon her life, so she boarded a train to keep a preaching engagement. Her choice cost her the marriage, for her husband divorced her and she has never heard from him since.

While she pastored in Franklin, Pennsylvania, members of her congregation began to experience spontaneous healings during the services. Kuhlman then began to preach sermons on divine healing; her present services evolved from this setting. Oddly enough, medical doctors occasionally grace the platform during her services. In a ministry that resembles William Branham's, many in the audience receive healings while seated, untouched by the evangelist. Like Pentecostal Branham, Kuhlman calls out to various afflicted people one after another with the startling news that divine healing is theirs. She states simply, "The Spirit bears witness to my spirit that you have just been healed. . . . I know these things but I do not pretend to understand why or how I know."[43]

The healings in her meetings have covered the gamut of human ills and afflictions. Box seats are reserved for those confined to wheelchairs. People willingly come forward on both sides of the stage to share their responses to the supernatural. Theological students from Harvard's Divinity School in Boston once came "to observe and scoff, but went away believing."[44] Most of those with testimonies of healing are from the historic Protestant denominations, but Catholics, Eastern Orthodox, Jews, and even agnostics find their way to Kuhlman's services. One atheist who hadn't attended a church service for twenty-five years walked to the stage and bluntly stated, "My ear just opened and I do not believe!"[45] Instances such as these leave Miss Kuhlman convinced that healing is the sovereign act of God. Numerous individuals in her meetings have readily admitted the healings they received were unexpected. She comments, "Until we have a way of defining it, all that I can tell you is that these are mercy healings."[46]

At times healings come unattended by prayer or the calling out of the affliction by Miss Kuhlman and she is just as delighted. One Southern Baptist young woman confined to a wheelchair for two years walked to the front of the line escorted by a staff member. She wept as she realized that God had healed her. The trim evangelist beamed, "She was healed and no one knew it but the Holy Spirit."

One of her associates, Gene Martin, envies Kuhlman's ability to place herself completely in the care of the Holy Spirit. He told me of a blind man accompanied by his seeing-eye dog who was healed while in the rear of the auditorium. Thrilled to be able to see, he came forward to testify. Of course the German shepherd was right by his side. As he reached Miss Kuhlman she was aware of the devil warning her not to touch the man. Instead of yielding to fear, she put forth her hands upon his head. Bystanders on the platform were gripped with the fear of a dog leaping to protect its master. Instead, as the healed man fell to the floor under the power of God, the dog first checked his breathing and then sat by his feet wagging his tail. To the shocked wife the greater miracle of the meeting was not her husband's healing. The calm, contented canine baffled her more.

Puzzling to many and disturbing to others is the phenomenon of people crumbling to the floor as Miss Kuhlman's hands are placed upon them in prayer. It resembles the "falling under the power" evidenced in the great revivals in America and witnessed in some Pentecostal services. During one of Kuhlman's services a Methodist minister, convinced of the supernatural dynamic in her ministry, came forward to frankly and humbly declare, "Miss Kuhlman, I do not have the power of the Holy Spirit in my life and ministry. Please pray that I will.[47] No sooner did she pray than he collapsed to the floor. Kuhlman explained the phenomenon as the power of God and invited other pastors who desired more of the Spirit in their ministry to also come forward. A number from various denominations did so, unashamed to acknowledge their needs openly, despite the fact that some of their own parishioners were seated in the audience.

In one of her rare local church appearances, Kuhlman came to Springfield Missouri's Central Assembly of God. My wife, Nadja, and I watched scores of people fall under the power of God at the hands of this Baptist. The pastor, associate pastors, choir members, a police captain, and Catholic nuns went down. Elderly folks and young boys and girls did too—one and all. It was May 2, 1971, and she was still unable to explain the strange phenomenon. "If I had to give a fuller explanation about being slain by the Spirit I could not. I've had psychologists back me to the wall. I can't tell you more. I don't know. I only know I believe this book," she stated as she firmly held a large Bible, "and I stake everything on it."

Kuhlman urged people not to come to the platform unless they were healed. With the Sunday afternoon overflow crowd necessitating the use of closed circuit television in an adjoining auditorium, the evangelist called out diseases and afflictions which included heart conditions, bursitis, deafness, arthritis of the spine, varicose veins, emphysema, fractured vertebrae, deterioration of leg muscles, and cancers.

A five-year-old boy healed of deafness in his left ear called to his grandmother seated in the balcony to tell her the good news. A man sixty years of age returned to the auditorium after removing a truss to report that a hernia that had plagued him for twelve years had disappeared. Many denominations were represented, and the radiant evangelist remarked, as she prayed for one lady, "My, all these Baptists getting healed in this Assembly of God church!" Almost three hours after the opening hymn, without a benediction, the service was over.

187

Kuhlman urges those who claim healings in her regular meetings to obtain medical verifications. Robert S. Hoyt, a medical doctor, headed for Pittsburgh to personally examine and interview some of these people who testified of healings in past years. "I checked, I examined, I interviewed," he reported. "I came away absolutely convinced that God is still performing miracles."[48]

Kathryn Kuhlman was instrumental in a relatively rare type of healing in the case of Billie, the seventh daughter in the Fischer family, who was afflicted with hydrocephalus, usually referred to as water on the brain. Her mother wrote a prayer request which Kuhlman read during her radio program before praying specifically for the healing. Within a short time Billie's head miraculously lost ten inches of its monstrous size and a scheduled operation was postponed. Week after week the mother hurried to the meetings in Pittsburgh's Carnegie Hall Auditorium with little Billie. The child's head continued to decrease. When Billie first began to react normally, the Fischers were delighted. When a few months later, Billie was brought to the Allegheny General Hospital the brain specialist remarked, "The Man Upstairs gets the full credit for this."[49]

Kathryn Kuhlman tries to convince the unconvinced that she has nothing to do with what happens. "The Holy Spirit, the Third Person of the Trinity, comes in power and He uses the vessel yielded unto Him," she explains. "I cannot use the Holy Spirit, He must use me. . . ."[50] She realizes from unforgettable experiences that it is precisely when she is most aware of her own helplessness that she has observed some of the greatest displays of God's power. However, she does not avoid human social responsibilities. As President of the Kathryn Kuhlman Foundation and its staff of eighteen, she maintains a Revolving Loan Fund at Wheaton College and has subsidized many costly missionary

188

projects. Even Dave Wilkerson's rehabilitation work among New York's addicts has been gifted sixty thousand dollars by the Foundation while more than forty thousand dollars was directed to the Western Pennsylvania School for Blind Children.[51] Part of her theology is simply "Love is something you do."

While many continue to misunderstand and misinterpret her work, a great host of people rise to call her blessed. As a Spirit-filled woman whose mind is surrendered to the Holy Spirit, she claims to "know the exact body being healed; the sickness, the affliction, and in some instances, the very sin in their lives."[52] Although she cannot fathom the why and how of it all, Kuhlman is absolutely certain that the power of the Holy Spirit, the same power that raised Jesus from the dead, is the "Resurrection power that flows through our physical bodies today, healing and sanctifying." She adds that while it is this power which performs the actual healing, "Jesus made it perfectly clear that we are to look to Him, the Son, in faith, for He is the One who has made all these things possible."[53]

A 1965 message from the Presidents of the World Council of Churches reminded world Christendom that the early Christians learned to know Jesus as Lord and believed in His resurrection. They were promised empowerment to become witnesses of this to the world. "That promise was fulfilled at Pentecost. Out from Jerusalem they went, reaching for the farthest corner of the world. . . . The church today is losing much of the power that it had. But God has never canceled the promise or withdrawn the gift He gave at Pentecost. The power is always available to the church which wants it enough to pay the price."[54] I can still hear the challenging words of the feminine Baptist evangelist in Springfield: "What's happening here today should be happening in every church in America."

XI

Catholic Charismatics

COUNTLESS PENTECOSTAL preachers down through the years of the twentieth century have quoted the promise found in the Old Testament Book of Joel, that in the last days God would pour out His Spirit upon all flesh.[1] But most of them were quite sure that this did not include Catholic flesh. The papal Church in Rome was cast in the despicable role of the "whore of Babylon" in prophetical sermons dealing with the end of the age. Persecution of Pentecostals in Italy and South America served to reinforce their position. After all, could anything good come out of Rome?

In the past Catholics have been looked on with favor only as a fertile field of evangelism by many Pentecostals. An executive minister of one of the Pentecostal denominations was on a tour in South America, traveling by train in a tropical region of the British Guiana. A Jesuit priest who was a missionary from England and the Pentecostal sat together for many a mile, chatting and even discussing their differences. The priest was asked, "Why do you Catholics so often obstruct our evangelistic and missionary work?" The answer was not without a touch of irony as the Jesuit replied, "We don't object to non-Catholic missions, but, my God, man! You Pentecostal people are bulldozers. You move into a village and take over."[2]

The Pentecostals felt that the Gospel seed surely would produce a good harvest if planted among the many Catholics who were far better acquainted with

Catholic Church tradition than with the Bible itself. Then along came an elderly humble man chosen to be the Supreme Pontiff of the world's Catholic population. He was Pope John XXIII, a man sensitive to the Holy Spirit, who will ever be remembered for summoning the Second Vatican Council. As nothing else could, this Council brought about change and opened the windows of the Roman Catholic Church to the invasion of the Holy Spirit. Catholicism hasn't been the same since.

The Second Vatican Council, which convened from 1962 to 1965, made many far-reaching decisions, affecting both internal and external matters. For instance, the Mass is now celebrated in the vernacular, readily understood for the first time by millions. The Orthodox and Protestant Christians, no longer denounced as schismatics and heretics, are now addressed as "separated brethren." And the growing spirit of ecumenism in some areas is nibbling away at the word "separated." The Catholic Church is now cooperating in Bible translations in various countries such as Costa Rica, where monks have labored closely with the Bible Society and Protestants in distributing a popular version of the New Testament. It may seem strange that at the very time when a large segment of Protestant liberals is doubting and discarding revelations found in the Bible, the Roman Catholics are entering into a new awareness and appreciation of the Scriptures.

Another reform coming out of the Vatican Council was the removal of the corporate guilt of the Jews for the crucifixion of Jesus Christ. Long overdue! Pentecostals have preached that the sins of all mankind placed Jesus on the cross and that each person individually must answer the probing question, "What will you do with Jesus, who is the Christ?"

With increasing pressures for change, two issues seemed to gain popular support—abolishing enforced celibacy for the clergy and obtaining general approval for birth control. But there has been no compromise by Pope John's successor, Pope Paul VI, as he reaffirmed the Church traditions in the face of growing defections and protests from the clergy and the laity.

No doubt the many changes that did take place prepared the way for what may prove to be the most significant change since Vatican II. To a number of the faithful it seemed that many of the laws which helped to establish a Catholic's righteousness had been discarded and little or nothing provided to fill the spiritual vacuum. This left an intense need to feel the acceptance of God, and as a result many hearts were opened to the Pentecostal experience. Other Catholics received the dictates of the Council as directives to seek the guidance and fire of the Holy Spirit as at the first Pentecost.

By the spring of 1967 Pentecostalism appeared as a movement within the Catholic Church in the United States. The bishops were puzzled and upset, but they proved to be more tolerant to the Pentecostal penetration than most historical Protestant denominations. In contrast even with earlier Catholic hierarchical reactions, no roadblocks were placed in the way of Catholics pursuing a renewal of Pentecost in the late 1960s. Strangely enough, most Catholics who have since experienced the baptism in the Spirit and speaking in tongues are proving loyal to the Church, so much so that one bishop remarked, "May their tribe increase." Father McDonnell observed that a number of priests and sisters who were "uncertain of their perseverance have been reconfirmed in their vocation" because of their Pentecostal involvement. Thus Father Henri Nouwen, a Dutch priest, had this to say about American Catholic Pentecostals: "In no way does Pentecostalism seem to threaten the Catholic orthodoxy. The opposite seems true. In the eyes of many, it seems to point to a reinforcing of the basic Roman Catholic doctrines and beliefs."[3]

Decades before the current charismatic renewal,

thousands of Roman Catholics adherents knelt at Pentecostal altars—in churches, storefront locations, and tent meetings, in order to receive Jesus Christ as their personal Savior. Pentecostal revival services preach for crisis experiences and public decisions. Most of these Catholics who responded then prayed on for the baptism in the Spirit, expecting tangible assurance that they truly had received this spiritual baptism by the physical evidence of speaking in tongues. Many subsequently joined local Pentecostal churches—in contrast to the current trend of remaining loyal Catholics. At the same time these early Spirit-filled Catholics made every attempt to influence other Catholics to try the Pentecostal way of life. To most of these former Catholics it was an either-or decision, for how was it possible to remain Catholic and at the same time be Pentecostal?

In the *Journal of Ecumenical Studies,* Catholic scholar Kilian McDonnell agreed that much could be said in criticism of the Pentecostal movement, such as the "superficiality of some of its manifestations, the noisy disorder of its worship services, the naive supernaturalism of its credulity, the exaggerated accounts of its own growth, the poverty of its intellectual range." He added, however, that whatever its faults, it was a movement to be reckoned with. "It must be taken seriously not simply as a threat, but as a significant theological reality. Even as a threat, one would think that Roman Catholic theologians would have given it more attention, since literally millions of former Catholics, especially in Latin America, are now to be found within the ranks of Pentecostal churches."[4]

Surprisingly candid, Jesuit Prudencia Damboriena claims for the Pentecostals a decisive victory amidst Catholicism in Latin America. Citing statistics from the *World Christian Handbook,* he notes that 80 percent of Chile's Protestant population is Pentecostal while there are four million Pentecostal followers in Brazil.[5] McDonnell, who functioned as a theologian with a team of scientists studying Pentecostalism for three years, added some more disturbing statistics for concerned Catholics. After a two-week visit to David Wilkerson's Teen Challenge Center in Brooklyn, he learned that almost all the drug addicts seeking deliverance were nominal Catholics and that most became members of Pentecostal churches upon completion of the lengthy program of rehabilitation. How this came about may be better understood by Father McDonnell's statement that, "At no time did I hear anything I would have to reject as a Roman Catholic. Quite the opposite. Everything I heard I was bound in conscience as a Catholic to accept. If the staff members had preached on the nature of the Church or authority in the Church, or the sacraments, there would surely have been doctrinal positions that I would not have been able to accept."[6] He found Teen Challenge to be an effective center because it preached the whole of the biblical message as the Pentecostals saw it and because it was staffed by Spirit-filled men who had taken seriously the imitation of Christ.

While the Pentecostals zealously evangelized and enlisted Catholics, those who responded and especially who spoke in tongues were ostracized and condemned for heresy and fanaticism. Before the Second Vatican Council, Pope John XXIII in his *Humanae Salutis* prayed, "Renew your wonders in our time, as though for a new Pentecost. . . ." Today in scores of American cities and towns, in convents, monasteries, and on campuses, in church basements and private homes, Catholics are praising God in other tongues as the Spirit gives them utterance. And they remain loyal, concerned Catholics, conservatively estimated at anywhere from thirty to fifty thousand.

How did it happen? Stirrings began among some

faculty members of Duquesne University in Pittsburgh who were already deeply concerned about the problems of renewal in the Catholic Church. It was the fall of 1966 and a divine discontent gripped these dedicated instructors. The vacuum left by their human endeavors was soon to be filled as their search narrowed down to two significant books. They had been urged by staff members of a student parish in Michigan to read *The Cross and the Switchblade* by the Pentecostal preacher, David Wilkerson.[7] They learned that because of Wilkerson's sensitivity and obedience to the leadings of the Holy Spirit, many gang members and dope addicts were transformed upon encountering the living Christ. The Scriptural references that pointed to Christ as Baptizer in the Holy Spirit were studied by one of the faculty.

The Duquesne professors keenly realized their lack of spiritual power as they wrestled with the apathy and unbelief among the college students. They recognized that Wilkerson had received divine power equal to his mission impossible. The men discussed and prayed about the book for two months. Meanwhile, one of them read John Sherrill's story, *They Speak With Other Tongues,* which recounted a journalist's research into Pentecost and, subsequently, his own experience of Pentecost.[8] These two books are best-sellers and "must" readings among Catholic prayer groups. This triggered the faculty's decision to look for outside aid in their spiritual quest. They located a Protestant Neo-Pentecostal prayer group instead of seeking out a Classic Pentecostal church. Somehow the latter conjured up images of fanaticism as well as the possible risk of encountering anti-Catholic feelings. Their second visit to the prayer group was a red letter day. Ralph Keifer and Patrick Bourgeois asked for prayer to receive the baptism in the Holy Spirit, and they both became recipients and spoke in tongues. Ralph writes, "They simply

195

asked me to make an act of faith for the power of the Spirit to work in me. I prayed in tongues rather quickly. It was not a particularly soaring or spectacular thing at all. I felt a certain peace. . . ."[9]

Several days later Ralph prayed for two other Duquesne men with the laying on of hands, and they also received the baptism in the Spirit. One of them later remarked that there was now "a much more spontaneous welling up of these aspirations and this power from within." He wisely observed that the Pentecostal experience was not mechanical but volitional and cooperative. He was confident that God would not have granted this gift unless faith were being exercised. [10]

By February 1967 the Pentecostal fire was burning in the lives of four Roman Catholics and the flames were about to spread rapidly. The men discovered a new boldness to witness in answer to Christ's promise to supply greater power. They spoke up for Christ to friends without embarrassment. A spiritual retreat was arranged that month and the attendant students and faculty members numbered about thirty for what Kevin and Dorothy Ranaghan call the "Duquesne weekend."[11] Most had read David Wilkerson's book before the retreat and they used this opportunity to probe into the first four chapters of the Book of Acts. The group met all day for prayer and Bible study while the evening was to be free for relaxation. Instead, one or two frequently would slip into the chapel and pray continuously until five in the morning. Some praised God in new tongues while others wept quietly for joy. During the remainder of the spring semester Duquesne students continued to receive the gifts of the Spirit and shared the new experiences with many Catholics in the area.

More baffling to Classic Pentecostals than the phenomenon of Catholics speaking in tongues is their remaining in the Roman Catholic Church. Pentecostals have been conditioned to believe that Catholics are steeped in doctrinal error, that they trust in a time-honored tradition which is contrary to Scripture. In short, they suspect that most Catholics are not born-again, regenerated Christians.

A coed present at the Duquesne weekend admitted her spiritual bankruptcy and provided some helpful insights that Protestant evangelicals and Pentecostals need to consider objectively. Patricia Gallagher writes: "About a year ago I realized that my ideal of being a 'good Catholic' was very weak because I didn't have a real, personal relationship with Christ. He was important to me, I prayed, even attended daily mass, but He was not the very center of my life." However, following the baptism in the Holy Spirit, Patricia experienced the great richness of Christ as Lord of her life. She continues: "Because of the victory of the Cross, we no longer need to fear Satan. I believe this, and ask Christ to protect and guard me with His precious blood when temptations come. He does."[12] Pentecostals would say a hearty "Amen" to this testimony, yet they remain amazed that a practicing Catholic actually could speak this way.

The Catholic Pentecostal flames then spread to the intellectuals at Notre Dame, nearby St. Mary's, Michigan State, Iowa State, and Holy Cross. During March of 1967 nine Catholics gathered at the home of an Assemblies of God deacon who was involved in Full Gospel Business Men's Fellowship International activities. In a suburb of South Bend, Indiana, eight of the nine were baptized in the Spirit before the evening gathering was over. Among those who spoke in tongues were clergymen, students, and laymen; some even sang in tongues.[13] Weeks later, what was planned to be a quiet retreat for about twenty students at Notre Dame came to be known as the "Michigan State weekend."

At the first session forty students from Michigan State University were matched by forty from Notre Dame and St. Mary's, meeting in the oldest building on the Notre Dame campus.

Doug Mead, a young Pentecostal preacher, attended in order to observe for the first time a meeting conducted by Pentecostal Catholics. He heard students, teachers, priests, and nuns giving lengthy testimonies, saturated with scriptural references. Many others present who had not previously been involved listened with rapt attention. Frequently people from the audience would ask if they could, right then and there, receive the baptism in the Holy Spirit. Unmoved, the moderator instead extended the time of sharing. At the conclusion of another testimony, a nun seated in the front stepped forward and knelt, saying, "I'd like to receive the gifts of the Holy Spirit." The leader had her return to her seat as others continued with testimonies.

Finally, with the seekers' anticipation and expectancy at its height, a circle of chairs was arranged in the center of the room. This was followed by an explanation of the gifts of the Spirit and the purposes for which they were given. Candidates for the experience were invited to come forward and sit in each of the chairs. Chairman Ranaghan explained and promised, "And those of us who have received, will lay our hands on you and 'speak in tongues' . . . and when we touch you, you will receive the gifts of the Holy Spirit!" Then the voices of Catholics who had already experienced tongues were heard by those who hastily occupied every available chair. Some seekers began to speak in tongues at once, and the presence of God permeated the entire room. The young Pentecostal observer could not hold back the tears as he burst forth in praise to God for what he was witnessing. One young lady prayed with great intensity for nearly an hour. Prayer continued for several hours before the seekers were divided

198

into small groups that continued to meet in various rooms throughout the building. As prayer went on into the early hours of the next morning, many received the baptism in the Spirit.

The Pentecostal observer was shaken, for he had been raised among Classic Pentecostals where the "fire" had waned. He felt uncomfortably cold as he viewed the blaze of Catholic Pentecostalism all about him. Never was he made more aware of his low spiritual temperature than that night in the Notre Dame prayer meeting. "Oh God," he prayed, "do something, set me on fire again!" His petition was abundantly answered as the gifts of the Holy Spirit became operative in his life within the next few months. That very summer Doug Mead entered into full-time evangelism and was to witness hundreds of Catholics being baptized in the Spirit and speaking in tongues in his services as they came to hear his impressions of the Notre Dame revival. Another overflow blessing of the Notre Dame visit for this Classic Pentecostal was his ministry in awakening Pentecostals to the power that the Holy Spirit had already given them. "I discovered thousands of young people like myself who needed a visualization of what the Holy Spirit can do," he remarked.[14] The fact of the matter is that the third generation of Pentecostals raised in Pentecostal churches cannot be sustained by the experiences of their parents and grandparents. Pentecost must be intensely personal, as is salvation.

During that same year groups of graduate students composed of nuns, priests, and brothers from every part of the United States arrived at Notre Dame for the 1967 summer session. A panel discussion on the Pentecostal movement was arranged by the new Catholic tongues-speakers and over three hundred responded. Healthy debate followed the presentations and subsequent prayer meetings were arranged. Strong interest was maintained as some two hundred packed into a classroom twice a week during the semester seeking the gifts of the Holy Spirit.

Upon completion of the summer session, the charismatic Catholics took the fire with them to their home towns and sparked further spiritual renewals. By 1969 Ranaghan estimated that there were at least five thousand Catholic Pentecostals.[15] The spiritual momentum continued and within two additional years a dramatic increase was visible. One expert who attended the Second Vatican Council recommended to 120 churchmen at Dayton University that speaking in tongues should be "running at the very heart of the church" simply because "the life of the church is the life of the Spirit."[16]

At a Notre Dame renewal conference held in March 1968, some one hundred Catholic Pentecostals shared what the Holy Spirit had been accomplishing in the various communities represented. In addition to Scripture readings, prayers of praise, and testimonies, there were also gifts of prophecy and the word of wisdom. These gave direction for the practical application of the spiritual blessings, bringing home the important truth that the responsibility of the participants to the needs of society was as great as the power of the Spirit who moved them. By the weekend attendance had doubled as the Holy Spirit continued to move among the spiritually hungry *within* the Catholic Church. Ranaghan asserts that "The Pentecostal movement has not separated or excluded Catholics from their church. Rather it has renewed their love of the church and has built up a lively faith in the Catholic community."[17]

If the entry of members of the historic Protestant churches into the current stream of Pentecostalism has introduced several doctrinal differences, how much more difficult is it to reconcile the old-line Pentecostal beliefs with those of charismatic Catholics? Despite the difficulties, however, the fact is that the prominence given to the Holy Spirit in the Catholic Church antedates Pope John's prayer for a new Pentecost. In the late nineteenth century, Pope Leo XIII circulated three important letters to the entire church, the third of which deals with the Holy Spirit. Notre Dame's professor Josephine Massingberd Ford believes that this letter prepared the way for special charismatic leaders in the Catholic Church.[18] Leo XIII pointed out that "there is only a difference of degree between the historical charismatic leaders and every member of the Church. We all have the same gifts but we do not always use them in the most economical and dynamic way."[19] Today these words have added meaning and evoke a new response.

After two and a half years of observation in the wake of the initial "Duquesne weekend," a report was submitted on November 14, 1969, to the semi-annual meeting of the U.S. Catholic Bishops in Washington, D.C. Entitled "The Pentecostal Movement in the Catholic Church in the U.S.A.," it was a candid, carefully worded report prepared by the chairman of the Committee on Doctrine of the National Conference of Catholic Bishops, Alexander N. Zaleski of Lansing, Michigan. Because of its permissive tone and its importance in the early development of American Catholic Pentecostalism, I quote it in its entirety:

Beginning in 1967, the so-called Pentecostal Movement has spread among our Catholic faithful. It has attracted especially college students. This report will restrict itself to the phenomenon among Catholics. It does not intend to treat classic Pentecostalism as it appears in certain Protestant ecclesial communities.

In the Catholic Church the reaction to this movement seems to be one of caution and somewhat unhappy. Judgments are often based on superficial knowledge. It seems to be too soon to draw

201

definitive conclusions regarding the phenomenon
and more scholarly research is needed. For one
reason or another the understanding of this movement is colored by emotionalism. For this there
is some historical justification and we live with a
suspicion of unusual religious experience. We are
also face to face with socially somewhat unac-
ceptable norms of religious behavior. It should be
kept in mind that this phenomenon is not a movement in the full sense of the word. It has no national structure and each individual prayer meeting may differ from another.

Many would prefer to speak of it as a charismatic renewal. In calling it a Pentecostal Movement we
must be careful to disassociate it from classic
Pentecostalism as it appears in Protestant denominations, such as the Assemblies of God, the
United Pentecostal Church and others. The Pentecostal Movement in the Catholic Church is not the
acceptance of the ideology or practices of any
denomination, but likes to consider itself a renewal in the spirit of the first Pentecost. It would
be an error to suppose that the emotional, demon-
strative style of prayer characteristic of the Protestant denominations [has] been adopted by
Catholic Pentecostals. The Catholic prayer groups
tend to be quiet and somewhat reserved.

It is true that in some cases it has attracted emotion-
ally unstable people. Those who come with such
a disposition usually do not continue. Participants
in these prayer meetings can also exclude them.
In this they are not always successful.

It must be admitted that theologically the movement
has legitimate reasons for existence. It has a
strong biblical basis. It would be difficult to in-
hibit the working of the Spirit which manifested
itself so abundantly in the early Church. The

participants in the Catholic Pentecostal Movement claim that they receive certain charismatic gifts. Admittedly, there have been abuses, but the cure is not a denial of their existence but their proper use. We still need further research on the matter of charismatic gifts. Certainly, the recent Vatican Council presumes that the Spirit is active continuously in the Church.

Perhaps our most prudent way to judge the validity of the claims of the Pentecostal Movement is to observe the effects on those who participate in the prayer meetings. There are many indications that this participation leads to a better understanding of the role the Christian plays in the Church. Many have experienced progress in their spiritual life. They are attracted to the reading of the Scriptures and a deeper understanding of their faith. They seem to grow in their attachment to certain established devotional patterns such as devotion to the Real Presence and the Rosary.

It is the conclusion to the Committee on Doctrine that the movement should at this point not be inhibited but allowed to develop. Certain cautions, however, must be expressed. Proper supervision can be effectively exercised only if the bishops keep in mind their pastoral responsibility to oversee and guide this movement in the Church. We must be on guard that they avoid the mistakes of classic Pentecostalism. It must be recognized that in our culture there is a tendency to substitute religious experience for religious doctrine. In practice we recommend that bishops involve prudent priests to be associated with this movement. Such involvement and guidance would be welcome by the Catholic Pentecostals.[20]

Doctrinal and traditional guidelines for Catholic Pentecostals are now beginning to appear. Let's look over some shoulders and see the position taken by responsible theologians within the Catholic Church regarding the proper use of the gifts of the Spirit.

First, the Catholic view of the baptism in the Holy Spirit differs from that of most Classic Pentecostals in that the Catholics do not necessarily include speaking in tongues as the initial physical evidence of this baptism. Notre Dame's Josephine Ford explains, "So nowadays when Catholics say they have received the 'baptism of the Spirit' they are saying that they have experienced God in a truly living way. This is usually accompanied by a great love for Holy Scripture, a deep appreciation of the fatherhood of God and sometimes of the motherhood of Our Lady, a love for the eucharist and the sacraments, an apostolic zeal but one which is not immoderate in nature, and above all, a great hunger for prayer."[21]

Ford is alert to the dangers of fanaticism, spiritual pride, and independent leadership. She calls for responsible leadership over the spontaneous prayer groups and recommends that the "chairman" and "chairwoman" be rotated lest some people become prominent and "begin to vie with the authority of the hierarchy." Cautious about the great ministry of healing, Professor Ford suggests "better to exercise the gift of healing very quietly . . . ask people to pray first for healing from the eucharist, or let prayers for healing come among prayers for other petitions." Again she expresses her fear of popular personalities who may be tempted to become independents, by observing that "While many incidents of healing have occurred within Catholic Pentecostal groups, God does not seem to wish at the moment to raise up great healers."[22]

Cautioning those who receive the release experienced in the baptism in the Spirit, Ford reminds her Catholic friends that "When it comes to those who have little practice in spiritual life, it may cause them to be thrown off their feet, as it were, with the joy and beauty and grandeur of the experience. They may go to extremes. . . ."[23] The possibilities of extremism within a spontaneous prayer group of Catholics can be minimized by wise leadership and the exercise of careful judgment by the group with regard to the genuineness of the gifts such as prophecy and the interpretation of tongues. This is measured by the peace, love, and joy which are produced in the hearts of those present. In short, the edification of the group rather than merely the individual must be a primary criterion.

The pattern used by the prayer groups is found in Apostle Paul's first letter to the Corinthians: "What then, brethren? When you come together, each one has a hymn, a lesson, a revelation, a tongue, or an interpretation. Let all things be done for edification. If any speak in a tongue, let there be only two or at most three, and each in turn; and let one interpret. But if there is no one to interpret, let each of them keep silence in church and speak to himself and to God. Let two or three prophets speak, and let the others weigh what is said. If a revelation is made to another sitting by, let the first be silent. For you can all prophesy one by one, so that all may learn and be encouraged; and the spirits of the prophets are subject to the prophets. For God is not a God of confusion but of peace."[24]

Dr. Ford, an associate professor in Sacred Scripture at Notre Dame University, has been a member of a Catholic Pentecostal group in South Bend. Although the meetings are unstructured, their pattern is based on the preceding quotation from the Apostle Paul.

Among such groups, the hymns sung are replete with praise, often accompanied by guitars and sometimes even tambourines. In a Williamston, Michigan, meeting many of the hymns were of the rhythmic kind that became popular at folk masses in recent years. At that meeting, one of at least fifteen held in various Michigan communities, about 150 Catholics gathered in the parish hall of St. Mary's Church for a monthly day of renewal. A University of Akron professor reported a striking instance of singing in tongues which began and ended spontaneously by about eight individuals present,". . . . their voices rising and falling in perfect counterpoint as though they were trained singers performing a motet by Palestrina."[25] Similar singing was heard in some of Parham's Azusa Street meetings and has been experienced by Pentecostals in many countries. One has to hear it to realize it is actually happening, and even then it is almost unbelievable.

The lesson, or Bible reading, may take the form of "praying for a text"—that is, expressing a desire for divine guidance to a passage especially pertinent to the group. Dr. Ford testifies to the remarkable manner in which a single meeting's theme is unfolded as "most of the passages read might revolve around love, joy, and peace, or all around apostolic works."[26] This method's dangerous extreme may be illustrated, tongue in cheek, by the story of the believer seeking instant guidance who flips open his Bible, pokes his finger on the page, and reads the words, "Judas went out and hanged himself." Suspicious that this has absolutely no relation to his need, he quickly turns the pages for another passage and his eyes light upon the verse, "Go, and do thou likewise." Seriously though, I along with many others have received direction and comfort and courage in critical situations by prayerfully seeking the Spirit's illumination. But I do not make this a practice.

Some elements of the pattern shown in I Corinthians 14 are present at these Catholic prayer meetings but all do not occur at every meeting. Ford speaks of the gift of revelation as the intellectual knowledge that "a Presence is experienced and the recipient of this

206

experience usually knows with great certitude whether this is Jesus, The Blessed Mother, or a saint." She believes a revelation may take the form of an image seen by the spiritual sight. For example, "A lady received an image of a narrow straight path at the end of which stood our Lord; it seemed that she could run swiftly along the path but if she withdrew her eyes from Christ the path was shrouded in darkness."[27] The effect of this upon the group caused many minds to be focused upon Christ in greater measure than before.

Regarding tongues and the interpretation of tongues the Catholic Pentecostals held that these companion gifts are to be placed at the service of the group. Their functions are subject to community judgment and should produce peace, love, and joy. If two or three receive the same interpretation, greater assurance results. The prayer gift of tongues without interpretation is given validity by the Catholics only when prayed in private. "The prayer language is used when one is at a loss to find words to praise God, or when one does not know how to intercede for other people, as a powerful weapon against sin, and to give one joy in the Holy Spirit. Although the words are not understood, the "gist of the prayer is often conveyed."[28]

Prophecies serve for general encouragement in the Christian life and are considered to be more a forthtelling than a foretelling. Ford encourages members to speak forth if the Holy Spirit gives a few words which keep recurring. This gift is considered akin to the gift of utterances of the word of wisdom and knowledge. Theologian Ford believes that prophecy may be given either in the vernacular or in tongues.[29] The Apostle Paul made the distinction clear to the Corinthian Pentecostals when he stated that "I would like you all to speak with 'tongues,' but I would prefer you to prophesy."[30] The gift of prophecy is in the language of the local worshipers and is greater than "tongues" unless

207

the interpretation in the vernacular follows, so that the church may be edified.

Silence plays an important role among Catholic charismatics and is considered "one of the chief characteristics of a good Catholic prayer meeting."[31] I'm afraid that many Pentecostals would be ill at ease or become drowsy if silence were to reign for more than a few minutes, while others probably would conclude that the prayer meeting was over. Voluminous congregational prayer is enjoyed without apology by many Classic Pentecostals because they are confident that "God is not nervous," while Neo-Pentecostals and Catholics prefer quiet prayer, confident that "neither is God deaf."

The value of the Catholic prayer meetings lies in the refreshing fact that each member, regardless of sex, age, or religious difference, may venture into following the inspiration of the Holy Spirit, for each "has a part to play in the great orchestra of prayer and praise."[32] This permissive atmosphere, permeated by love and respect, makes it easier to participate than to hold back. All are reminded, however, that the prayer session is to produce love toward God and one's neighbor, a love which extends beyond the confines of the gathering. Ford believes that God has fulfilled Leo XIII's and John XXIII's prayers that "the spiritual gifts may be manifest in the main body of the Church, not merely among her saints. If the gifts are given they must not lie unused and concealed; the talent must accrue interest when the Master comes for the reckoning."[33] Surely here is an approach to the operation of the gifts of the Spirit which Classic Pentecostals need to take. Too often the larger congregational gatherings limit the exercise of the gifts to a very few members. It may be well to reactivate cottage prayer meetings in various homes throughout the cities where large Pentecostal churches are located.

The Pentecostal experience has opened new doors of

fellowship and sharing between charismatic Catholics and Pentecostals. Both are open to the fulness of life in the Spirit and to the exercise of all the gifts of the Spirit. Catholic Pentecostals are reading their Bibles as never before, and in worship they are being drawn to Christ more than ever before. The Holy Spirit is the author of the Holy Scriptures and He ever seeks to glorify Christ. But Classic Pentecostals are puzzled about some Catholic doctrines and would like to think that Spirit-filled Catholics will be seeking to modify or even discard some traditional beliefs which apparently do not square with Scripture. Some modification along these lines is hinted at by Notre Dame's theologian Edward D. O'Connor, who notes that contemporary Catholic theological approaches to the sacraments "are being viewed as personal encounters with God (and especially with the Holy Spirit), and not merely as sacred rites. . . ." He goes on to reveal that, "There is a clamor for the hierarchy to lay aside its material trappings in order to be more transparent to the Spirit. Never in the past has theology been so acutely conscious of the charismatic dimension of Christianity."[34]

A professor at a Catholic university suggests one possible departure from literalism regarding Catholic dogmas when he analyzes the Assumption (the bodily resurrection of Mary) as "a strong mythic endorsement of corporality"; the Immaculate Conception (the birth of Mary free from original sin) as an expression of Christian joy and hopefulness in the appearance of life in a world that has heard God's voice"; purgatory (the intermediate state of suffering where one atones for one's venial sins before entry into heaven) as "touching the great scriptural truths of God's holiness and man's radical sinfulness, and expressing the need for purification before union"; and Infallibility (the doctrine that papal utterances are binding upon all Catholics when spoken ex cathedra—that is, by virtue of the exercise of

209

the Pope's office) as "an appreciation of the power of God's truth and the already-begun victory of his Spirit." Daniel Maguire understands the dogmas as "deeply felt words from man's religious past, words which may represent peak experiences."[35]

By and large, Classic Pentecostals are inclined to be far more rigid in their approach to basic doctrines than is Professor Maguire toward Catholic dogmas. Church tradition is not considered inspired and Pentecostals do not equate it with the Bible. From the Bible the assurance of salvation from judgment and hell is accepted as a reality, not after death but for the present moment by Pentecostals. But Dr. Ford does not hedge in stating, "We can never be certain of our salvation. . . . Never until we reach heaven can we be certain that we are saved."[36] The doctrinal waters become muddier at this turn, for the Pentecostals would accept all who have experienced the baptism in the Spirit and speak in tongues as individuals who are saved, who possess salvation, for tongues are God-given, subsequent to salvation. The logical conclusion is that Catholic Pentecostals must be saved individuals and each should now be rejoicing in the assurance of salvation. "Truly, truly, I say to you, he who hears my word and believes him who sent me, has eternal life; he does not come into judgment, but has passed from death to life."[37]

Another example of the polarity which exists at present is illustrated by Dr. John S. Phillipson, who was present at a Full Gospel Business Men's Fellowship seminar on "The Work of the Holy Spirit" in which a panel answered questions submitted in writing from the audience. One question was: "Must a born-again Catholic discard belief in purgatory?" The answer was blunt. "Purgatory doesn't exist. A mature Christian accepts salvation through the sacrificial death of Jesus Christ on the cross. We don't need purgatory to get to heaven." At this meeting Dr. Phillipson found no anti-Catholic literature distributed; instead, he heard friendly references made to "our Catholic brethren."[38]

During the 1970 spring semester at Oral Roberts University, several Dominican priests were visiting the campus and I invited them to address a class I was teaching on "The Dynamics of the Christian Ministry." Fathers Gerdes and Cleeter were most gracious guests as they shared their faith with about eighty students in the classroom. After some introductory remarks, they opened the session for questions. The students, mostly freshmen with backgrounds from dozens of denominations, indicated their limited knowledge of Catholicism. A few queried about the subject of conversion and the call to the ministry. Gerdes answered, "I find it very difficult to pin conversion to a moment of time because I'm involved with the sacraments. I see it as a process, a whole life. When I learn something new, I say yes at the first moment of awareness. I've learned that the Spirit is not limited by my preconceptions. I knew also that my earlier preconceptions precluded a common Pentecostal experience that made such a meeting possible, one which would be impossible before the Duquesne weekend."

The devotion given to Mary by Catholics is disturbing to Pentecostals who hold a strong conviction that the only way to God is through Christ. How far Catholics are from this position may be seen in a prayer of St. Alphonsus from the "Little Flower Prayer Book" directed to Mary, which includes this passage: "I worship thee, great Queen, and give thanks to thee for the many favors thou hast bestowed on me in the past; most of all do I thank thee for having saved me from hell, which I had so often deserved. . . ." In this context, Pentecostals often answer Catholics by quoting this verse from Paul's first letter to Timothy: "There is one God, and one mediator between God and men, the man Christ Jesus."

211

Paul W. Witte, a Catholic living among the Andoque Indians of Colombia, has been busily engaged in translating the Bible into their language. Regarding Mary he exclaimed, "I have found myself agreeing with many evangelical arguments against the Catholic Mariological stand (especially as it is manifested in Latin America) for the simple reason that it often has no scriptural basis."[39]

Catholics such as Jesuit Prudencia Damboriena are dismayed at the informal services enjoyed by Classic Pentecostals. He is convinced that the main weakness of the Pentecostals is their poverty of theological doctrines related to the church and the sacraments. Yet most Catholics who received the Pentecostal experience before the Vatican Council abandoned Catholicism's sacraments, rosary, and other ritual elements. So did the Pentecostals formerly in the Eastern Orthodox Church. When my mother, a Russian Orthodox, had experienced her personal Pentecost, among the first possessions she discarded were the icons of Jesus and Mary, for these were considered idolatrous by Russian Pentecostals. They could not even remain in the home as pieces of art, so they were relegated to the apartment incinerator. Because she had observed these religious symbols through the years, not as a bridge of faith but as a barrier of false security, the parting was not difficult. Nor was it defiant. It was definite and decisive, for Jesus Christ had become so real that nothing less than worshiping God in spirit and in truth would suffice.

Dr. Ford also deals with the sacrament of penance or confession, admitting that it is declining in popularity, perhaps due to "too negative an approach." Protestant evangelical ministers administer only two ordinances, or sacraments (water baptism and the Lord's Supper), and their nearest approach to the confessional is pastoral counseling. Ford radically urges that the sacrament

212

of confession be viewed "as a Pentecostal experience" wherein the priest is "officially given by the Church the power of spiritually healing those who ask for it with the right disposition." Thus penance is a working of the Holy Spirit "bringing creative life and peace." Dr. Ford believes that other gifts of the Spirit may well function during confession. To substantiate this belief she refers to some confessors of the past who exercised the word of knowledge, the word of wisdom, and the discernment of spirits as they heard confession. She conceives of penance as "The minister and his patient" praying together "for an outpouring of the Holy Spirit, a release or absolution from the obstacles which quench the Holy Spirit in the spiritual patient." She tells of one priest "suddenly inspired to recite verbatim a passage from the Old Testament Book of Ezekiel which he had read two weeks before, and this passage gave the penitent the precise counsel he needed. Another priest stretched out his hand to give absolution and his penitent was "baptized in the Spirit."[40] Such incidents puzzle Pentecostals who have their anti-Catholic doctrines neatly packaged and sealed in airtight compartments.

Even the sacrament of extreme unction may not be inconsistent with Pentecostal beliefs if it is accompanied by an exercise of faith for healing, as suggested by the epistle of James. Ford states positively, "There has been a new emphasis on the sacrament of unction. Once again, this sacrament should be administered with a lively expectation that God will heal the recipient."[41] Most Pentecostal pulpits are supplied with a vial of oil for the purpose of anointing the sick, and for decades many healings have occurred during this common practice in their churches.

What direction will the Catholic Pentecostal movement take in the days ahead? Although its appearance among Catholic professors and collegians was unex-

213

pected, it has now proliferated among lay Catholic members in numerous parts of the country as well as among the various orders in religious communities. They have found no credibility gap between the charismatic revival and structural forms, which for Catholic Pentecostals, go hand in hand. Classic Pentecostals accept the validity of the Catholic's reception of the supernatural gifts of the Holy Spirit, although they still tend to be amazed at the very existence of such a thing as a Catholic Pentecostal. In the Pentecostal camp are some who feel that ultimately many charismatics will leave the Catholic Church because of its continued adherence to nonbiblical doctrines. But Catholics are conditioned to submit to authoritarianism; if this were not the case there would be by now a variety of schismatic Catholic Pentecostals.

In one diocese a newly formed prayer group was given orders by the bishop to cease speaking in tongues and laying on of hands at their meetings. It hit them hard, but the group obeyed and their numbers increased noticeably. After a few months the restrictions were lifted. In another diocese not only were speaking in tongues and the laying on of hands forbidden, but there was to be no exorcisms and "asking for a text." Prophecy was the only charismatic practice not censored. Here also the group submitted to the regulations as announced, and before that very meeting ended, prophecy came forth for the first time in that group. Two prophecies were written down by a member and read as follows: "Bear in all patience what has happened to you. Obey those I have put over you. See the care I have for my flock," and "Fear not, for the wonders I have worked among you shall not cease." Here too the group was eventually allowed complete freedom in its prayer meeting.[42]

The movement does not aim to form an exclusive community apart from the Church. A Jesuit priest described Catholic charismatics as those who seek the gifts of the Spirit to ". . . become more holy in Christ . . . become freer, more supple apostles, instruments of the power of love which is the Spirit of Jesus Christ."[43]

The Catholic Pentecostal movement continues to grow. Charismatic prayer groups meet in every state but Wyoming and Alaska. From the small 1967 gathering known as the Michigan State Weekend there is now an annual National Conference on Charismatic Renewal in the Catholic Church. In 1970 a total of 1,279 registered for the weekend convocation, coming from all parts of the United States and Canada. The final service was preceded by Catholics "witnessing to what God had done in their lives; their testimonies, together with the thunderous and enthusiastic singing, made an impression that would not soon be forgotten." The closing Mass was attended by more than 1,400 and was concelebrated by about thirty priests.[44] The 1971 Conference doubled this response, and exploded to 11,000 in 1972.

As long as the drive of Pentecostal Catholics is directed toward exalting Jesus Christ and as long as the desire of these charismatics is to be available channels through which the Holy Spirit will prove Christ alive to their contemporaries, so long will the movement expand and be an awakening force for world Catholicism.

XII

Pentecostals Under the Hammer and Sickle

MY GRANDFATHER Samson Durasoff was a Russian priest among the Old Believers, a schismatic group that had withdrawn from the Russian Orthodox Church back in 1666. This group differed from the parent church over such minutiae as whether an individual should cross himself with three fingers (symbolizing the Trinity) or two (symbolizing the dual nature of Christ). The adamant Avvakum kept the faith of the *Staraya briatsi* (Old Believers) to the very end. As leader of the dissidents, he defiantly crossed himself with two fingers as he was engulfed in flames at the stake in 1682—courtesy of the Church.

Evidently grandfather's religion had little effect on my father, Gregory Samsonovich. Dad served in the tsar's navy, and as a crew member of the mutinous warship *Potemkin* he was on the wanted list of the tsar's autocracy. On the other hand, the seamen were later lauded by the Soviets, who claimed they held the only unoccupied territory in the first Russian revolution. Lenin labeled the uprising a dress rehearsal for the 1917 revolution. Following the mutiny on the Black Sea, the *Potemkin* left Odessa with several slain officers onboard and sped toward Constanta, Rumania. The seamen debarked, scrambling in several directions; some sailed to South America while others just waited, optimistically hoping to return to Russia. Learning that imprisonment was the fate of any who set foot on Russian soil, my father decided to leave Rumania for New York City, U.S.A.

216

Evdochia Durasoff, an illiterate childhood sweetheart raised in Saratov on the Volga and married there to Gregory at the age of sixteen, never lost hope of being reunited with her husband. Her hope was deferred for five long years, but her happiness knew no bounds as she joined him in the new country and they quickly settled down in a Brooklyn apartment. For over twenty-five years, however, she was to live with a Jekyll-Hyde husband who mistreated her while on his frequent drunken binges.

My dad lived as though God didn't exist. But at fifty-two he was to experience a cataclysmic conversion in a tiny Brooklyn Russian Pentecostal church. There he met Jesus Christ and as a result his former craving for vodka was gone, no longer to rule over the lost weekends—and weeks on end. If I ever learned the potency of Apostle Paul's words, "If any man be in Christ, he is a new creature, old things are passed away, behold, all things are new,"[1] it was as I witnessed the remarkable transformation in the life of Gregory Samsonovich. Evdochia found it impossible to believe that Gregory had truly experienced a genuine conversion and would remain sober. But it was so, and when she was finally convinced of the miracle, she too sought and met the same Jesus who had transformed her husband's life.

Shortly after his confrontation with Christ as his Savior, my father met Him as his baptizer. Alone on his knees in prayer one evening, he received his personal Pentecost and spoke in other tongues for an extended period of hours—in praise and worship to his newfound Lord.

Wonderful events continued to happen. Upon awakening one morning, my mother related a dream she had, repeating several phrases in Russian which she recalled. "It sounds like it might be in the Bible," remarked Gregory. Excited, he began flipping the pages of his new Russian Bible and searched for these words among

217

the Gospels. Finally he located a passage in the eleventh chapter of the Book of Matthew. "Evdochia, repeat those words." She did—quoting the invitation of Jesus word for word: "Come unto me all ye that labor and are heavy laden, and I will give you rest. Take my yoke upon you, and learn of me; for I am meek and lowly in heart; and ye shall find rest unto your souls. For my yoke is easy, and my burden is light."[2] Inspired and determined to know more of this living Word, she learned to read the Scriptures for herself.

These events happened in the lives of two Russians in Brooklyn. But how and when did Pentecostalism appear in Russia? How many Pentecostal believers are now to be found in the U.S.S.R.? Are Soviet Pentecostals permitted to conduct their charismatic form of worship under the hammer and sickle?

Before these and other related questions are answered, it will help to catch a glimpse of the development of Russian sectarianism as it emerged at the close of the seventeenth century. In a broad sense, Russian Protestantism can be traced back to the late fourteenth century, long before Martin Luther nailed his theses on the Wittenburg church door in 1517. These were the first Russians to exhibit signs of protest against the authoritarian posture of the Russian Orthodox Church. In spurning the hierarchy and repudiating most of the Orthodox rites, they attempted to return to the fundamentals of early apostolic Christianity. Executions soon erased the *Strigol'niki* leaders and this "heresy" was eliminated early in the fifteenth century.

It wasn't until 1639 that the Russian Orthodox Church even made a distinction between the doctrinal beliefs of the Protestants and the Catholics residing in Russia. All their teachings were simply lumped together as "Latin heresy." The imported versions of Protestantism which appeared in Russia after the *Strigol'niki* dissenters were gone, included Lutheranism, Reformed Calvinism, Methodism, and Anglicanism. The Lutherans actually received permission to build a church within a mile of the Kremlin in 1575 by none other than Ivan the Terrible, while the Reformed Church opened its doors in 1629 to worshipers in Moscow. Methodists were located at one time in St. Petersburg (now Leningrad) and Bielorussia, but now exist only in Estonia under the Soviet regime. Only a small number of Englishmen lived in Russia during the reign of the tsars, but they worshiped in Anglican churches located not only in Moscow and St. Petersburg, but in cities as distant as Odessa and Archangel.

Right up to the October Revolution the Lutherans embraced eight consistorial districts. More than a million members attended services in the two largest districts, Moscow and St. Petersburg. The majority of them were Germans and the remainder, about 30 percent, were made up of Finns, Estonians, Latvians, Swedes, Armenians, and some Russians. The once flourishing Lutheran churches have vanished since the last General Synod was held in 1928. The Reformed Church would have had a similar fate were it not for later Soviet annexations in Transcarpathian Ukraine and Galicia, where Hungarian and Ukrainian congregations were active.[3]

Meanwhile, some form of speaking in tongues was evidenced in Russia at the close of the seventeenth century among a sect of flagellants called Khlysti. As they whipped themselves, jumped, shrieked, and cried, they also were reported to prophesy and speak in other tongues. Many Khlysti hymns were the product of these utterances and their interpretations were collected together to form the *Book of the Dove*. For these mortifiers of the flesh, the *Book of the Dove* surpassed the inspiration of the Bible and was given the position of highest authority.

In the nineteenth century the Pryguni, or Jumpers,

appeared in the Ukraine, firmly believing that the Holy Spirit would fall upon them as they danced vigorously. Reports paralleling those which occurred during the exhaustive dancing of the Khlysti claimed that the adherents uttered "unintelligible words in various tongues" during their rites.

Other glossolalists to emerge in the twentieth century were the Smorodintsi and the Murashkovtsi, both named after their leaders. The Smorodintsi denied the doctrine of the Trinity, adhering to the Jesus Only, or Oneness, doctrine. The Murashkovtsi sect championed the prophecies of Ivan Murashkov, the "Father of Zion," who warned of impending judgment. So convincing was he that his followers believed he would create a new "Zion" and one hundred families sold their homes and offered the proceeds for the purchase of land near Sarnom. Instead of remaining with the flock until the given prophesied date, Murashkov and his wife absconded to Argentina with all the funds.

This sporadic disarray of fanatical Russian sects displaying some elements of glossolalia cast suspicion upon anyone who claimed the supernatural gifts of the Spirit. So it was that most Russian Baptists suspected and feared the man who introduced biblical Pentecostalism on a large scale within the Soviet Union. Ivan Voronaev founded hundreds of Pentecostal churches during the 1920s, despite the scathing denunciations, oddly enough, of both the Baptists and the Communists.[4]

Who was Ivan Efimovich Voronaev and why was he so successful in launching the phenomenal growth of Pentecostalism in the U.S.S.R.?

After serving with the Cossacks under the tsar, Voronaev became a Baptist preacher in Irkutsk, Siberia. Following a period of relentless religious persecution under the state church, the twenty-five-year-old minister decided to leave Russia via Harbin, Manchuria, for the United States. Several years later, while pastoring a Russian Baptist Church on Henry Street in New York City, Voronaev faced a spiritual crisis. His young daughter Vera, who had been attending a Pentecostal Sunday School with her teenage neighbor Ann Siritz, had just received the baptism in the Holy Spirit and spoke in other tongues. The mid-afternoon church schedule at Glad Tidings Tabernacle enabled Vera to attend the Pentecostal meetings without missing any of her father's Russian services. But the news reached the Russian Baptists and it created an awkward situation. Voronaev was embarrassed and his members were upset. Several Baptist deacons and members determined to personally investigate the Pentecostal services in midtown Manhattan where Robert and Marie Brown were pastors.

Meanwhile, the cautious and reserved Voronaev inwardly hungered for the supernatural moving of the Holy Spirit in his own life. Shortly thereafter, while in prayer, he received the Pentecostal experience. His leadership as pastor of the Russian Baptist church now seemed untenable, so Voronaev resigned, arranged to rent the facilities of the Emmanuel Presbyterian Church on East Sixth Street, and founded the first Russian Pentecostal Church in New York City on July 1, 1919. To his surprise almost twenty of his Baptist members made the same move—they had already become glossolalists and insisted on charter membership in the Pentecostal Church!

These services were blessed of God, as Russians, Ukrainians, and Poles were converted and filled with the Holy Spirit. Many Slavic believers from other cities and states converged upon Sixth Street to investigate, and departed convinced that the movement was of the Lord, for they personally had experienced glossolalia there. Several of these visitors were Baptist ministers.

The growing congregation worked loyally with its

221

energetic pastor. They learned to emulate his persistence in house-to-house evangelism, even though opposition came in the forms of threatening brooms and douses of water. Amidst the joy of Christian activity and significant growth, the congregation was not ready for an unexpected turn of events. Voronaev announced God's definite call upon his life to return to Soviet Russia in order to share the Full Gospel with his beloved people. The initial summons came during a prayer meeting in the home of a member named Anna Koltovich. She related to me how hurt she was when Voronaev refused to accept her utterance during a small prayer meeting. It was brief and to the point: "Voronaev, Voronaev, journey to Russia." Too serious a step to take without receiving a personal revelation, Voronaev sought God's will in earnest prayer. The answer directly to his heart was identical: "Voronaev, Voronaev, journey to Russia." That was enough. He immediately planned his return, believing that God would supply all his needs. Voronaev forsook his beloved adopted land of America and set his face to serve Jesus Christ in the land of his birth. Now under atheist rule, Soviet Russia was facing famine after the terrible toll of a Civil War.

On July 15, 1920, Ivan, Katerina, and their children sailed for the Soviet Union, debarking first at Varna, Bulgaria. There he preached for a fruitful period of months, founding Pentecostal churches before journeying on to Odessa, U.S.S.R.

Voronaev was well received by the Baptists and Evangelical Christians in Odessa, a thriving seaport on the Black Sea. Well received, that is, until he began preaching the message of Pentecost and the gifts of the Spirit. The line of separation was quickly and sharply drawn. The Baptists obviously respected Voronaev's ministerial and administrative abilities and sensed the danger of both his personal popularity and the dynamic of his doctrines. Jakob Zhidkov, later the first president

of the Union of Evangelical Christians-Baptists, admitted that the Pentecostals in the Ukraine alone had
quickly grown to almost twenty thousand in number.
The other churchmen had cause to be upset. When
Voronaev founded the first Pentecostal Church in
Odessa, fully half of his eager congregation came from
the Baptists and Evangelical Christians. Voronaev became the special target of the two fundamental denominations during the decade of the twenties, a period of
phenomenal growth of Pentecostalism within the
Soviet Union. Before the enactment of the anti-
religious law of 1929, most of the Protestant evangelical
believers enjoyed unparalleled opportunities to propagate the Gospel in Soviet Russia.

Even as his headquarters church in Odessa approached
a membership of a thousand, Voronaev traveled extensively on evangelistic tours. In the three-month
itineraries which drew him as far north as Leningrad,
Voronaev founded Pentecostal assemblies composed of
a nucleus of believers who embraced the new message.
Within a few short years the labors of this pioneer of
Pentecost were rewarded with the birth of 350 assemblies, growing like mushrooms after a Russian rain.

Voronaev and several of his key workers received
financial aid each month from Glad Tidings Tabernacle
and the Russian Eastern European Mission, then in
Chicago. Under missionary appointment of the Assemblies of God, the largest American Pentecostal group,
Voronaev submitted routine reports on the disburse-
ment of the funds received. It was this generous American support which enabled the Russian evangelist and
his co-laborers to give their undivided attention to the
propagation of the Full Gospel. In retrospect, it is
amazing that even this was permitted to take place in
Soviet Russia during this unbelievable decade. In one
of his services an agent of the Cheka (the Russian secret
police, now KGB) heard him preach, was converted,

and later filled with the Spirit! However, such unexpected liberties were to be short-lived. Foreign financial aid, a source of blessing, was to become a curse in the form of trumped-up Soviet charges against Ivan Voronaev. He was accused of serving the "American imperialists" in espionage activities against the U.S.S.R. Arrest and imprisonment followed. Soviet writers concocted articles framing Voronaev as an apostate.

The days of legal propagation of the Gospel were numbered. The luxury of vying for the confused converts who strayed in and out of Baptist and Pentecostal folds was suddenly discontinued at the height of its indulgence. As the stock market crash of 1929 stunned Americans and revolutionized many lives, so the antireligious Law of April 8, 1929, had a crushing effect upon all Russian believers. It denied legal existence to all churches in the Soviet Union and permitted no activity other than the performance of worship. What religious freedom they did have was on its way out for good. Whereas two thousand churches, almost all Orthodox, had been closed during the entire decade of the twenties, the fateful year of 1929 alone saw 1,370 houses of worship shut down. In this vicious vise the Russian Pentecostals were all but squeezed out of existence. Courageous masters at propagating the Gospel, the Pentecostal believers continued to spread the good news of Jesus Christ in the slave labor camps and Siberian areas of exile. Voronaev did so to his dying day.

Then came the Hitlerian threat, a life-and-death struggle of the Russian nation against the invaders and their *blitzkreig* warfare. Stalin, shrewd and pragmatic, courted the religious leaders to rally behind "Mother Russia" by discontinuing the atheist publications *Bezbozhniki* (Godless) and *Antireligioznik.* Stalin's New Religious Policy also brought about the demise of the League of the Militant Godless, while concessions were granted to religious groups. The evangelicals were permitted to form a union, to publish a bi-monthly periodical, and to build prayer halls.

During the holocaust of World War II evangelical believers in the Soviet Union raised 400,000 rubles for a medical plane called *The Good Samaritan*. Helpless war orphans raised in atheist homes were adopted and brought up in the nurture and admonition of the Holy Scriptures. This mass adoption program was strongly promoted by the evangelical churches despite the restrictions of the Law of 1929 which prohibited church activity in any area not specifically connected with public congregational worship. No doubt many of these are today faithfully serving God in Soviet Russia because believers cared enough to practice their religion. This is a good example of the inconsistency and duplicity of the Soviets in the face of problems with which they cannot fully cope. At any time they choose, pressures to carry out the letter of the Law of 1929 are applied with a passion.

In 1944, the Baptists and the Evangelical Christians, two fundamental groups almost identical in doctrinal beliefs, merged to form a single union—the All-Union Council of Evangelical Christians-Baptists—with headquarters in Moscow. Pentecostal believers, once again active and expanding rapidly, were invited to become the third denomination to join the Union—if they would agree to forbid the speaking of tongues in all public services. That was like asking Baptists to cease immersing new believers and settle for sprinkling.

Despite this restriction, four recognized Pentecostal leaders signed a document with the Baptists known as the August Agreement. A strange alliance indeed, because many Baptists were strongly indoctrinated against the Pentecostals and resented the invitation, convinced that it would only court dissension within the Union. Then how, one wonders, did this unlikely alliance ever come about? Some Soviet authors claim

225

that a majority of the Pentecostals joined the Union so they could enjoy government recognition by belonging to the registered churches, after which they planned to take advantage of the situation by infiltration within the Union. Indeed, Pentecostal doctrines were shared with fellow members and many warmly responded.

What was the alternate choice for the Pentecostals? It was impossible for them to form an independent union, for the Soviet regime forbade it, fearing the Pentecostals as fanatics who supposedly gravitated toward anti-Soviet activities. Therefore, all Pentecostals meeting outside the merger union were subject to arrest and imprisonment. Because of this the Soviet Union became the only country where Pentecostals joined with Baptists. They have already celebrated their twenty-fifth anniversary and are still working at it! What is more amazing is the scope of success enjoyed by the Union in the early years, despite the polarity of views on the gifts of the Spirit and the practice of speaking in tongues. Most Baptists in Soviet Russia rejected the Pentecostal posture, making it obvious that they had little choice but to accept the Pentecostals into the Union. In spite of these tensions, *Bratskii Vestnik* (Fraternal Messenger), the official bimonthly publication of the Union, showed a growth of almost 200,000 additional members during the first decade of the merger![5]

Early pressures on the part of Pentecostal believers, however, caused Jakob Zhidkov, president of the All-Union Council of Evangelical Christians-Baptists, to publish the following statement: "They say, 'The Spirit arouses us to prayer and you quench our spirits and thus destroy the Word of God.' We do not quench the Spirit, but we strive to suppress noise and disorder."[6]

The crux of the matter was to be found in the non-Scriptural logic to which the four Pentecostal leaders acquiesced when they signed the August Agreement.

The document included two articles that rendered impossible any practice of the gift of tongues and its companion gift, the interpretation of tongues. Article 7 reads: "Both sides acknowledge that unknown tongues without interpretation are fruitless, concerning which the Apostle Paul explicitly states, 'If there be no interpreter, then keep silent in the church' (I Cor. 14:6-9,28). Both sides uphold this as a rule given by God, through Apostle Paul." So far this is fair enough. Responsible groups of Pentecostal believers adhere to this biblical restriction of congregational tongues without interpretation. But the gift of tongues and the interpretation of tongues are operative on the principle of believers exercising faith for the supernatural at any service. There must always be the essential freedom of a divine-human relationship. The Holy Spirit bestows the gifts as He determines the need, but man must be able to respond. This is the heart of the matter. If Article 7 seems to be reasonable, Article 8 closed the door to the sovereign manifestation of the Holy Spirit once and for all: "Considering the words of Apostle Paul about the fruitlessness of unknown tongues in the absence of an interpreter, both sides agreed to abstain from unknown tongues in general meetings."[7]

Is it possible that the four Pentecostal signators did not see this article? How else could they justify their position as Pentecostal leaders? Suggestions of duress and confusion at the time of the August Agreement seem reasonable, because two of the four Pentecostal leaders soon abandoned the Union. In fact, the dissatisfaction of one of them with this compromise led him to spearhead an early exodus movement. A. I. Bidash chose to be counted among the nonregistered, illegal Pentecostals, rather than to continue denying his Pentecostal heritage of liberty in exercising the gifts of the Spirit. In 1948 Bidash and others founded an independent Pentecostal center in opposition to the Union merger.

One of those who remained in the Union was D. I. Ponomarchuk, who had labored together with the Pentecostal founder Voronaev. He was instrumental in convincing many Pentecostal believers to abandon their illegal gatherings and make the transition into the Union churches. But Ponomarchuk previously pastored in Baptist, then Evangelical Christian churches before joining hands with Voronaev. Was he a man of conviction or an opportunist, attaching himself to the group currently evidencing the greatest momentum? What we do know is that Ponomarchuk was in a key position to link these believers in a bond of strong Christian interdenominational fellowship. He was elected a Council member and appointed to be the aide to the senior presbyter over all the Ukraine, the stronghold of both Baptists and Pentecostals in the Soviet Union. Ponomarchuk visited many Pentecostal churches, officially known in the U.S.S.R. as the Christians of Evangelical Faith. In this capacity he influenced entire assemblies to follow his example in joining the Union. In his appeal to the Pentecostals, Ponomarchuk pointed out that the merger would grant them full rights as equal members in the Union. The evangelical brotherhood had "no stepsons, but each member was accorded equal status by faith in Jesus Christ." His positive approach reassured them that God would purify all the members within the Union and that downgrading of any believer for his personal convictions would not be tolerated. Thus many Pentecostals joined the Union churches because they felt they had nothing to lose and much to gain. Of course, Articles 7 and 8 must have been soft-pedaled or omitted in the approach to the independent Pentecostal assemblies, because the new members would not readily have agreed to abandon the spiritual exercise so precious to them. They continued to speak in tongues. Where entire churches joined the Union, this presented

228

no problem so long as the Pentecostal membership composed a dominant majority. Russian Pentecostals and Baptists agree on most evangelical doctrines. For instance, they believe in the plenary inspiration of the canonical Scriptures, man's sinful condition, his need of salvation, the revelation of God's love and forgiveness in Jesus Christ, and the virgin birth of the Son of God. They maintain that it is imperative for a sinner to have a conversion experience, called the new birth, which must be followed by public profession in baptism by immersion. The doctrine of eternal security—a doctrine held by many American Baptists that allows no room for departing from the faith or final apostasy—presented no problem in the Russion Union, for these Baptists rejected it, as did the Pentecostals. A. V. Karev, called the Russian Charles Spurgeon, taught the possibility of apostasy based upon man's free will after salvation as well as before. A believer could turn his back upon God and forfeit his salvation.

Despite agreement on a number of issues, problems kept coming to the fore. The persistent Pentecostals simply could not keep from sharing the glories of the glossolalia and the firm belief that the experience was for all believers in the twentieth century. The Pentecostal penetration within the Union was admitted when a drastic change was inserted in the August Agreement nine years after its inception. In 1954 all Pentecostals not only were reminded to refrain from speaking in tongues in public services but also were ordered to discontinue sharing their personal experiences of the glossolalia with individual Baptist members upon threat of excommunication! To add insult to injury, the Union executives claimed that this rule had been in the original August Agreement! I have gone through each and every copy of the *Bratskii Vestnik* published since the merger of 1944 and can ascertain that no such provision was even implied in the August Agreement of

1945. Why then did they attempt to silence the Pente-costals? Clearly for two reasons: the growing success experienced by the Pentecostals and the increased fear and anger of Baptist leaders. Shades of Ivan Voronaev! The loss of Baptists and Evangelical Christians to Pente-costal persuasions—which had been all too distressing to the two latter groups during the 1920s—was again being repeated in the forties and fifties.

Voronaev died in Siberian exile after many years of cruel slave labor, but he successfully pioneered the trail for all subsequent Pentecostal believers in the Soviet Union. Multiplied thousands continue to be-lieve that the baptism in the Spirit is proven by the subsequent sign of speaking in tongues.

Baptists and Pentecostals in Russia as elsewhere are unable to agree on the meaning of the baptism in the Spirit. For the Baptists this experience occurs at the time a person accepts Christ as Savior. But Voronaev and his followers insisted that the spiritual baptism John spoke about in all four gospels took place *after* the experience of conversion. At this point the Russian Pentecostals aggravated the Baptists no end as they dogmatically insisted that whoever did not speak in tongues simply did not possess the indwelling Holy Spirit and surely would not be ready to meet Christ at His second coming. With the validity of their salvation itself at stake, the Baptists were indignant. In refuta-tion, I. Motorin wrote: ". . . nowhere is it stated that one possessing the gift of healing, the gift of tongues, or the gift of the interpretation of tongues has eternal life. The opposite is declared by Jesus Christ—'I never knew you' (Matt. 7:22, 23)—a warning to those Christians who think more about miracles and tongues, than of a wholesome life in Jesus Christ."[8]

Another Baptist leader reasoned that the necessity for tongues disappeared because the Scriptures had been translated in more than a thousand languages.

Karev hit closer to home by stating that there were preachers who spoke so much of the Holy Spirit and so little of Christ that he doubted that they were filled with the Spirit, for the Holy Spirit's ministry was to glorify Christ and lead the believer into a preeminent love for Jesus Christ.

From the very beginning the Pentecostals had disregarded the August Agreement. Their violation of Article 8 continued for a decade and finally triggered President Zhidkov to vigorous action against those who continued to speak in tongues during worship services. He ordered all pastors to "expel them from the church, not because they are Pentecostals, but for their violation of our fraternal agreement." I wonder if the majority of the Pentecostal laity were aware of the basic restrictions in the August Agreement when they joined the Union churches.

In 1957 this internal revolt precipitated a special Moscow conference of the key pastors now in the Union who formerly held positions of leadership among the Pentecostal churches. Together they hammered out principles aimed at correcting local church leaders who continued to disregard the Council regulations.

The Conference went on record declaring that every Christian possessed the indwelling Spirit of God and priority was to be given to the daily life and walk in the Spirit. Christ, not the gifts, was to be preeminent. In itself this was excellent, but a basic contradiction nullified this statement. They claimed that spiritual gifts could be exercised provided they edified the believers. In their words, "Spiritual gifts are granted in order to edify everyone. They can be used as such only when believers do not place themselves above others or force them upon others."[9] In fact, however, the August Agreement forced the Pentecostals to violate the Scriptures by completely banning the exercise of the gift of tongues and the interpretation of tongues.

231

The Conference solved nothing. Instead, the Ukrainian Pentecostals in the Union, numbering about forty thousand, saw their eastern portion withdraw itself from the Union because of the suppression of Pentecostal teaching by the Baptists.[10] Evidently the Scriptural solution of the abuse of charismatic gifts was to be found not in their suppression but in the correct exercise of the gifts as outlined by Apostle Paul.

The problem took another turn in 1958 with an increase in Soviet anti-religious pressures, especially aimed at the nonregistered evangelicals—all of them—Baptists, Evangelical Christians, and Pentecostals. There were many thousands of each outside the Union. This may very well have had a quieting effect upon the glossolalists, who felt that the restrictions within the Union churches could not compare with the dangers of arrest and imprisonment which faced the nonregistered illegal independents.

I remember the first time I met several of the executive leaders of the Russian evangelicals in the Union headquarters, located in the church building on Maly Vuzovski Pereulok, within walking distance of the Kremlin. My companion was Demian Matysuk, the man who had pastored the New York church founded by Ivan Voronaev, serving for twenty-three years as the shepherd of this flock. The Muscovites were delighted to meet us, the first Pentecostal preachers they had ever met from America. That was in 1959. Following a barrage of questions on the beliefs and practices of American Pentecostals, I came away with mixed impressions. They recounted a grotesque example of wild fanaticism reported among some Pentecostals in the Ukraine—the usual approach of Soviet anti-religious propagandists! The Russian Baptists seemed surprised to hear that Scriptural order was practiced in most American Pentecostal services, such as the interpretation of tongues following an utterance in tongues.

232

A greater surprise was theirs when they learned of the large response to divine healing services conducted across America and in many cities around the world. When Oral Roberts visited Moscow's one and only Protestant church in 1960, about a dozen church leaders eagerly questioned him about the exercise of the gifts of the Spirit. For four long hours they poured out their probing questions, such as: "Why did godly Job have to suffer so?" and "Why was not Paul delivered from his thorn in the flesh?" Responding to their difficult questions with thought-provoking answers, Oral Roberts then asked the Russian clergymen why they did not minister to the sick with the laying on of hands. "Have you no hands?" he asked. Perhaps in their silence they were thinking of the hostile anti-religious articles slanted against those who dared do this publicly, charging them with the practice of medicine without a license!

Before Oral Roberts left he offered prayer for each Russian minister with the laying on of hands. While praying for one of these ministers the supernatural word of knowledge came forth and Roberts stated that God had been dealing with this person to pray for the sick. Later, when he could see the American evangelist alone, the preacher admitted that God indeed had been prompting him to use his hands in a ministry of prayer for the sick, and now, by God's grace, he would obey.

The Soviet press has not overlooked the work of famous American evangelists such as Billy Graham and Oral Roberts. Regarding Graham's New York City crusade, *Nauka i Religiia* (Science and Religion) ran a long article which was accompanied by seven derogatory cartoons depicting Graham as a bald-headed, unshaven gangster counting an enormous amount of money on an abacus. The Soviet writer charged that Graham "sanctimoniously carries out the orders of his earthly master—the lord of the dollar."[11]

Oral Roberts was scored in the Soviet political-literary magazine *Rovesnik* for publishing an illustrated message in Russian called "Happiness and Healing For You." They declared that rather than offering happiness he was disseminating destruction by attempting to alienate believers from the truly happy Soviet society.[12] In one propaganda film designed to castigate the Pentecostals in the U.S.S.R., they actually inserted the photograph of Oral Roberts as a Pentecostal leader, accusing him of employing ideological diversionary tactics in order to camouflage his true intentions—supposedly the spread of anti-Soviet propaganda! The Assemblies of God was also scored for its production of religious broadcasts in Russian and Ukrainian which are beamed into the Soviet Union via powerful transmitters. They were also disturbed by the tons of literature printed by the American Pentecostals, including a Russian journal called *Strannik*. The intent of the atheist writers was to cast a bad light upon the Russian Pentecostals, inferring that they shared guilt by association with the American attempt to "slander . . . the Soviet Union and countries of the socialist camp."[13]

The tough-skinned Pentecostals in Russia were already hardened to the Soviet slander hurled against them. The Soviets conducted a study under the auspices of the Section of the History of Religion and Atheism, a branch of the Institute of History, Academy of Sciences, in which they noted the Pentecostals' "extreme mysticism," expressed in the "knowability of God" and the accessibility of God to man via the sense organs, or glossolalia. As a result, Pentecostalism was listed among the most "virulent species of religious opium."[14] Another Soviet writer must have picked up some copy from American anti-Pentecostal writers when he referred to the followers of Voronaev as psychologically unstable. He said, ". . . this incoherency is called 'angelic' tongues by Pentecostals. People with sound

234

nervous systems cannot enter such a state at all. . . .
People with weak nervous systems fall into the ritual so
devastating to the nerves that they end up in a mental
asylum." He dismissed the miracles, healings, and
prophecies of the pastors as nothing more than manip-
ulated acts put on in their meetings in order to reinforce their religious doctrines upon the Pentecostal
believers. With disdain he added that there was no lack
of "prophets or prophetesses who interpreted the incoherent muttering of the glossolalia."

He went on to say that the Pentecostal prophets
foretold Christ's return to earth in the year 2000. Although few believed such prophets, he complained that
"the harm of such 'predictions' lies in this, that the
sermons of 'terrible judgment' often tie in with the
imperialistic propaganda of World War III initiated by
the enemies of peace. . . ."[15]

Bizarre charges were heaped upon the Pentecostals
in the Soviet press for the benefit of credulous readers.
British author J. C. Pollack, with clear insight, declared,
"If the reports of court cases in the early nineteen-
sixties are taken at face value, Russian Pentecostals
behave utterly unlike their brethren elsewhere in the
world, being not only enthusiasts but grim, harsh, violent and malevolent. . . . And when Pentecostals are
further said to thieve, embezzle and even incite to
murder and suicide, the detached observer is at once
confused and blinded by the impossibility of sorting
truth from deliberate misrepresentation."[16] Six Pentecostals received sentences of three and five years imprisonment and the loss of parental rights for "crimes"
such as the distribution of "reactionary American publications," which included translations of booklets by
Oral Roberts, R. A. Torrey, and Bible portions published by the Scripture Gift Mission in London.[17]

In January 1963 press releases outlined the exciting
and heart-rending story of thirty-two believers who had

traveled from Siberia to Moscow. They reached the American Embassy by actually passing the flabbergasted Soviet militiaman, whose main duty it is to keep Soviet citizens from entering. Later identified as Pentecostals, the group was composed of six men, twelve women, and fourteen children whose goal was to escape religious persecution once and for all by emigrating to Israel. How difficult must have been the task of the American Embassy personnel to refuse their request and turn them right back into the hands of the Soviet officials. What a tragic sight to see them herded into a bus for shipment back to Siberia. Six weeks later, during an English-language broadcast from Moscow beamed toward North American listeners, a listener's letter from Texas was answered. The announcer informed his audience that the group was returned in comfortable sleeping cars to their homes in Siberia, repudiating any claim that they had been punished.[18]

The militant atheists work all the angles. Their article in *Nauka i Religiia* lampooned the Baptists for stating that God had discontinued performing miracles and incisively wrote, "Why? Only Mitskevich knows. However, to spread religious superstitions without believing in miracles is very difficult even for experts such as the Baptist theologians." The article was accompanied by a cartoon depicting a bald, white-bearded man asleep on a pillowy cloud next to a sign which read, "I no longer perform miracles."[19]

Of course, the nonregistered Pentecostals were subject to far greater pressures than those whom they called "their compromising brethren," meaning the members of the Union churches. An atheist hack writer stereotyped all Pentecostal preachers as obscurantists who forbade the reading of newspapers, journals, and books (except the Bible), attendance at the cinema, theater, concerts, dances, and social organizations. He charged some of them with instructing fellow Pente-

236

costals not to vote or work in governmental establishments and to refuse to be drafted in the army. Others were seared for convincing members not to participate in professional unions or join in the Soviet holiday celebrations, nor to allow their children to be members of the Pioneers or Komsomols (Communist Youth League). In the eyes of the Soviets such teachings were counter-revolutionary, designed to sabotage their great goal of producing the new Soviet man. How could religion die with the old people if these Pentecostals continued to meddle with young, impressionable minds? Pentecostal leaders who insisted on the freedom to continue influencing others received warnings and fines, followed by sentences of one to five years of imprisonment. The special wrath of the Soviets is incurred upon all those, be they Pentecostal, Baptist, or whatever, who dare to assemble groups of children in order to teach them Bible stories or hymns. Freedom of conscience in the Soviet Union means the freedom to keep your faith to yourself. Despite the fact that Lenin's decree of 1918 gave room for evangelistic endeavors and religious propaganda, Stalin's repressive Law of 1929 permitted only anti-religious propaganda designed to eradicate every vestige of belief in God from the minds and hearts of all Soviet citizens.

Special films were produced to warn and alert the Soviet public against the inroads of the Pentecostals. These productions are added to the arsenal of anti-religious propaganda. *Clouds Over Borsk* was designed to "show the influence of Pentecostal preachers on the souls of young people and how they harmonize the preaching of love for one's neighbor with the revolution of fanaticism." In *The Road from Obscurity,* a supposedly factual Alma Ata documentary, the "true face of the 'sacred healers' and 'miracle workers' " was exposed. Both films emphasized the fanaticism of the Pentecostals. Why all the fuss and budgetary expendi-

237

ture? Admittedly because of the dangerous influence, constantly growing, of dynamic Pentecostals intent on winning youth in the Soviet Union to Jesus Christ. These films were designed to shock the apathetic and indifferent Soviet comrades into active membership in the ever struggling ranks of militant atheism.

The newspaper *Komsomol'skaia pravda* published a provocative article entitled "Komsomol Leaders Must Play a Greater Role in Atheistic Propaganda." The author's frustration was readily apparent. After hurling all the accusations against the Pentecostals he could muster up, he asked his readers, "Why do the sectarians find so many followers? Where do they get their strength?" Between his caustic remarks about a Pentecostal engineer named Shevchenko, the Soviet writer was unable to omit several reasons for the believer's success among the young people in the city of Krasnoiarsk. He admitted that the Pentecostal was "powerful, clever . . . kind . . . tearful prayers and fiery sermons were the methods which Shevchenko used beautifully." Finally, in a fit of anti-religious missionary fervor, he pleaded with his readers, "Why such irresponsibility and complacency among the Komsomol leaders? . . . People are lost . . . and it does not bother the Komsomol workers?"[20] He had reason to complain. In this Siberian city of half a million, only fifteen Komsomol members were found to be actively engaged in atheist propaganda. Ironically, an inaccurate editorial in the following morning's *Pravda* back in Moscow lauded Krasnoiarsk for its intensification of scientific atheist education.[21]

In a recent book *Who Are These Pentecostals?* Soviet author Nikolai Koltsov makes the sweeping declaration that during the brief period of its twentieth-century existence, "Pentecostalism has grown into one of the strongest religious movements at a rate unknown in any other." He recognized that its worldwide unity was cemented by its teaching of "the baptism in the 'Holy Spirit' in other languages." Soviet readers were able to learn the extent of the global growth of the Pentecostals in this popular paperback, and despite the fact that it was designed to downgrade Russian Pentecostals, many readers must have been impressed to learn how many Scandinavian neighbors had embraced the Pentecostal message. The author singled out Italy, a nation with strong Communist Party membership, as a country where "Pentecostals are the largest and strongest Protestant group.[22]

Koltsov focused upon the special attention given to recruiting Soviet youth to Pentecostalism. Organized trips for this purpose rally young people to the countryside, forests, and lakes for prayer meetings and singing sessions. The songs they sing in these gatherings attract many young unbelievers for they are based on popular Soviet tunes. Tape-recorded songs composed by young Pentecostals are transcribed to these popular melodies and only when visitors are among the circle of believers do they realize that the words focus upon faith in God and His goodness. Young people dropping in to the "Evenings of Love" will hear discussions of the world's greatest love story—God's love for all men. Then there is the attraction, adventure, and romantic atmosphere of the clandestine meetings in semi-dark buildings on the outskirts of town.

Other tactics of evangelism are employed by the Russian Pentecostals in contemporary Soviet society. In Krivoi Rog they were reported to have purchased television sets—taboo for most Pentecostals there—to serve as a smokescreen for their religious meetings. The set is switched on during the service to drown out the worship sounds. The set is also a convenient excuse in case the meeting is discovered—"just watching a television program." Family celebrations such as birthdays and weddings provide fine occasions for general worship.

239

Success with Soviet youth inevitably brings a crackdown by the authorities. *Nauka i Religiia* reports a courtroom scene in Enakievo in which the Pentecostal Kondrakov was criminally tried and prosecuted. The mine workers had warned him to discontinue his home gatherings in more than five towns, but he continued. They declared in court that, "He lied, dodged, gave no direct answers to questions, tried various aphorisms from 'Holy Scripture' to evade responsibility of judgment of crippling lives." The City Court carried out the will and desire of the people by sentencing him with eight years' "deprivation of freedom." The verdict brought forth "stormy applause" both in the overcrowded courtroom and from anti-Pentecostals on the street.

It was my privilege to visit in the home of a Pentecostal family a thousand miles from Moscow. Although I identified myself as a Pentecostal brother, I met with nothing but a guarded reserve. The father and grown son evidenced no warmth. In a few minutes we knelt to pray and after a brief session of prayer which included utterances in other tongues, the father embraced me with the Russian kiss of fellowship. He stiffened when I asked how many Pentecostals there were outside the Union churches. He simply referred to the punishment King David received from God after numbering the Israelites.

In another Soviet city I met a pastor of a Union church who was Pentecostal. Members were made up of both Baptists and Pentecostals and the order of the midweek service was Baptistic, with no evidence of Pentecostal worship whatsoever. I had forwarded a note to the pulpit, identifying myself as a believer, a professor from Oral Roberts University, and a person acquainted with a number of the executive brethren from Moscow. The Russian pastor invited me to come forward and be seated with the preachers—every church has five or more. After a few choral renditions and sermonettes by three preachers, the pastor introduced me to the congregation. He whispered to me not to be hurried, but to take a half hour. I did just that, speaking in my Brooklynese Russian, which appeared to be quite acceptable. The pastor tried to have me remain in the city for their next service on Sunday morning but I was already scheduled to be in another city. He begged me to return at some future time, adding that he believed many would receive gifts of the Spirit in his congregation.

While visiting another Union church in the area I was invited by the Baptist pastor to join the preachers on the platform during a standing-room-only Sunday evening service. To my surprise several young people quoted religious poetry during the meeting. Again I had the liberty of sharing with the congregation for half an hour. I told of my father's cataclysmic conversion, bringing attention to a thought on the God of Isaac as the God who performs miracles. Illustrations followed, to demonstrate that the God of Isaac performs miracles today. These intent Russian believers seemed to hang on every word and to pull the best out of you. At the close of the service, immediately after the benediction, a number of people came forward to have a word with me. Among them were those who wished me to accompany them to pray for afflicted loved ones. If this were not possible, they were determined to get cabs and bring them to the church without delay. As a guest I referred them to their pastor and stated that whatever he decided would be fine. I had not expected such active response and realized that I had placed the Baptist pastor in an awkward position. But even as he was trying to make the best of the situation, some had hurried off to bring these relatives for prayer. Soon they returned with an afflicted child. The pastor had the people seated and announced that there would be no laying on of hands, but that everyone would instead kneel and pray that if it was God's will, He would bring forth the healing. We all prayed but no visible healing was manifested. I clearly remember the pleading eyes of the mother directed my way as I was escorted back to the center of town. Not two streets from the church a Soviet cab came to a screeching halt in the middle of the street. A believer had brought an aged mother for prayer! With the cabbie eyeing me quizzically, I prayed for the woman, stretching forth my hand on her right shoulder as I stood in the street. They warmly thanked me and the cabbie drove on. I don't know the result, but I must admit to mixed emotions as I prayed. You see, I remembered reading the Soviet account of a Pentecostal woman holding healing services in the Saratov region. The authorities stepped in, reminding her that Soviet law "categorically forbids similar kinds of 'medical' activity."[23] I'm glad that physical contact is not necessary for divine healing to be experienced—be it in Soviet Russia, in China, or in the good old U.S.A.

XIII

Pentecostal Perspectives

JESUS IS COMING soon!

Pentecostals are not looking for the undertaker, but the Uppertaker. They believe in the imminent return of the very same Christ who departed from the Mount of Olives, half a mile from Jerusalem on Ascension Day. "This Jesus, who was taken up from you into heaven, will come back in the same way that you saw him go to heaven," was the message to the apostles as their eyes were still fixed on the sky.[1]

Christians have looked for Christ's return ever since. The second coming of Jesus is mentioned more than three hundred times in the New Testament. Entire books (I and II Thessalonians) and chapters (Matthew 24 and Mark 13) picture His second coming to earth. The Apostle Paul refers to this dramatic theme more than fifty times.

In attempting to explain Pentecostalism, I have repeatedly referred to three basic tenets firmly believed by all Pentecostals—that Jesus Christ is the Savior, the Healer, and the Baptizer in the Spirit. The fourth fundamental belief is that Jesus is the soon-coming King. This concept, coupled with the witnessing power received when baptized in the Spirit, adds a sense of urgency and haste to winning as many people to Christ as possible, for "in such an hour as you think not the Son of Man cometh."[2] A few Pentecostal groups have felt so strongly about the relationship of the baptism in the Spirit and the return of Christ that they have wrongly insisted that only Spirit-filled Christians who speak in tongues will be ready to meet the Lord at His return.

Jesus is coming soon! This message has been heralded by Pentecostals in every decade of this century. They believe the return of Christ will be visible and personal. They discount interpretations which endeavor to avoid a personal and literal view of Christ's coming, such as those that explain that Christ comes at the Christian's death, or others which spiritualize it and say that Christ comes when a person is converted. Pentecostals believe this exciting promise to mean Christ's outward and visible physical return.

Most Classic Pentecostals believe that Jesus will suddenly arrive to call Christians who look for His appearance and that in a moment's time they will be launched into His presence for a judgment which will determine rewards for faithful service. This *parousia* (Greek for "appearing") is commonly called the "Rapture" among Pentecostals, a catching away of Christians. It is dramatized in Paul's first letter to the Thessalonians: "The Lord himself will descend from heaven with a cry of command, with the archangel's call, and with the sound of the trumpet of God. And the dead in Christ will rise first; then we who are alive, who are left, shall be caught up together with them in the clouds to meet the Lord in the air; and so we shall always be with the Lord."[3]

Pentecostals are Pre-Millenialists for they believe that this instantaneous disappearance of Christians from the planet earth for a brief period will precede Christ's thousand-year-reign upon the earth. How well do I remember the many vivid Pentecostal sermons that described the plight of those left behind to face the Great Tribulation foretold in the last book of the New Testament, the Revelation. Following the preacher's fiery presentation, an invitation was extended to accept Christ and escape the vials of wrath to be unleashed upon the world. A lingering altar call, often

244

given in tears, was aimed at getting decisions then and there. Stubborn and world-loving, I resisted many altar calls and inner tugs over a period of three years, although I was miserable and under conviction. As a fence-sitting teenager I could enjoy neither the world nor the Pentecostal services. Finally, at seventeen, I responded to a message on "Where Will You Spend Eternity?" deciding that eternal values far outweighed the trivia of time.

A common expression used by Pentecostals is "the Lord tarrying." If the preacher announced revival meetings the following month, he would add, "The Lord tarrying." The Lord's coming was no abstraction. Those who thought they would miss the "Rapture" because they hadn't spoken in tongues prayed all the more fervently. Because they prayed in fear they strained in prayer. In spite of these psychological barriers, most received the experience and were greatly relieved. In the 1920s, when the Pentecostals in Soviet Russia preached that the doctrine of the "Rapture" included only Spirit-filled believers, the indignation of the Russian Baptists was heaped upon them. Most Pentecostals do not hold this view.

The pioneer American Pentecostals rejected society even as they were rejected. Scarcely any institution, pleasure, business, vice, or social group escaped the condemnation of many Pentecostal preachers. The social sin list included: "tobacco in all its forms, secret societies, life insurance, doctors, medicine, liquor, dance halls, theaters, movies, Coca Cola, public swimming, professional sports, beauty parlors, jewelry, church bazaars, and makeup."[4] This period of rejection continued from 1906 to 1923, when Aimee Semple McPherson showed another face of Pentecostalism and caused it to receive widespread acceptance. Through the many outreaches of her five-thousand-seat Angelus Temple she did much to promote a tolerant attitude toward the Pentecostals as she shared the headlines with evangelist Billy Sunday during the twenties and thirties.[5]

Pentecostal denominational growth from the mid-twenties to the mid-sixties was ninefold in the Church of God (Cleveland), twelvefold in the Assemblies of God, and fourteenfold in the black-membered Church of God in Christ.[6] Storefront churches metamorphosed into sanctuaries seating up to a thousand. The Pentecostals appealed to and served the common people gladly. Missionaries hastened to foreign shores to share the good news of salvation before Jesus' return. Scores of Pentecostal Bible Institutes were founded in the first half of the twentieth century to prepare pastors and missionaries to put in the sickle for a harvest of souls. As late as World War II few of the instructors in the Assemblies of God schools were college graduates themselves.[7] Many early Pentecostals were suspicious of a liberal arts education within their denominational schools, fearing that the fires of revival would be smothered and die out. In 1949, although in the vanguard among Pentecostals in the number of schools, the Assemblies of God went on record as opposed to academic degrees ever being required for ordination in the ministry.[8] Donald Gee struck a balance when he said, "An educated ministry is good; an inspired ministry is better; but an inspired educated ministry is best of all."[9]

As the economic level of many Pentecostals rose, television invaded many Pentecostal homes in the fifties and a decline in the attendance at the Sunday night evangelistic services disturbed many pastors. With the quickening pace of life, revival services formerly held nightly for two- and three-week periods were now streamlined to a week or just a weekend. As believers approached affluence, apathy began to lull some Pentecostal churches to sleep. And where the trumpet sound

246

of the Second Coming was muted, evangelistic fervor waned. But the overall picture of Pentecostals in America was one of satisfying growth and advance.

Since World War II a greater formality in worship practices within the Classic Pentecostal churches has emerged. In earlier decades the services were readily identified by their fervency in most locales and the regular zealous participation of lay members was taken for granted. Services were strikingly informal, including testimonies, songs, exhortations, and the exercise of the gifts of the Spirit.[10] This is the general format of services now enjoyed, but with a more subdued tone, by the prayer groups among the Protestant Neo-Pentecostals and the Catholic charismatics. Equally surprising is the finding that within one Classic Pentecostal denomination (the Assemblies of God), an authority indicated that at least three general categories of worship could be found in most parts of the country in recent years. The first category attempts "to perpetuate the image of unrestrained, exuberant worship" while the second reacts violently to the first "with a resultant formalism that has little typically Pentecostal remaining." The greater part of the churches lie "somewhere in between, attempting to maintain a balance between freedom and discipline in worship."[11]

If Pentecostals within one denomination are so different in their manner of worship and yet work together on common goals in order to hasten the return of Christ, why should it be thought unlikely that as the coming of Jesus draws nearer, all Spirit-filled people will come closer together? Man divides, but the Spirit of God unites, for He desires to fulfill the prayer of Jesus "That they may all be one."

Pentecostalism is highly adaptable to all Christian forms of worship and is accepted and appreciated by people of many nations, from the conservative Swedes to the emotional Brazilians. Even among deaf wor-

247

shipers using sign language, the baptism in the Spirit
has been followed by speaking in tongues. There are no
stereotype Pentecostals! The unifying factors capable
of drawing all Christians together in fellowship are
Jesus Christ and His baptism in the Holy Spirit. Whether
a person prefers to worship as an exuberant Pentecostal
or as a calm Charismatic does not matter. He is spoiled
for anything less than the supernatural presence and
leadership of God the Spirit in the midst of a receptive
body of believers. And where the Holy Spirit reigns
supreme, the truth of the Second Coming of Christ
burns brighter.

While the sword of Damocles has taken the shape of
the mushroom cloud with its overkill capacities, the
Spirit of God is breathing upon the youth of the world:
"This is what I will do in the last days, God says: I will
pour out my Spirit upon all men; Your sons and your
daughters will prophesy, Your young men will see
visions. . . ."[12]

The Spirit of God upon the young! *Look* and *Time*,
among many magazines, have featured extensive articles
on the "Jesus Movement" and the "Jesus Revolution,"
both coming in the strength and fervor of youth. Young
people have turned on to Jesus and believe He is coming soon.[13] The movement has special momentum in
California—where the Azusa Street revival of 1906 and
the Van Nuys Charismatic renewal began. Now instead
of a copping out with sex, drugs, and violence, young
people can be heard with a "New Rebel Cry: Jesus Is
Coming!"[14] Charismatic Chuck Smith baptized more
than two thousand in the Pacific Ocean in one year.
Converts from Smith's Calvary Chapel become activists
for Jesus, proving the song they sing is true: "They'll
know we are Christians by our love."[15] The Los
Angeles Teen Challenge Center expresses that love by
winning over young people involved in drugs, without
caring "what they look like, how they smell, or where

they come from." In Orange County an entire motor-
cycle gang came to Christ.[16] Across from Disneyland is
the huge complex called Melodyland, headed by Pentecostal Ralph Wilkerson. His Anaheim center has a
twenty-four-hour emergency phone service manned by
youthful volunteers who handle thousands of calls
every month. This is a movement that has puzzled
many adults, but at least they're sure it beats drugs.
The multitudes of young people, both poor and upper-
middle-class, insist that "Jesus is coming. Praise God!"[17]
Speaking of the Jesus revolution, the *Time*'s writer says
that "Its strong Pentecostalism emphasized such
esoteric spiritual gifts as speaking in tongues and healing
by faith. For many, there exists a firm conviction that
Jesus' Second Coming is literally at hand."[18]

A young lady who got her boot training at Dave
Wilkerson's Brooklyn Teen Challenge Center working
with addicts runs the large coffeehouse, "The Cata-
combs," across from Seattle's Space Needle. Hundreds
are attracted on weekend nights to hear gospel rock
and to engage in Jesus "rapping." During a huge out-
door rock festival she dropped ten thousand copies
of her underground paper *Agape* on the crowd from a
small chartered plane. The Jesus Movement reports
frequent miraculous healings and demon exorcisms,
and when heroin addicts discard the drugs they say
they experience no withdrawal symptoms. Is it any
wonder that two traveling photographers covering the
Movement for *Look* received Christ while on assign-
ment![19]

The "Children of God," one of the more radical of
the new young believers groups, offered their unique
life-style to students on the Oral Roberts University
campus. This group rarely presents panel discussions at
college campuses because of their critical attitude
toward the educational systems and churches. Instead,
they encourage students to drop out of school and live

totally for Christ by joining their communes. Nevertheless, their discussion made an impact and a group of ORU students visited their Texas colony during an Easter break. Two students decided to remain. Their approach resembles that of the twentieth-century pioneer Pentecostals who felt that school was a waste of time and that students should instead be ministering to a needy world.[20] But the pioneer Pentecostals, although strong believers in the Second Coming, soon recognized the need and value of serious study under trained Spirit-filled teachers. This was followed by a vastly greater service for God on the field. Will communal life succeed under the Children of God? Failures of such movements in Christian history augur poorly for its lasting success, but there is no questioning their sincerity.

Twenty years before the Jesus Movement of today, Presbyterian statesman John A. Mackay learned both by experience and observation this important lesson: "Never be afraid of a young fanatic or of what appears to be a fanatical movement, if Jesus Christ is the supreme object of devotion. On the other hand, I am terribly afraid of a cold, frigid, professionally-aired Christianity which is interested only in form. The young fanatic, if wisely dealt with, can be toned down and mellowed. However, nothing short of the sepulchre awaits those who identify conventional order and aesthetic devotion with spiritual life."[21]

Certainly those who have been zealous without knowledge, as were some pioneers of the Pentecostal movement, need to be broad enough to understand and flexible enough to make room in the three-generation-old movement for the prophetic zeal and joyful abandonment of the Jesus Movement. David Wilkerson, the well-known author of *The Cross and the Switchblade,* calls it the "Jesus Revolution," sponsored by the Holy Spirit. He calls for love, patience, pity, and forgiveness by God's people in order to reach this volatile generation of youth. He is convinced that the many thousands of searching teenagers and students want reality and a deeper religious experience found in the baptism in the Spirit. When that inner "revolution" begins, Wilkerson is convinced that "Addicts kick the habit and start preaching Jesus. Blacks and whites join hands and praise God. Rebels lay down their weapons and preach peace. Children are reunited with their parents. Prodigals return home. Gang leaders prophesy."[22]

The more closely revival movements resemble the early pattern of Pentecostalism, the greater are both the dangers and the rewards. A lively expectation of the imminent return of Jesus does not produce slothful Christians. As violence, hatred, degeneration, and perversion abound on every hand, the Pentecostals can not be yawning for lack of a challenge. The early Christians lived with the keen expectancy of Christ's return, so much so that they greeted each other with the watchword *Maranatha,* "Lord, come!" No true Pentecostal excludes the very real possibility that Jesus will come during his lifetime. He gauges his life accordingly and is a wise steward of any material blessings which may come his way. He gives liberally to make possible the speedy dispatch of many missionaries to share the good news with those who have not yet heard the old, old story of Jesus and His love. He is also alert to the real possibility that Jesus may come today! This concept provides the zeal and fearlessness of apostolic faith. And it ensures practical holiness, a daily walk which is pleasing to God. The Apostle John said it this way: ". . . when Christ appears, we shall become like him, because we shall see him as he really is. Everyone who has this hope in Christ keeps himself pure, just as Christ is pure."[23]

Pentecostals recognize the signs of the time and become ever more convinced that Jesus is coming soon. Wars and rumors of wars, earthquakes in diverse places, distress of nations, men's hearts failing them for fear, the increase of iniquity, and a falling away of believers in apostasy are among these signs. But the most striking sign is the reappearance of the nation Israel fulfilling ancient prophecy which foretold this restoration. Not since the destruction of Jerusalem in A.D. 70 had Israel existed as a nation. Then, in 1948, against unbelievable odds, this country experienced its rebirth and has since developed rapidly. The Six-Day War in 1967 enabled Israel's Holy City to be united for the first time in almost two thousand years. Hebrew has been restored to popular usage and the Old Testament is taught in its schools while the New Testament is read as religious literature. Israelis may be found at the Wailing Wall praying daily for the coming of the Messiah. Although the Israelis do not recognize the coming Messiah to be Jesus of Nazareth, Pentecostals believe that world conditions are rapidly shaping up for the acceptance of Jesus Christ by Israel when he returns to reign from the world capital in Jerusalem. But Pentecostals know better than to predict the time of Christ's arrival, for Jesus said, "Watch out, then, because you do not know the day or hour."[24]

Pentecostalism represents radical Christianity and if it chooses to be at ease and to compromise it will fail miserably. This dying world desperately needs its distinctive testimony. The Pentecostals have been persecuted, but they have grown and prospered whenever they were more concerned about courting God's favor than man's, whenever they feared God's displeasure more than failure. If Pentecostalism ceases to be a movement it will be carving its own monument. But God is never without a people who want nothing more than to live for Him and if necessary die for Him, simply because they love Him. Call them what you will—Classic Pentecostals, Protestant Neo-Pentecostals, Catholic Charismatics, Full Gospel Business Men, Jesus' Children, or what have you—God will bless and use those who will be as pliable in His hands as were the first Christians who experienced the Pentecostal outpouring.

Pentecostalism will never be computerized to maintain an atmosphere of faith in which the gifts of the Spirit constantly function. There is the ever-present danger of man getting in the way, despising the gifts because of some extravagances and regulating them excessively, leaving nothing but a dry shell of professed Pentecost. Long ago someone coined the phrase, "There is no Pentecost without Plentycost." The price is death to the proud self-life, death to the delight in the power and prestige of organizational position, death to the egotistical concept that shuts Pentecostals within small mutual admiration cells. The price is humility—to God alone belongs the glory; honesty—but for the grace of God the Pentecostal is weaker than all men; and holiness—the happy, wholesome kind that never repels, but always attracts people to Jesus.

The Holy Spirit is the initiator of the Pentecostal renewal and He is faithful to His task of preparing a body of people from all nations and from all walks of life to make up the Body of Christ. The universal church is composed of redeemed men and women who worship and work as they watch for the soon return of Jesus Christ.

"Even so, come, Lord Jesus."

Pentecostals—Who Are They?

1   Donald Gee, ed., *The Fifth World Pentecostal Conference* (Toronto: Testimony Press, 1958), p. 94

2   National Broadcasting Company, "First Tuesday" (telecast), January 4, 1971.

3   Prudencia Damboriena, *Tongues As of Fire* (Washington, D.C.: Corpus Books, 1969), p. 87.

4   Matthew 3:11, Mark 1:8, Luke 3:16, John 1:33.

5   I Corinthians 12:8-10.

6   George B. Cutten, *Speaking with Tongues Historically and Psychologically Considered* (New Haven: Yale University Press, 1927).

7   Frank Stagg, Glenn E. Hinson, and Wayne E. Oates, *Glossolalia: Tongue Speaking in Biblical, Historical, and Psychological Perspective* (Nashville: Abingdon Press, 1967), p. 12.

8   *The Nation,* September 28, 1963, p. 173.

9   *Melodyland Messenger* (Anaheim, Calif, n.d.), special edition.

10 *Ave Maria,* June 3, 1967.

11 David J. du Plessis, *The Spirit Bade Me Go,* rev. ed. (Plainfield, N.J.: Logos International, 1970), p. 40.

12 Acts 2:1,4.

13 *U.S. News & World Report,* October 19, 1970, p. 86.

14 Acts 1:8.

15 Du Plessis, op. cit., pp. 14-15.

16 *America,* March 30, 1968, p. 406.

17 *Christian Life,* November 1969, p. 60.

18 *Tulsa Daily World,* April 1, 1971.

19 *Commonweal,* November 8, 1968, p. 203.

Where It All Started

1   John 20:21-22 (Revised Standard Version [New York: Thomas Nelson & Sons, 1953]). Hereafter cited as RSV.

2   Acts 1:4,5,8,9,12-14 (RSV).

3   Acts 1:26 (RSV).

4   John 1:17 (RSV).

5   Matthew 10:8 (RSV).

6   Luke 10:17 (RSV).

7   Acts 2:1-4 (RSV).

8   Acts 2:38-39 (RSV).

9   Acts 8:8 (*The New Testament in Modern English,* translated by
     J. B. Phillips [New York: The Macmillan Company, 1958]).

10   Acts 8:20 (*The Twentieth Century New Testament* [New York:
     Fleming H. Revell Co., 1964]).

11   Acts 10:44-46 (RSV).

12   Acts 10:47 (RSV).

13   Acts 11:15-17 (RSV).

14   Acts 19:6 (RSV).

15   Acts 15.

16   Acts 21 (*Good News for Modern Man; Today's English Version of
     the New Testament* [New York: The Macmillan Company, 1966]).

17   Acts 9 and 20.

18   Acts 19:13-20 (*Good News for Modern Man*).

19   Acts 16:17-23 (*Good News for Modern Man*).

20   I Corinthians 14:12-28.

21   I Corinthians 14:39 and 18 (RSV).

22   I Corinthians 14:2 (RSV).

23   Ira Jay Martin III, *Glossolalia in the Apostolic Church* (Berla,
     Kentucky: 1960), p. 38-39.

24   *Pentecostal Evangel,* May 10, 1959.

NOTES   *CHAPTER III*

Supernatural Traces Through the Centuries

1   Bernard L. Bresson, *Studies in Ecstasy* (New York: Vantage Press,
     1966; and *Encyclopaedia Britannica,* 1944 ed., XXII, 283.

2   I Corinthians 13:8 (King James Version).

3   Robert Glenn Gromacki, *The Modern Tongues Movement* (Philadelphia: Presbyterian and Reformed Publishing Company, 1967), p. 12.

4   Alexander Roberts and James Donaldson, eds., *Ante-Nicene Fathers* (Grand Rapids: Wm. B. Eerdmans Publishing Co., 1885), 1, 531.

5   Frank Stagg, Glenn E. Hinson, and Wayne E. Oates, *Glossolalia: Tongue Speaking in Biblical, Historical, and Psychological Perspective* (Nashville: Abingdon Press, 1967), p. 47.

6   *Ecclesiastical History,* C. F. Cruse, trans. (London: Bell and Daldy, 1870), p. 184.

7   Acts 2,9;I Corinthians 14:2.

8   Sauer, *History of the Christian Church,* III, 406, quoted in Gordon F. Atter, *The Third Force* (Peterborough, Ontario: The College Press, 1962), p. 12.

9   L. M. Van Eetvelot Vivier, *Glossolalia* (Johannesburg: University of Witwatersrand doctoral thesis, 1960), p. 95.

10   *John Wesley's Journal* (London: Epworth Press reprint, 1949), p. 98.

11   Vivier, *op. cit.,* p. 111.

12   Jean Christie Root, *Edward Irving: Man, Preacher, Prophet* (Boston: Sherman, French and Co., 1912), p. 94.

13   Vivier, *op. cit.,* p. 115.

14   Root, *op. cit.,* p. 109.

15   Atter, *op. cit.,* p. 16.

16. Root, *op. cit.,* p. 131.

17. Atter, *op. cit.,* p. 17.

NOTES   *CHAPTER IV*

The Rediscovery of Pentecostal Power

1   Quoted in Harold V. Synan, *The Pentecostal Movement in the United States* (unpublished doctoral thesis, University of Georgia, 1967), p. 11.

2   Williston Walker, *A History of the Christian Church* (New York: Charles Scribner's Sons, 1959), p. 459.

3   E. T. Clark, *Small Sects in America* (New York: Abingdon-Cokesbury Press, 1949), pp. 88-89.

4   Peter Cartright, *Autobiography of Peter Cartright* (New York: Abingdon Press, 1956), p. 46.

256

5   Synan, *op. cit.*, p. 34.

6   *Ibid.*, p. 35.

7   *Ibid.*, p. 57.

8   R. A. Torrey, *Person and Work of the Holy Spirit* (Grand Rapids: Zondervan, 1968), p. 244.

9   Stanley H. Frodsham, *With Signs Following* (Springfield, Mo: Gospel Publishing House, 1946), pp. 9, 10.

10 *Ibid.*, pp. 16-17.

11 James Gordon Lindsay, *The Life of John Alexander Dowie* (Shreveport: Voice of Healing Pub. Co., 1951), p. 4.

12 *Ibid.*, p. 117.

13 *Ibid.*, pp. 137-45.

14 *Ibid.*, p. 151.

15 *Ibid.*, pp. 203-5.

16 Sarah E. Parham, *The Life of Charles F. Parham* (Joplin, Mo: The Tri-State Printing Company, 1930), p. 51.

17 *Ibid.*, p. 47.

18 *Ibid.*, p. 52.

19 *Ibid.*

20 *Ibid.*

21 *Ibid.*, p. 53.

22 *Ibid.*, p. 66.

23 *Ibid.*, p. 53.

24 *Ibid.*, p. 55.

25 Nils Bloch-Hoell, *The Pentecostal Movement: Its Origin, Development, and Distinctive Character* (Oslo: Universitetforlaget, 1964), p. 21.

26 *Ibid.*, pp. 21-23.

27 *Ibid.*, p. 24.

28 *Ibid.*, p. 25.

29 Quoted in Frodsham, *op. cit.*, p. 19.

30 Parham, *op. cit.* p. 62.

31 *Ibid.*

32 *Ibid.*, p. 81.

Miracles in the Early Twentieth Century

1 Claude Kendrick, *The Promise Fulfilled,* p. 56, quoting Charles F. Parham, "The Latter Rain," *Apostolic Faith,* July 1926, p. 3.

2 Stanley H. Frodsham, *With Signs Following* (Springfield, Mo.: Gospel Publishing House, 1946), p. 26.

3 Frank Bartleman, *What Really Happened at "Azusa Street"?* (Northridge, Calif.: Voice Christian Publications, Inc., 1962), p. 25.

4 *Pentecost,* No. 29, September 1954, p. 8.

5 Bartleman, *op. cit.,* p. 26.

6 Sarah E. Parham, *The Life of Charles F. Parham* (Joplin, Mo.: The Tri-State Printing Company, 1930), pp. 163-66.

7 Harold V. Synan, *The Pentecostal Movement in the United States* (unpublished doctoral thesis, University of Georgia, 1967), p. 230.

8 *Ibid.,* p. 139.

9 Parham, *op. cit.,* p. 176.

10 *Ibid.,* p. 201.

11 *Ibid.,* p. 413.

12 *Ibid.,* pp. 416, 418.

13 *Ibid.,* p. 415.

14 *Pentecost,* No. 30, December 1954, p. 15.

15 Aimee Semple McPherson, *This Is That* (Los Angeles: Echo Park Evangelistic Association, 1923), p. 45.

16 *Ibid.,* pp. 50, 51.

17 *Ibid.,* p. 162.

18 *Ibid.,* pp. 197, 304, 309.

19 *Ibid.,* p. 318.

20 *Ibid.,* pp. 319-32.

21 *Ibid.,* pp. 222, 223, 398.

22 *World Pentecost,* No. 1, 1971, p. 15.

23 McPherson, *op. cit.,* pp. 532, 539, 587 and *Pentecost,* December 1958, p. 12.

24   Aimee Semple McPherson, *The Story of My Life* (In Memoriam)
      (Hollywood: An International Correspondent's Publication, 1951),
      chapters XXII and XXIII; and "It's Time That the Truth Be Told"
      (Los Angeles: Statement by International Church of the Four-
      square Gospel).

25   Letter from Rolf K. McPherson, December 20, 1971.

26   *Pentecost,* No. 64, June-August 1963, p. 5.

CHAPTER VI

The Global Explosion of Pentecostalism

1   Zechariah 4:6 (RSV).

2   John 16:13, 14 (RSV).

3   Acts 8:19 (RSV).

4   Genesis 1:2; Romans 8:11 (RSV).

5   John 14:15-17 (RSV).

6   Harold V. Synan, *The Pentecostal Movement in the United States*
      (unpublished doctoral thesis, University of Georgia, 1967), p. 195.

7   *Ibid.,* p. 197.

8   *Pentecostal Fellowship of North America* (Springfield: PFNA
      News, 1968), circular.

9   John T. Nichol, *Pentecostalism* (New York: Harper & Row,
      Publisher, Inc., 1966), p. 87.

10   Acts 6:16, 8:14, 15; Titus 1:5.

11   Joseph E. Campbell, *The Pentecostal Holiness Church* (Franklin
      Springs, Ga.: Pentecostal Holiness Church, 1951), p. 251.

12   Nichol, *op. cit.,* pp. 93, 102.

13   Synan, *op. cit.,* p. 227.

14   *Ibid.,* p. 228.

15   *Ibid.,* p. 229.

16   *Pentecost,* No. 47, March 1959, p. 3.

17   Nichol, *op. cit.,* p. 92.

18   *Pentecost,* No. 48, June 1959, p. 16.

19   Carl Brumbach, *Suddenly . . . From Heaven* (Springfield, Mo.:
      Gospel Publishing House, 1961), pp. 282, 283.

20   Nichol, *op. cit.,* p. 209, quoting Donald Gee.

21   *Ibid.,* p. 210.

22   D. P. Gaines, *The World Council of Churches* (Peterborough, N.H.: Richard R. Smith Co., 1966), p. 1011.

23   William Menzies, *Anointed to Serve* (Springfield, Mo: Gospel Publishing House, 1971), p. 221.

24   David du Plessis, *The Spirit Bade Me Go,* revised ed. (Plainfield, N.J.: Logos International, 1970), p. 13.

25   *Ibid.,* p. 26.

26   *Ibid.,* pp. 112-18.

27   *Ibid.,* p. 4.

28   *Christian Life,* July 1966, p. 27.

29   David J. du Plessis, *The Spirit Bade Me Go,* revised ed. (Plainfield, N.J.: Logos International, 1971), p. 50.

30   *Pentecost,* No. 1, September 1947, p. 11; No. 2., December 1947, p. 8.

31   *Ibid.,* No. 21, September 1952, p. 10.

32   *Ibid.,* March 1948, p. 4.

33   *Ibid.,* No. 19, September, 1949, p. 10.

34.   *Ibid.,* No. 22, December 1952, pp. 1-2.

35   *Ibid.,* No. 26, December 1953, p. 15.

36   *Ibid.,* No. 52, June-August 1960, p. 11.; No. 53, September-November 1960, p. 15; No. 27, March 1953, p. 7.

37   *Ibid.,* No. 58, December 1961-February 1962, p. 2.

38   *Ibid.,* No. 76, June-August 1966, pp. 2-3.

39   *Ibid.,* No. 10, 1949, p. 11, and Nichol, *op. cit.,* p. 163.

40   *Ibid.,* No. 37, September 1956, inside cover; No. 65, September-November 1963, p. 1.

41   *Ibid.,* No. 9, September 1949, pp. 1-2.

42   *Ibid.,* No. 56, June-August 1961, pp. 8-10.

43   *Pentecostal Evangel,* September 17, 1967, pp. 8-10; October 1, 1967, p. 9.

44   *Pentecost,* No. 57, September-November 1961, p. 1.

45   *Ibid.,* No. 22, December 1952, pp. 4-5.

46   *Ibid.,* No. 25, September 1953, back cover.

47   *World Vision Magazine,* May 1971, p. 31.

48   *Pentecost,* No. 57, September-November 1961, p. 15.

49   *World Pentecost,* No. 1, 1971, pp. 19, 20, 30, 31.

50   Quoted in *Pentecost,* No. 51, March 1960, p. 1.

51   *Ibid.,* No. 43, March 1958, p. 2.

52   *Ibid.,* No. 22, December 1952, p. 7.

53   *Voice,* Vol. 12, July-August 1964, p. 29.

54   *Pentecost,* No. 59, March-May 1962, p. 7.

55   *Ibid.,* No. 31, March 1955, p. 11.

56   *Ibid.,* No. 25, September 1953, p. 1.

57   *Faith Digest,* February 1956, pp. 4-7.

58   *Ibid.,* March 1956, pp. 2-5.

59   *Pentecost,* No. 29, September 1954, p. 3.

60   *Ibid.,* No. 40, June 1957, p. 8.

61   *Ibid.,* No. 46, December 1958, p. 9.

62   *Ibid.,* No. 47, March 1959, p. 21.

63   *Ibid.,* No. 56, June-August 1961, pp. 3, 7.

64   *Faith Digest,* July 1971, pp. 10-13.

65   *Pentecost,* No. 19, March 1952, p. 3.

66   *Ibid.,* No. 19, March 1952, p. 3.

67   *Ibid.,* No. 22, December 1952, p. 7.

68   *Ibid.,* No. 19, March 1952, p. 2.

69   *Ibid.,* No. 19, March 1952, inside cover.

70   *Ibid.,* No. 13, September 1950, pp. 8, 9.

NOTES   *CHAPTER VII*

Oral Roberts, Evangelist Extraordinaire

1   Oral Roberts, *Oral Roberts' Life Story* (Garden City, N.Y.: Country Life Press, 1952), pp. 49-51.

2   *Ibid.,* pp. 57, 58.

3   E. M. and Claudius Roberts, *Our Ministry and Our Son Oral* (Tulsa: Oral Roberts, 1960), pp. 70, 71.

4   *Oral Roberts' Life Story*, p. 73.

5   Acts 10:38.

6   Luke 9:56.

7   John 10:10.

8   *Our Ministry and Our Son Oral,* p. 64.

9   *Tulsa Tribune,* August 2, 1962.

10   E. M. and Claudius Roberts, *op. cit.,* pp. 67, 68.

11   Prudencia Damboriena, *Tongues As of Fire* (Washington, D.C.: Corpus Books, 1969), p. 134.

12   *Abundant Life,* May 1963.

13   Mike Douglas Show, National Broadcasting Company, September 28, 1970.

14   Dick Cavett Show, American Broadcasting Company, March 24, 1970.

15   Cf. Hebrews 9:27.

16   International Seminar, Oral Roberts University, November 12, 1963.

NOTES   *CHAPTER VIII*

University President and Charismatic Methodist

1   Oral Roberts, *Miracle of Seed-Faith,* (Tulsa, Okla.: Oral Roberts, 1970), pp. 13-34, 163-66.

2   *Sports Illustrated,* November 30, 1970, pp. 64-65.

3   *Abundant Life Magazine,* February 1970, pp. 7-8.

4   James D. G. Dunn, *The Scottish Journal of Theology,* November 1970, p. 403.

5   Video Lecture at Oral Roberts University, Fall 1971.

6   *Christianity Today,* March 28, 1969, p. 40.

NOTES   *CHAPTER IX*

Pentecostal Merchants on the March

1   *Full Gospel Business Men's Voice* (hereafter cited as *Voice*), October 1953, p. 4.

2   *Voice,* February 1953, p. 3.

3   *Ibid.,* p. 12.

4   *Voice,* June 1969, pp. 26-28.

5   *Voice,* February 1961, p. 33.

6   *Voice,* September 1953, p. 4.

7   Letter from FGBMFI, 1971.

8   *Christianity Today,* November 24, 1967, p. 39.

9   Kevin Ranaghan, *Logos Journal* Vol. 39, No. 10 (November-December 1971), p. 22.

10 *Christian Life,* August 1967, pp. 22, 42.

11 *Voice,* November 1954, p. 7.

12 *Ibid.*

13 *Voice,* 1959, p. 40.

14 *Voice,* September 1963, pp. 4-9; *God's Formula for Success and Prosperity* (Tulsa, Okla.: Abundant Life Publication), pp. 38-39.

15 *Voice,* March 1971, pp. 5-6.

16 *Voice,* June 1966, pp. 12-13.

17 *God's Formula for Success and Prosperity,* pp. 102-4.

18 *Voice,* October 1963, pp. 21-22.

19 *Voice,* April 1954, p. 4.

20 *Voice,* July-August 1954, p. 14.

21 *Voice,* September 1954, p. 8.

22 *Ibid.,* p. 10.

23 *Voice,* December 1954, p. 9.

24 *Voice,* February 1958, p. 4.

25 *Voice,* June-July 1955, p. 5.

26 *Voice,* July 1957, p. 5.

27 *Ibid.,* pp. 5-6.

28 *Voice,* October 1969, p. 35.

29 *Voice,* April 1971, pp. 11, 29, 30.

30 *Voice,* February 1959, pp. 4-5.

31 *Voice,* March 1959, pp. 19, 20.

32 *Voice,* March 1960, pp. 13-22; May 1960, p. 8.

263

33   *Voice,* October 1961, pp. 1-3, 10, 11.

34   *Voice,* July-August 1961, p. 18.

35   *Pentecost,* September-November 1961, p. 4.

36   *Voice,* October 1963, p. 2.

37   *Voice,* January-February 1971, pp. 33-34.

NOTES   CHAPTER X

Protestant Neo-Pentecostals

1   *Christian Life,* July 1966, p. 32.

2   *Ibid.*

3   *Ibid.,* p. 27.

4   *Pentecost,* June 1949.

5   *Ibid.,* p. 16.

6   Dennis J. Bennett, *Nine O'Clock in the Morning* (Plainfield, N.J.: Logos International, 1970), p. 5.

7   *Ibid.,* p. 21.

8   *Ibid.,* p. 46.

9   *Ibid.,* p. 51.

10 *Ibid.,* p. 58.

11 *Ibid.,* p. 60.

12 *Ibid.,* p. 61.

13 *The Nation,* September 28, 1963, p. 173.

14 *Ibid.,* p. 175.

15 *Time,* August 15, 1960, p. 55.

16 Donald S. Metz, *Speaking in Tongues* (Kansas City, Mo.: Nazarene Publishing House, 1964), p. 38.

17 *Eternity,* July 1963, p. 10.

18 H. J. Stolee, *Speaking in Tongues* (Minneapolis: Augsburg Publishing House, 1963), p. 7.

19 *Time,* August 15, 1960, p. 55.

20 Bennett, *op. cit.,* p. 201.

21 *Pentecostal Evangel,* May 10, 1959.

22   Kilian McDonnell, "Catholic Pentecostalism: Problems in Evaluation," *Dialogue*, Winter 1970. (reprint).

23   *Scottish Journal of Theology*, November 1970, p. 407, Ibid. of p. 3.

24   *Christianity Today*, September 13, 1963, p. 4.

25   *Christian Herald*, May 1964, p. 10.

26   *Ibid.*, p. 22.

27   *Reader's Digest*, January 1957, p. 128-29.

28   *Ibid.*, p. 131.

29   *Ibid.*, p. 129.

30   *Ibid.*, pp. 129-30.

31   *Christian Century*, August 28, 1957, p. 1012.

32   *Presbyterian Life*, February 1, 1965, p. 14.

33   *Ibid.*

34   *Ibid.*, p. 13.

35   *Pulpit Digest*, January 1966, p. 27.

36   *Ibid.*

37   *Reader's Digest*, September 1960, p. 5.

38   *Christianity Today*, January 30, 1961, pp. 13, 14.

39   *Reader's Digest*, September 1960, p. 52.

40   *Ibid.*

41   *Ibid.*

42   *Time*, September 14, 1970, pp. 62, 64.

43   Kathryn Kuhlman, *God Can Do It Again* (Englewood Cliffs, N.J.: Prentice-Hall, Inc., 1969), p. 18.

44   *Ibid.*, p. 8.

45   *Ibid.*, p. 254.

46   *Ibid.*, p. 255.

47   *Ibid.*, p. 23.

48   *Ibid.*, p. 140.

49   Kathryn Kuhlman, *I Believe in Miracles* (Englewood Cliffs, N.J.: Prentice-Hall, Inc., 1968), pp. 80, 83.

50   Kathryn Kuhlman, *God Can Do It Again*, p. 5.

51   Interview with Kuhlman associate Gene Martin, May 2, 1971, Springfield, Missouri.

52   Kathryn Kuhlman, *I Believe in Miracles*, p. 199.

53   *Ibid.*, p. 200.

54   *Christian Century*, June 2, 1965, p. 699.

NOTES   *CHAPTER XI*

Catholic Charismatics

1   Joel 2:28.

2   *Christian Life*, July 1966, p. 30.

3   *Pentecostal Evangel*, September 24, 1967, p. 7.

4   *Journal of Ecumenical Studies*, Vol. 5, No. 1 (1968), p. 125.

5   Prudencia Damboriena, *Tongues As of Fire* (Washington, D.C.: Corpus Books, 1969), pp. 156-59.

6   *America*, March 30, 1968, p. 405.

7   David Wilkerson, *Cross and the Switchblade* (New York: Random House, 1963).

8   John Sherrill, *They Speak With Other Tongues* (New York: McGraw-Hill Book Company, 1964).

9   Kevin and Dorothy Ranaghan, *Catholic Pentecostals* (Paramus, N.J.: Paulist Press Deus Books, 1969), p. 15.

10   *Ibid.*, p. 17.

11   *Ibid.*, p. 21.

12   *Ibid.*, pp. 35-37.

13   Interview with Kevin Ranaghan at Oral Roberts University, January 26, 1971.

14   Douglas and Gloria Wead, eds., *Testimonies of the Notre Dame Revival Story* (South Bend, Indiana, n.d.), plus chapel service at Oral Roberts University.

15   Ranaghan, *op. cit.*, p. 50.

16   *Ibid.*, p. 51.

17   *Ibid.*, p. 55.

18   J. Massingberd Ford, *The Pentecostal Experience* (Paramus, N.J.: Paulist Press, 1970), pp. 15-17.

19   *Ibid.*, p. 15.

20   From the Report of the American Bishops as quoted by Edward D. O'Connor, C.S.C., in *The Pentecostal Movement in the Catholic Church*, (Notre Dame: Ave Maria Press, 1971), pp. 291-93.

21 Ford, *op. cit.*, pp. 22-23.

22 *Ibid.*, p. 47.

23 *Ibid.*, p. 24.

24 I Cor. 14:26-33 (Revised Standard Version).

25 *America,* March 29, 1969, p. 363.

26 Ford, *op. cit.*, p. 32.

27 *Ibid.*, p. 33.

28 *Ibid.*, pp. 33, 34.

29 *Ibid.*, p. 35.

30 I Cor. 14:5 (James Moffatt translation).

31 Ford, *op. cit.*, p. 36.

32 *Ibid.*, p. 37.

33 *Ibid.*, p. 38.

34 *Commonweal,* November 8, 1968, p. 185; *America,* March 29, 1969, p. 36.

35 *Commonweal,* November 8, 1968, p. 220.

36 Ford, *op. cit.*, p. 48.

37 John 5:24 (Revised Standard Version).

38 *America,* March 29, 1969, pp. 361-62.

39 *Christianity Today,* December 18, 1970, p. 269.

40 Ford, *op. cit.*, pp. 39, 40.

41 *Ibid.*, p. 46.

42 E. D. O'Connor, *The Pentecostal Movement in the Catholic Church* (*Notre Dame*: Ave Maria Press, 1971), pp. 168-170.

43 James F. Powers at the Bergarno Center for Renewal.

44 O'Connor, *op. cit.*, pp. 100, 101.

NOTES   *CHAPTER XII*

Pentecostals Under the Hammer and Sickle

1 II Corinthians 5:17 (King James Version).

2 Matthew 11:28, 29 (King James Version).

3 Walter Kolarz, *Religion in the Soviet Union* (New York: St. Martin's Press, 1962), pp. 245-73.

4   Steve Durasoff, *Russian Protestants* (Cranbury, N.J.: Fairleigh Dickinson University Press, 1969).

5   *Bratskii Vestnik,* 1958, No. 1, p. 29.

6   *Bratskii Vestnik,* 1949, No. 2, p. 8.

7   *Bratskii Vestnik,* 1957, No. 4, p. 36.

8   *Bratskii Vestnik,* 1961, No. 3, p. 15.

9   *Bratskii Vestnik,* 1957, No. 1, p. 79.

10   *Pentecost,* March 1957.

11   *Nauka i Religiia,* No. 9 (1961), pp. 40-43.

12   *Rovesnik,* No. 8, 1963, p. 2.

13   V. M. Kalugin, *Contemporary Religious Sectarianism* (Moskva, 1962), p. 19.

14   I. A. Malakhova, "Historians Study Modern Religious Trends," *Istoria U.S.S.R.,* No. 2, 1961, pp. 233-35.

15   F. I. Garkavenko, *What Religious Sectarianism Is* (Moskva, 1961), p. 82.

16   J. C. Pollock, *Faith of the Russian Evangelicals* (New York: McGraw-Hill Book Company, 1964), pp. 146-47.

17   *Ibid.,* p. 162.

18   *Ibid.,* pp. 180-84.

19   *Nauka i Religiia,* No. 12 (1961), pp. 18-20.

20   *Komsomol'skaia pravda,* September 25, 1962.

21   *Pravda,* September 26, 1962.

22   Nikolai Koltsov, *Who Are These Pentecostals?* (Moskva, 1965).

23   *Nauka i Religiia,* No. 9 (1961), pp. 73-74.

NOTES   *CHAPTER XIII*

Pentecostal Perspectives

1   Acts 1:11 (*Good News for Modern Man: Today's English Version of the New Testament* [New York: The Macmillan Company, 1966]).

2   Matthew 24:44 (King James Version).

3   I Thessalonians 4:16,17 (Revised Standard Version).

4   Harold V. Synan, *The Pentecostal Movement in the United States* (unpublished doctoral thesis, University of Georgia, 1967), p. 242.

5   *Ibid.,* p. 256.

6   *Ibid.,* p. 260.

7   William Menzies, *Anointed to Serve* (Springfield, Mo.: Gospel Publishing House, 1970), p. 103.

8   *Ibid.,* p. 105.

9   *Pentecost,* No. 58, December 1961-February 1962, Editorial page.

10   Menzies, *op. cit.,* p. 99.

11   *Ibid.,* pp. 100-101.

12   Acts 2:17 (*Good News for Modern Man*).

13   *Look,* February 1970, pp. 15-20; *Time,* June 21, 1971, pp. 56-63.

14   *Time, loc. cit.,* p. 56.

15   *Christianity Today,* January 29, 1971, p. 21.

16   *Decision,* February 1971, p. 7.

17   *Look, loc. cit.,* pp. 16, 19.

18.   *Time, loc. cit.,* p. 59.

19   *Christianity Today,* January 29, 1971, p. 35.

20   *Oracle,* April 16, 1971, p. 3.

21   *Pentecost,* June 1951, No. 16.

22   *The Cross and the Switchblade,* Vol. 9, No. 2 (April 1971), p. 5.

23   I John 3:2,3 (*Good News for Modern Man*).

24   Matthew 25:13 (*Good News for Modern Man*).

BIBLIOGRAPHY

Atter, Gordon Francis. *The Third Force.* Peterborough, Ontario: The College Press, 1962.

Bartleman, Frank. *What Really Happened at "Azusa Street"?* Edited by John Walker. Northridge, California: Voice Christian Publications, Inc., 1962.

Bennett, Dennis J. *Nine O'Clock In The Morning.* Plainfield, New Jersey: Logos International, 1971.

Bloch-Hoell, Nils. *The Pentecostal Movement*, Its Origin, Development And Distinctive Character. New York: Humanities Press, 1964.

Brumback, Carl. *Suddenly . . . . From Heaven*, A History of the Assemblies Of God. Springfield, Missouri: Gospel Publishing House, 1961.

Damboriena, Prudencia. *Tongues As Of Fire.* Washington, D.C.: Corpus Books, 1969.

du Plessis, David J. *The Spirit Bade Me Go.* Plainfield, New Jersey: Logos International, 1970, Revised Edition.

Durasoff, Steve. *The Russian Protestants.* Cranbury, New Jersey: Fairleigh Dickinson University Press, 1969.

Ervin, Howard M. *These Are Not Drunken As Ye Suppose.* Plainfield, New Jersey: Logos International, 1968.

Ford, J. Massingberd. *The Pentecostal Experience.* A New Direction For American Catholics. New York: Paulist Press, 1970.

Frodsham, Stanley Howard. *With Signs Following*, The Story Of The Pentecostal Revival in the Twentieth Century. Springfield, Missouri: Gospel Publishing House, 1946, Revised Edition.

Gee, Donald. *Wind and Flame.* Croydon, England: Heath Press Ltd., 1967.

Gee, Donald. *The Pentecostal Movement.* London: Elim Publishing Company, Ltd., 1959, Revised Edition.

Kuhlman, Kathryn. *I Believe In Miracles.* Englewood Cliffs, New Jersey: Prentice-Hall, Inc., 1968.

Kuhlman, Kathryn. *God Can Do It Again.* Englewood Cliffs, New Jersey: Prentice-Hall, Inc., 1969.

Lindsay, James Gordon. *The Life of John Alexander Dowie.* Shreveport, La.: Voice of Healing Publishing Company, 1951.

McPherson, Aimee Semple. *This Is That.* Los Angeles, California: Echo Park Evangelistic Association, Inc., 1923.

Menzies, William. *Anointed To Serve.* Springfield, Missouri: Gospel Publishing House, 1971.

Nichol, John Thomas. *Pentecostalism.* New York: Harper and Row Publishers, 1966.

O'Connor, E. D. *The Pentecostal Movement In The Catholic Church.* Notre Dame: Ave Maria Press, 1971.

Parham, Sarah E. *The Life of Charles F. Parham.* Joplin, Missouri: The Tri-State Printing Company, 1930.

Ranaghan, Kevin and Dorothy. *Catholic Pentecostals.* New York: Paulist Press Deus Books, 1969.

Roberts, Oral. *Miracle Of Seed-Faith.* Tulsa, Oklahoma: Oral Roberts, 1970.

Sherrill, John L. *They Speak With Other Tongues.* New York: McGraw-Hill Book Company, 1964.

Stagg, Frank; Hinson, E. Glenn and Oates, Wayne E. *Glossolalia: Tongue Speaking in Biblical, Historical and Psychological Perspective.* Nashville, Tennessee: Abingdon Press, 1967.

Synan, Harold Vinson. *The Pentecostal Movement In The United States.* Doctoral Thesis, University of Georgia, 1967.

Vivier, L. M. Van Eetvelot. *Glossolalia.* Doctoral Thesis, University of Witwatersrand, Johannesburg, 1960.

Wilkerson, David. *The Cross And The Switchblade.* New York: Random House, 1963.

Magazines and Periodicals

Abundant Life. Edited by Oral Roberts. Tulsa, Oklahoma.

Christian Life. Edited by Robert Walker. Wheaton, Illinois.

Full Gospel Business Men's Voice. Edited by Raymond W. Becker. Los Angeles, California.

Logos. Edited by Daniel Malachuk. Plainfield, New Jersey.

Pentecostal Evangel. Edited by Robert Cunningham. Springfield, Missouri.

World Pentecost. Edited by P. S. Brewster. Cardiff, Wales, Great Britain.

INDEX

273

275

276

Sabellianism, 79, 80
Safford, C. P., 153, 154
Scandinavia, 93, 98, 102, 161, 239
Second Vatican Council, 9, 191, 200, 203, 212
Seymour, William J., 62-66, 77, 82
Shakarian, Demos, 145-152, 156, 157, 162, 163
Simpson, A. B., 51
Smith, Angie, 142
Steidel, Florence, 69
Steiner, Leonard, 92
Sweden, 98, 102, 103, 162

Teamsters Union, 163, 164
Teen Challenge Center, 12, 194, 248, 249
Timko, Nick, 152
Tongues, 2-8, 10, 11, 13, 19, 20, 24, 25, 28, 34, 36-43, 46, 49, 50, 57-63, 65, 69, 71, 77, 84, 86, 89, 94, 99, 105, 112, 127, 146, 160, 166-170, 172-175, 178, 192-200, 205-207, 210, 214, 217, 219-221, 225-232, 234, 240, 245, 248, 249
Torrey, R. A., 50
Trasher, Lillian, 68, 69
Trinity, 19, 79-81, 87

United Lutheran Church, 181
United Pentecostal Church, 6, 81, 83, 202

Vietnam, 131
Voronaev, Ivan, 220-224, 228, 230, 234

Wainwright House, 182, 183
Wales, 131
Wesley, John, 35, 39, 44, 45, 50
Wesleyan Methodists, 49
Westmont College, 177
Wheaton College, 177, 188
Wilkerson, David, 12, 99, 189, 194-196, 249-251
World Council of Churches, 86-90
World Neighbors, 178
Wycliffe Bible Translators, 177

Xavier, Francis, 38

Yugoslavia, 12

Zhidkov, Jakob, 222, 226
Zimmerman, Thomas F., 86
Zion City, 53, 54, 65
Zurich Conference, 92, 93, 98

DATE DUE
